Also by Mary-Ann Tirone Smith

The Book of Phoebe
Lament for a Silver-Eyed Woman
The Port of Missing Men
Masters of Illusion: A Novel of the Great Hartford Circus Fire
An American Killing

The Poppy Rice Mysteries:

She Smiled Sweetly
She's Not There
Love Her Madly

Girls of Tender Age

A MEMOIR

Mary-Ann Tirone Smith

Free Press

NEW YORK LONDON TORONTO SYDNEY

*f*P

FREE PRESS
A Division of Simon & Schuster, Inc.
1230 Avenue of the Americas
New York, NY 10020

FREE PRESS and colophon are trademarks of Simon & Schuster, Inc.
For information about special discounts for bulk purchases,
please contact Simon & Schuster Special Sales:
1-800-456-6798 or business@simonandschuster.com

Book design by Ellen R. Sasahara

Manufactured in the United States of America

3   5   7   9   10   8   6   4   2

Library of Congress Cataloging-in-Publication Data
Smith, Mary-Ann Tirone.
Girls of tender age: a memoir/Mary-Ann Tirone Smith.
p. cm
1. Smith, Mary-Ann Tirone–Childhood and youth. 2. Smith, Mary-Ann Tirone–
Homes and haunts–Connecticut–Hartford. 3. Novelists,
American–Homes and haunts–Connecticut–Hartford. 4. Novelists, American–
20th century–Biography. 5. Hartford (Conn.)–Social life and customs.
6. Child molesters–Connecticut–Hartford. I. Title.
PS3569.M537736 Z465   2006
813'.54[B]–dc22   2005051376
ISBN-13: 978-0-7432-7977-2
ISBN-10:   0-7432-7977-8

A short one to you, Dad

THE NEIGHBORHOOD
Hartford, Connecticut, 1953

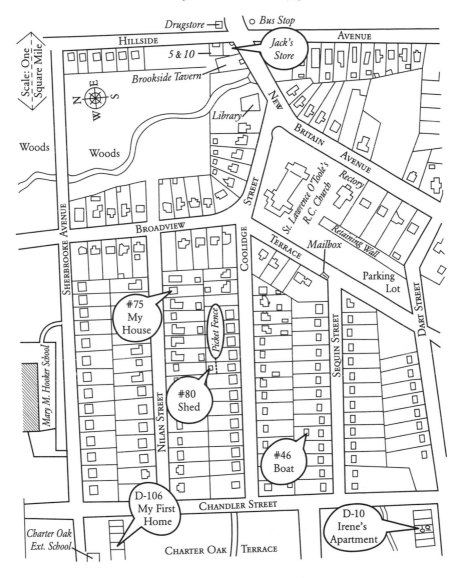

ten·der (ten'dœr) adj. **1. a.** Easily crushed or bruised; soft; fragile: a *tender* petal. **b.** Having a delicate quality: a *tender* song. **2.** Young and vulnerable: of *tender* age. **3.** Frail; weakly; delicate. **4.** Not hardy. **5. a.** Easily hurt; sensitive: a *tender* skin. **b.** Painful. **6. a.** Gentle and solicitous. **b.** Expressing gentle emotions; loving: a *tender* glance. **c.** Given to sympathy or sentimentality; soft: a *tender* heart.

Part I

Mortality

Mickey, Mother, and Tyler

one

*Dad and Mickey at Chalker Beach,
Old Saybrook, Connecticut*

HERE IS HOW my father describes our socioeconomic level: Working Stiffs.

We live in the D section of Charter Oak Terrace in Hartford, Connecticut. Hartford is a city where all manner of public buildings, bridges, restaurants, playgrounds, and gin mills are named after the oak tree where Captain Joseph Wadsworth hid the Charter of Independence granted by England in 1687. He hid it because England changed her mind. When James II assumed power, he sent an agent to seize it but the charter had gone missing and the agent didn't think to look in a squirrel's nest. Likely story.

Charter Oak Terrace was the first low-income housing project to be constructed in the United States. It was built for the GI's returning from war to give them a leg up while they put the Battle of the Bulge,

Anzio, Bataan, and Corregidor behind them and looked for jobs. My father's brother-in-law, Uncle Guido, was a WWII veteran so he got to live there, and my father, who wasn't, got to live there because of his job making ball bearings for the war effort. Also because Uncle Guido had pull.

At D-106, we have a coal furnace in its own little room, an alcove black with soot, between the front door and the kitchen. Our furnace utilizes a primitive heating system consisting of aluminum pipes and ducts and a narrow chimney that carries fumes, gases, and grime out through the roof while providing fitful outbreaks of warmth to our kitchen, living room, and two bedrooms. The vents in the walls have an aureole of coal dust. These heating details differentiate us, Working Stiffs, from the truly impoverished, who also work, but at the most menial of jobs—picking tobacco in the fields bordering the city's North End, sweeping factory floors, or risky jobs like running numbers. Their coal stoves have no alcove; they are in the kitchen.

The truly impoverished attach a rolled-up piece of sheet metal to their stoves that leads through a hole gouged out of the wall. Plus they gerry-rig hoses from the main shoot to bring heat into the other rooms. These hoses melt and then the houses catch fire and burn down.

Their children come to school with rags tied around their shaved heads because they have lice. The truly impoverished girl who sits next to me in first grade with her head wrapped in a rag has a name that intrigues me, Poo-Poo. When her house burns down, she moves to a new school district. Two days after she leaves, all the first-graders have lice. Since we're the children of Working Stiffs, not the truly impoverished, we don't have our heads shaved. Instead we are subject to foul-smelling shampoos, plus my mother combs my hair every night with a fine comb to remove the nits, which are lice eggs.

Got one! she goes, whereupon she carefully slides the nit out from the teeth of the comb and snaps it between her thumbnails.

Each morning my father fuels the furnace, shoveling coal into its belly as quietly as he can so as not to wake my mother, who is the prototype of the light sleeper. My mother can be wakened by the smell of cigarette smoke outside.

Yutchie, wake up. A *prowler!*

She's also awakened by Mrs. Alexander's radio even though it's late in the evening in the dead of winter and we're all sealed in tight with our coal dust. My mother can hear a field mouse in a nearby empty lot as well as Fluffy, the neighbor's cat, stalking it.

Later I will learn that fog comes on little cat feet. My mother can hear arriving fog too. Beyond that, she is just as easily awakened by the *absence* of sound; one spring night the freight train barreling through Hartford like clockwork at 2 A.M. doesn't send forth its dull blast at the Flatbush Avenue crossing three miles from D-106 at the northeast corner of Charter Oak Terrace. That's because it never reaches Flatbush Avenue.

She rouses my father. Yutchie, wake up! *The train has crashed.*

My father calls my Uncle Norbert, my mother's youngest brother, who is a fireman.

Early the next morning Uncle Norbert drops in.

What do you mean, Florence? he says to my mother. You couldn't have heard the crash. The goddamn train derailed in Meriden! (Meriden is twenty-five miles away.)

She says, I *didn't* hear the crash. What I heard was the train's horn not blast (which it always does when it crosses Flatbush).

My father says to my Uncle Norbert, How about a short one?

Word is that my mother has psychic powers based on her placement in her family of fourteen. She is the seventh daughter. When I ask my Auntie Coranna, the sixth daughter, what psychic powers are, Auntie Coranna says it's when people can see and hear what the rest of us can't. A devout Catholic, my mother eschews such nonsense. But the night the train derails in Meriden there is fire and destruction and death too, because in Meriden the train tracks run right down the middle of Main Street. Being a psychic, no matter that she denies it, is it any wonder she woke up?

Ten years later, my Uncle Eddie, my mother's brother born between her and Uncle Norbert, is staggering home from Alphone's Bar and Grill and is hit by the 2 A.M. train when he passes out on the tracks at the Flatbush Avenue crossing. The engineer never sees him, never applies his brakes, so my mother doesn't hear the train coming to a screeching halt, which would have really woken her up.

At six each morning, I force myself to open my eyes and climb out of my crib in the corner of my parents' bedroom, where I experience many horrific nightmares probably due to the sounds of sex a few feet away and my, no doubt, witnessing the shadowy tussles in the dark. When my father hears me whimpering, he comes over to the crib and says, You're having a nightmare, Mick. (My nickname is Mickey though I am a girl.) Go back to sleep.

He brings me a glass of water.

At 6 A.M., I scramble downstairs, take a right through the kitchen, and sit on a little rug by the front door in order to watch my father perform his daily, cold-weather ritual: he takes up a shovel leaning against the wall of the alcove and heaves coal out of a three-sided metal bin and into the fading pink interior of the furnace until its gaping black maw magically blooms into a wildly crimson glow. Then a tiny lick of flame leaps up above the coals signaling the end to my father's chore. The red glow is the most beautiful, most ethereal image that exists in my life. Sitting and watching, I think that if Our Lady ever appears to me (all little Catholic children are insanely envious of the children of Fatima) it won't be in a bush, it will be in our incantatory furnace.

When my father is finished shoveling coal, he gives me a piece of toast from the toaster on the kitchen floor. There is no counter space in our kitchen to speak of, just a sink against the wall and a white metal table next to it with one drawer packed tightly with Raleigh coupons. One day, I lean against the hot toaster acquired via Raleigh coupons and the first three letters of the name *WEAREVER* are branded onto the back of my calf. I am four and starting to read. *WEA* I know, is not a word. The toaster burn is my first memory of pain. I gag and press my hands to my mouth as I leap away from the toaster.

My mother says to my father, Look at what you've done!

This is the chronic response to crisis in my family. First, there can be no cry. That is because of Tyler. Tyler is my brother, five years older. We are all half-mad because my brother is autistic at a time when no one has ever heard of autism. (Today it is rampant.) Tyler cannot stand noise, which includes crying out or, in fact, just plain crying. The agony he feels when he hears such noise is extreme; when that pain comes, he bites his wrist. He grasps his left hand in his right and gnaws away like he's devouring a drumstick. He squeals hideously while he does this. His left wrist is covered by a thick, often oozing, callous. People will do terrible things to satisfy their compulsions and in Tyler's case, he does them to himself.

There is no one in the United States with the name Tyler except my brother. His name, like autism, is also rampant today. But then, my mother was psychic.

The second response to crisis follows immediately upon the heels of the first; my mother assigns blame and then won't forgive the guilty party even if it means carrying a grudge to the grave.

The third response is for her to light up a Raleigh then light up a second while stamping out the first until the ash tray is overflowing.

Until I am in first grade, I have no idea that when you are hurt, some people have the urge to hug and comfort you. In the first grade, my fingers get caught in the girls' lavatory door and my teacher, Miss Wells, takes me in her arms and hugs me to her big bosom. I don't understand what this is, a body surrounding mine, pressing sympathy from one heart into another. But my mother is the prototype of a woman on the verge of a nervous breakdown.

That is what I hear my aunts say to each other: *Florence is on the verge of a nervous breakdown.* They are familiar with such verging because it is the fifties when women were either on the verge or actually having one. Two of my aunts have nervous breakdowns themselves.

When I am five, my Auntie Mary, my mother's only unmarried sister, has a nervous breakdown and then gets shock treatments after which she comes and lives with us for three months. She sleeps on a cot in the living room. My Auntie Kekkie has one too; first she goes missing and then my father's brother, Uncle Johnnie, finds her behind the furnace and she won't come out. He calls my father to come help. My father assesses the situation and calls for a doctor. The doctor sends my father and Uncle Johnnie out for all the ice they can get. Then he has them dump the ice in the bathtub, add cold water almost to the top, whereupon my aunt is wrestled into the tub and submerged. (Perhaps there wasn't such a thing as a shot of tranquilizer back then.) Once subdued, Auntie Kekkie goes to the hospital and comes back a month later all better.

As young as I am, when I am burned by the toaster I know it isn't my father's fault. I know it isn't anyone's fault. It's the toaster's fault and the toaster didn't do it on purpose because it's an appliance. After I'm burned, my father smears the *WEA* on my calf with Vaseline and then he makes me smile by lighting up a Dutch Masters and blowing smoke rings into which I carefully insert my index finger. His record is six smoke rings from one inhalation on the cigar. Sometimes, a friend will give him a special treat, a cigar from Havana. He passes all his exotic cigar bands along to me for my treasure box, which is actually a humidor distributed on the fiftieth anniversary of the Dutch Masters Company. I think the picture on the humidor—a lot of men in a jolly group and sporting pointy beards—are Jesus's apostles only wearing pilgrim suits.

My father tells me the girl and boy on my prize Havana band are Romeo and Juliet.

He says, In Cuban, Mickey, that's *Romeo y Julieta.*

He tells me his rendition of the Shakespeare tragedy except he changes the ending and Romeo and Juliet get married and live happily ever after. I picture them dancing the polka at their wedding. I pretend my name is Juliet. After all, I have an uncle named Romeo, one of my mother's brothers. When I'm an adult, I watch Dick

Schaap interview Joe Namath on TV. Dick asks Joe what movies he's seen recently. Joe says, Some broad dragged me to see *Romeo and Juliet*. I didn't like it.

Why? asks Dick.

Because it was so sad.

There's a pause, and then Dick asks, You didn't know how it would end, did you, Joe?

No.

Poor Joe. Poor me; when I read the play in high school, I figure I know how it will end, my father's version.

A few days after I am burned by the toaster, I am sitting in the closet with a flashlight aimed at my leg, enjoying the delicious solitary pleasure of peeling the paper-thin scab off my skin. I look at the pieces of scab in the palm of my hand. They are me, but they are no longer me, a phenomenon I wonder at. I save the scab in my humidor. For the next few days I will have raw pink letters on my leg— *WEA*.

Each morning after my father stokes the furnace, I stand in the doorway and wave good-bye to him. He drives off in his black Ford coupe to the factory where he will keep many furnaces stoked all at once. He is a heat treater in the hardening room. The factory, the Abbott Ball Company, turns out millions of ball bearings punched from steel wire an inch in diameter, which are heat-treated in the furnaces and then polished to a high shine in huge vats of teeming chemicals, where they bounce up and down like Mexican jumping beans.

The Abbott Ball Company also produces ball bearings the size of poppy seeds punched from twenty-four-karat gold wire the diameter of a silk thread. My godmother, Auntie Doris, works at the Abbott Ball Company as an inspector. When she has to inspect the tiny gold ball bearings, she must be guarded and then inspected herself. The inspector knows Auntie Doris isn't a thief, but all the same he has to check very carefully under her fingernails, where the ball bearings might lodge without her even knowing it.

Auntie Doris studied opera when she was a girl. At all our family weddings she sings the "Ave Maria." (For my wedding, I ask her to sing the Miriam Makeba hit, "Kumbaya"; I have returned from Peace Corps service in an African country and I think it's an appropriate choice. But Auntie Doris sings the "Ave Maria.") As a child, I am convinced my godmother is an actual angel with her golden voice and the stray golden seeds lodged beneath her nails.

Auntie Doris is actually my cousin, but she is twenty years older than me so I think she is my aunt. No one corrects this. I do not know that she is my mother's oldest sister's daughter. My mother's oldest sister, Auntie Verna, whose real name was Zephyrina, died of breast cancer when she was in her early forties. My Auntie Mary, who is sister number three, tells me Verna was in so much pain she would lie on the floor and ask family members to jump on her. The pain of being jumped on is bearable while the cancer pain is not; the former takes her mind off the latter. I understand, then, why Tyler bites his wrist.

I STAND in the doorway and wave good-bye to my father until I can't see his black Ford anymore. One day, when I am three years old, I stand in the doorway whimpering because I do not manage to wake myself up in time to watch him feed the stove, or feed me my piece of toast, or worst of all, wave good-bye. He is gone and I must face the day without the ritual of his attention, which means a day without any attention whatsoever. It's winter, and my mother comes downstairs with a sweater wrapped around her.

Mickey, get in here and shut the door.

I don't move.

Get in here, Mary-Ann! She calls me Mary-Ann instead of Mickey when she is angry.

I still don't move. I am hoping my father forgot something and will come back and I don't want to take a chance of missing him. But it must be a morning when my mother is especially close to the verge of a nervous breakdown because she grabs my hand and yanks me in the door so hard my upper arm breaks. This is a pain I don't remember.

Mickey, age 4,
in kindergarten

What I do remember is my mother standing in the doctor's office arguing with him that my arm is broken.

He keeps saying, You can't break a child's arm by yanking her by the hand.

My mother says, I'm telling you, I heard it *snap.*

The broken arm is suddenly *his* fault. That is, until my father arrives, running into the examining room, Freddie Ravenel right behind him. Freddie is the colored man my father hired to sweep the floors at the Abbott Ball Company. The first colored man ever hired there. My father says on many occasions, Freddie Ravenel is the best man I've got. When my father becomes foreman, he promotes Freddie to stoker. My father's real name is Maurice, which his family pronounces Morris, but everyone calls him Yutch. Freddie Ravenel, though, insists on calling him Mr. Mawse because Freddie feels it's a due respect and my father can't convince him otherwise.

Freddie is so grateful for the job he is devoted to my father. When the news of my broken arm reaches the Abbott Ball Company, Freddie insists on driving my father to the doctor's office because he can see how upset my father is.

My mother's arms are folded across her chest. She says to my father, You didn't wave good-bye to her.

This is her explanation of how my arm came to be broken. I won't be waving good-bye to my father for some time. At least not with my right arm.

The doctor quits arguing with my mother and takes an X ray. Then he mixes a pot of plaster of paris. (In those days, there was no such thing as going to a specialist in orthopedics.) While he is soaking the strips of gauze, he is distracted by my brother, who is drawing a line of B-52s on the examining room wall.

The doctor turns to my mother. Can you not *do* something about that?

My mother says to my father, *You* do something.

Freddie Ravenel, like everyone else, knows my mother is on the verge of a nervous breakdown so he goes to my brother and says, Tyler, come stand over here by Freddie. Doctor say not to draw on his wall.

Tyler looks up in the vicinity of Freddie Ravenel, not directly into his eyes because that is something autistic people are unable to do, smiles his perfect Cheshire grin, and says, *Blackie.*

He loves Freddie Ravenel, who rolls his eyes, slaps his knee, and laughs heartily. Then Freddie Ravenel says to me, Don't you worry, Junior Miss, you be fine.

His words have a similar effect to Miss Wells's hug.

When I'm an adult attending a dinner party, I'm sitting next to a specialist from Yale–New Haven Hospital, a child abuse expert. He is one of the doctors who determines that Woody Allen's behavior toward his three-year-old daughter is inappropriate rather than sexually abusive. I find myself telling him about my mother breaking my arm.

He says to me, It's an accident when a child is yanked and her wrist breaks. But the *humerus?* You were treated very roughly. Today, that injury would be categorized as a direct result of physical abuse. The physician would be required by law to notify the police.

I say, My mother didn't really mean to break my arm.

He says, Oh?

She was on the verge of a nervous breakdown.

He's quiet and then he says, No intent then?

That's right.

He says, A nervous breakdown isn't a clinical term. In most cases, it's a psychotic episode of paranoia.

Really?

Yes, but the lay term conveys what a lay person might observe in the patient.

Then he says, Was it a wake-up call for your mother? Injuring you like that?

Yes.

She never hurt you again?

She never laid a hand on me.

He says, Sometimes, that's the case. I'm glad. He pauses before he says, Did she have a nervous breakdown?

No.

I'm glad for that, too. Then he says, My own mother had a nervous breakdown.

I say, Did you find her behind the furnace?

No. Up in the apple tree.

I'm sorry.

Thank you.

I don't explain to the doctor the reason my mother is on the verge of a nervous breakdown. Explaining Tyler would overly monopolize the man and he wouldn't be able to speak to the woman on his right.

WHEN TYLER is eight and I am three, sporting a cast from hand to shoulder, he has over five hundred books on the subject of WWII because he is obsessed with the war; his books cover battles, defense, weaponry. My mother says to the child psychiatrist at the Boston Children's Hospital, who deems him retarded, If he's retarded, how come he's reading *Arms and the Covenant* by Mr. Winston Churchill?

The doctor gives her a withering look. But my mother will not wither. She raises her chin and storms out of the child psychiatrist's office. This is how she fights people, storming out on them because, of course, she's powerless.

My mother learns she is powerless as a young woman at the Aetna Life Insurance Company where she is successful at a difficult job—processing data at a time when it is accomplished with a pencil. But this is during the Great Depression and the rule is that female employees are immediately fired upon marrying. Married men need work to support their families; how selfish for a woman to take up a job merely for frivolity.

However, when my mother is about to get married she is asked to keep the marriage a secret because the championship Aetna girls' basketball team is undefeated and they have been asked to take part in an exhibition game against the girls' Olympic basketball team. My mother, a fine athlete and the youngest member of a national championship bowling team, is Aetna's center, which today would translate to point guard. My mother agrees to keep her marriage a secret and gets to play in the big game. The center for the Olympic team is Babe Didrikson. The Aetna girls win. (Connecticut girls have been playing great basketball for a long, long time.)

Then my mother is fired.

two

O<small>N THE OTHER SIDE</small> of the country, Robert Nelson Malm was born in Walla Walla, Washington, on November 23, 1923. His mother died eight days later. There were three versions as to what happened to his father: One, he took off never to be heard from again; two, he killed himself; three, he was no good and why should he be expected to care for his motherless new son and two daughters? He was never seen or heard from again.

The children's aunt took possession of the baby and his two sisters and brought them to her home in Oakland, California. Four months afterward, she either felt she was unable to provide the care they required, or maybe decided she didn't want them after all. So she placed an ad in the *Rotarians'* magazine saying she had three orphaned children available for adoption and a Mr. and Mrs. Malm responded to her ad. They chose to take the younger of the two daughters and brought her home with them to San Francisco. The little girl was five, and she cried and cried for her baby brother so the couple decided they might as well go back and get the other two children.

The aunt told them she was sorry but the older daughter had been taken. The baby was still with her though. Would you want him? The Malms took him. They named him Robert Nelson Malm and called him Bob.

Bob never saw his oldest sister again, never found out what became of her, and was not told about his adoption until he was arrested at the age of twelve for molesting a little girl who lived on his street.

three

Joseph and Cleasse Deslauriers with the first six
of their dozen children, 1906

My French grandfather, my mother's father, immigrated to Hartford from Quebec in 1910 with his wife and six children, making a brief stop in Vermont, where the sixth baby, fifth daughter, was born, my Auntie Yvonne. The French Canadian diminutive for grandfather is *Pipier*, but we grandchildren, who are prevented from speaking French since we're Americans, call him Pippi. He is a Working Stiff. Pippi mans the assembly line at the Royal; he puts typewriter keys into typewriters. (I will grow up to be a writer but I do not read anything into that coincidence as I am not psychic.)

He and my grandmother, who will die long before I am born, have six more children. My grandmother gives birth every other year for twenty-four years except for a four-year gap between sister number six, Auntie Coranna, and my Uncle Romeo because, as a Canadian citizen, Pippi is drafted by the king to go to Africa and fight in the Boer War. When I am seven, I learn in school that Canada has no king.

I come home and say, Ma, how could Pippi have been drafted by the king of Canada? Canada doesn't have a king.

My mother says, after blowing two streams of Raleigh smoke out of her nostrils signaling irritation, The king of *England.*

She means Queen Elizabeth's father, who died a few years earlier.

I can't dope that out but the tone my mother takes with me teaches me to be content to just absorb what people say, and never question an adult pronouncement. So does my catechism priest, who tells us children that the greatest sin a child is capable of is to question his parents; to ask *why* is a direct refusal to obey the Fourth Commandment, Honor thy Father and thy Mother. So I absorb rather than question, and then go back to reading comic books.

Tyler and I love comic books. His favorite is *Blackhawk,* which I enjoy, and mine is *Archie,* which Tyler never so much as glances at. In Archie comics, unlike in the real world, the brunette girl, Veronica, is the beauty; Betty, the blond, is ordinary. The brunette even has the pretty name; the blond, the plain name. My hair is black like Veronica's. Every Saturday morning my father goes out to buy groceries and when he returns, he brings my brother and me one comic book apiece. My father, not my mother, does the grocery shopping and when he comes home she says, I wanted the *large* size peas.

Same tone as with, The king of England.

My French grandmother's name is Cleasse. One day, when I come to have a daughter, I want to name her Cleasse because I think it is a profound name. But my husband says that when our daughter reaches middle school, all the kids will call her *Clitoris.* I do have a

Mother (second from left, front row) and her seven sisters

cousin named after my grandmother, the daughter of my Auntie
Yvonne. Cleasse II is ten years older than me.

I ask her if her school chums called her *Clitoris* when she was growing up and she tells me no one ever heard of a clitoris when she was
growing up. She says, They called me *Ass*.

My French grandmother died of having babies. My cousin Marietta passes this information along to me. Her mother is the eighth and
final daughter, Auntie Margaret, my mother's best friend. When Auntie Margaret is sixteen, she is my mother's maid of honor. When Marietta is sixteen, she is mine. I love Auntie Margaret particularly
because she introduces me to politics. She is chairman of the Democratic Ward in the south end of Hartford. When I am seven she brings
me to a meeting. Instead of going into the building where the meeting
is taking place, she parks under a tree away from the streetlight. She is
wearing a babushka pulled low over her forehead. I want to wear a
babushka too. She figures no one will know who I am but she lets me
wear one of her ratty old babushkas, which she comes up with after

rummaging around on the car floor. Auntie Margaret gives me a note-book and pencil and whispers names to me as people file into the building for the meeting. I write down the names. I ask her who the people are.

She says, Traitors.

The traitors' choice loses and Ella Grasso is elected to the Con-necticut state legislature. Twenty years later, Auntie Margaret gets to go to the governor's ball. The governor is Ella Grasso, the first woman in the country ever to be elected governor.

My mother buys Auntie Margaret her ball gown; she has the money to buy the gown because she starts working again as soon as possible after the rule is changed that didn't allow married women to have a job.

The day of the ball, my mother wants to pay for Auntie Margaret's hair appointment but Auntie Margaret insists she will go to the Char-ter Oak School of Hairdressing, where she will only have to fork over fifty cents to get her hair set. When the director of the school hears where my aunt is going that night, she does Auntie Margaret's hair herself, giving her a cute poodle cut, a twenty-year-old style that looks really nice. Auntie Margaret is too proud to ask my mother for any-thing else beyond the gown so instead of a purse she carries a plastic bobby pin case to the ball. No one notices because Governor Ella Grasso, who is built like a linebacker, is wearing an inaugural gown de-scribed by the society editor of the *Hartford Courant* as a floor-length Princeton sweatshirt—it's orange and black. After Governor Grasso's reelection, she wears a cotton shirtwaist from the Sears catalog to her second inaugural ball, purportedly saying, If anyone doesn't like it, they can go fuck themselves.

My mother, who learns of the plastic bobby pin case, sees to it that Auntie Margaret carries a gold mesh purse on a chain to ball number two.

My cousin Marietta is also the one to pass along to me the legend of our grandmother's deathbed scene. Marietta and I are drinking sidecars at the time—our mothers' choice of cocktails—chasing them with Budweisers while we eat fried clams at Dock n' Dine in Old Saybrook on Long Island Sound, where we spend summers.

She says, So our grandmother went to confession after giving birth to her ninth child—your mother—and told the priest the doctor said it would kill her if she had another baby because childbirth damaged her insides so bad. She asked him to allow her to practice birth control. The priest went ballistic and he said to her, Birth control is a filthy, disgusting practice and a mortal sin besides.

Marietta imitates the priest really well, raising her finger in the air: *Cleasse, you will be doomed to eternal damnation if you commit such a grievous sin!*

Marietta says, He told her that birth control is what God was talking about when he gave us the last of the Seven Deadly Sins: Lust!

I raise my sidecar and I say to Marietta, To lust.

We toast. Then I say, Let's toast the other six.

She says, What *are* the other six?

I think. Gluttony!

Marietta says, Sloth!

We order another round of sidecars but we can't come up with the other four. Being drunk, I roll the three deadly sins we do remember into one; I say to her, Marietta, you lazy bitch, let's order some cherrystones and meanwhile have you checked out the unit on the bartender?

She checks it out before we order the cherrystones even though we're stuffed after the fried clams. Then she goes on with her story:

The priest said to our grandmother that she and Pippi would have to live as brother and sister. Or she could go back to the doctor to see if he would perform a hysterectomy, which would solve the problem. (The feminist movement fought the concept of unnecessary hysterectomies. But the practice of unnecessary hysterectomies came about from doctors who performed them out of compassion for their Catholic patients forced to have one baby after another.)

Then Marietta says to me that Pippi, naturally, wouldn't go along with the idea of living as brother and sister because he had conjugal rights. Marietta, who studied law, says, Conjugal rights? Now there's a contract no one ever signs.

Marietta also says, Trying to get Pippi to agree to living as his wife's brother was probably like trying to get Uncle Oscar to take a breather from hiding under the head table at all our weddings, barking.

My Uncle Oscar, the oldest of Pippi and Cleasse's four sons, can mimic with grand precision many breeds of dog. When my own wedding rolls along, Uncle Oscar will not only hide under tables but also under my train imitating the barking of an entire line of dogs from St. Bernards to Chihuahuas, and also, he will offer a toast: Stepping up to the microphone, raising his glass of Asti Spumanti, he says: To the pealing of the organ and the coming of the bride!

Half the guests laugh uproariously. The other half, my new husband's family, drop their jaws. Uncle Oscar's wedding present is a picture frame made of raw pine glued together with very little precision. He is pleased to tell us it was handmade by a friend of his who is serving time at the state prison for kiting checks. One of the first things my husband and I will do in our new apartment is throw away the gift from Uncle Oscar.

Marietta continues: After our grandmother's priest suggested she might look into a hysterectomy, she instead went on to have three more babies after your mother—Uncle Eddie, Uncle Norbert, and then, finally, *my* mother. And when our grandmother lay dying of hemorrhage brought on by her childbirth injuries plus an emergency hysterectomy, which only made matters worse, the family called the priest. Our grandmother told everyone she wouldn't see him. But he came anyway because his job was to give comfort to the dying and to administer Extreme Unction whether they wanted it or not.

Marietta leans closer, her sidecar waving about, and finishes her story: Now get this—the priest marches in, stands by her bed, and before he can administer anything she says to him, *I have been visited by a holy vision.* The whole family who are milling around stop in their tracks and stare at her. The priest asks her when she saw it. Mickey, can you imagine? Before the priest asks her *what* the vision was, he asks her *when* she saw it. *When!* As your mother would say, what has that got to do with the price of rice? Are all men idiots or what?

Yeah, they are. What did our grandmother say?

She said, *At dawn today.* So the priest asks her, What exactly did you see, my child?

Marietta's voice is now sotto: I saw the Virgin Mary, dressed all in blue and holding a beautiful white rose.

Marietta slides a cherrystone into her mouth.

Then what?

Then the priest goes down on his knees and takes her hand and he asks her if the Virgin spoke to her. Our grandmother said, Nooooo . . . So he says, Did she do anything? Noooo . . . goes our grandmother. Then the priest says, Well then, what happened? So our grandmother thinks for a little bit and then she says, The Holy Virgin Mary sat on the edge of my bed.

I say, You're shitting me, Marietta.

I'm serious. So the priest say to her, And then?

Now Marietta leans in close: Our grandmother gathered up the last of whatever strength she had left and shouted into his face at the top of her lungs, *I farted and blew her out the goddamned window!*

MY MOTHER ADMITS to me that Marietta's story is true because she was there when it happened. I am shocked. Who was my grandmother to commit such blasphemy? We are God-fearing Catholics, who believe in the one, true, holy, and apostolic Church, which is a damn good thing because I am brainwashed as a child into believing that everyone who isn't a Catholic is second-rate and won't get into heaven, even Protestants though the Pope recognizes their rite of baptism in eliminating Original Sin. Still the Protestants' chances are very slim since they eat meat on Fridays. I know by the time I am seven that Jews have absolutely no chance at all of getting into heaven because they don't get baptized. When I am eighteen, I go to college

The Deslauriers plus two brothers-in-law (Mother front row left), 1923

and learn that Jews don't believe in Jesus. I am appalled. This information has been successfully kept from me so that I won't think there is a choice when it comes to believing whether or not Jesus is God.

Buddhists and Muslims are a thing of myth so no one discusses their chances of getting into heaven.

I believe utterly that if I eat a cheeseburger on Friday and then get run over by a tractor-trailer an hour later, I will go straight to hell, where I will burn like those trick candles that don't go out when you blow on them. Also, worms will be feasting on my flesh as the devil is laughing his ass off.

So who was this woman from Canada, our grandmother, Cleasse Bessette Deslauriers, who defies the priest so unimaginably? I say to Marietta, Can you believe she really said such a thing?

Marietta says, I wouldn't if it weren't true.

• • •

Marietta

MY BELOVED COUSIN Marietta, my little buddy, the closest thing to a sister I've got, my maid of honor, dies of breast cancer in her early forties. My Auntie Margaret comforts me. She says, She won't be alone, Mickey.

It turns out that my Auntie Verna, is buried in a double plot. In Auntie Verna's day, when you got married, the first thing you did was buy your burial plot. After Auntie Verna died of breast cancer, her husband remarried and he is now buried in a plot with his second wife. So Marietta will be buried in the unused plot next to Auntie Verna.

The irony of it.

four

A T THREE, Robert Nelson Malm and his new family moved to Palo Alto when his father acquired a position at Stanford University. California state law required that a child had to live with foster parents for four years before they could be legally adopted. Bob and his sister were formally adopted by the Malms in 1927.

When Bob was ten years old, his father began to experience periods of paralysis, the early symptoms of polio. When he was twelve, his parents and sister moved to Los Angeles for two reasons: The first was that his father believed the best medicine available would be found there; the second—the reason Bob didn't go with them—was because of Bob's sexual molestation charge. He had been sent to a juvenile home for three months. The Malms were pariahs.

In Los Angeles, at age fifteen, Bob attempted to rape a ten-year-old girl. Since it was a second offense, he was sent to reform school for a year.

Bob was returned to his family when he was sixteen. His parents decided it was best for him to go to work instead of school since the school was so full of little girls to tempt him.

five

Francesco and Giulia Tirone and six children (Dad far right), 1921

MY OTHER GRANDPARENTS are Italian. My Italian grandfather left the north of Italy for America as a young man because he
was a vocal anti-Fascista. His male family members serve in the *Apen-
nini* and sing *"Viva Italia"* when they are drunk. My grandfather's
nickname is Visconti, pronounced *Viscu* in the Piedmontese dialect,
because as a teenager he worked for the bishop of Turin, who was also
a viscount. My grandfather, who we grandchildren call Gramps, wore
the bishop's fine clothes to dances when the bishop was out of town
and that is how he acquired his nickname.

My grandfather and the few other North Italians in Hartford form

26

a social club. They buy an eighth of an acre of swamp, fill it in, and build a brick meetinghouse. (They are all bricklayers, a skill they agreed to learn in order to get into the United States.) They call the meetinghouse the Luna Club in honor of their favorite song which goes: *C'e la luna mezz-o mare, mama mia me maritari . . .*" They form their club because they want to differentiate themselves from most Italian immigrants living in Hartford who are *Sicilianos,* considered to be Africans, not Italians, by my grandfather. When my grandfather and his friends sing *Viva Italia* they aren't singing about Sicilians, they are singing about the Piedmontese.

Every year the club holds a Christmas party for members' children and grandchildren. My godfather, Uncle Jimmy, plays Santa. I know there is no such thing as Santa at my first Luna Club Christmas party since I am not stupid enough to think Santa would look like Uncle Jimmy and wear a beard made of cotton batting. My mother makes me dance in front of all the other children wearing my costume from my dancing school's recital held the previous June, which means the costume, by December, is too small.

My Italian grandmother—who died long before I was born just like my French grandmother—produced six children, half the number of Cleasse. When my Italian grandmother died, my father was thirteen and his two little sisters were five and seven. It was decided that the girls should be sent back to Torino to be raised by my grandmother's sister. But my father, who had just suffered the realization that he would never see his mother again, was not about to see his sisters lost to him. So he insisted he would manage their care and he did. He found a babysitter for Auntie Alice, the younger one, and he took my Auntie Palma—who was born on Palm Sunday—to school with him every day and saw that she got to her classroom, where he picked her up in the afternoon and walked her to the babysitter to retrieve their little sister. Then he walked both girls home, and they cooked the family's dinner.

My Auntie Palma still says to me on many occasions, Every morning your father would braid our hair.

Dad (in middle) with brothers and sisters

Every morning my father would make me a piece of toast.

My dead Italian grandmother's name was Giulia. There are no j's in the Italian alphabet. She died in the hospital of hemorrhage, same cause of death as my other grandmother.

When I ask my father about his mother, he says, They took her away and she never came back.

Gramps remarries before I am born. He marries Ann, whom I think is my actual grandmother until I'm a teenager. She has a son, Jimmy, who will be my godfather. Tyler allows Uncle Jimmy to babysit for him. Every Easter, Uncle Jimmy brings me a chocolate bunny. As an adult, when I return home from my Peace Corps service, Uncle Jimmy brings me a welcome-home gift. A chocolate bunny though it isn't Easter.

*Dad (center rear), Gramps, brothers, stepbrother, and their wives,
Mother on far left*

six

WHEN BOB MALM was returned to his family at sixteen, it was agreed that he should take part in a training program with the Texaco Oil Company and learn how to lubricate automobile engines. He completed the program successfully and was then hired by a local Texaco station near his home. He gave his mother his paychecks and she gave him a small allowance. Pearl Harbor was attacked and within days, Bob's father died. He quit his job and enlisted in the Navy on November 3, 1942.

The Navy sent him to their massive base in San Diego where he was in boot camp with Henry Fonda, who turned all the men into avid movie fans. (After service, Bob made sure to see every Henry Fonda movie within a week of its debut at theaters.)

At the conclusion of boot camp, Bob was sent to Occupational Landing Force School at Balboa Park outside San Diego. Those seamen who successfully completed the school became known as commandos. Following that, he was also trained at fleet signal school so that he would have signalman skills. This last was considered one of the most dangerous duties for an enlisted seaman. A signalman was a sitting duck, patrolling the deck of a ship, searching the sky for enemy "signals," i.e., aircraft fire. There was never time for a signalman who spotted aircraft fire to find cover. In May 1943, Bob reported for duty at Treasure Island, San Francisco.

He was originally assigned to a landing craft and then to a destroyer, the *Charles F. Osborne,* patrolling Espéritu Santo Island in the New Hebrides. He served on board for three years in the South Pacific. The *Osborne* engaged with Japanese forces in the Central

Solomons, New Guinea, New Britain, New Ireland, the Marshall Islands, the Bonin Islands, the Marianas, the Philippines, and Okinawa.

Bob received the Asiatic-Pacific Theater of War ribbon with ten battle stars. All the men on board the *Osborne* were honored with the Presidential Citation. From the Philippine government, Bob was awarded the Philippine Liberation Medal with a battle star.

The only known glitch in his service was when Bob was absent over leave for two hours in Pearl Harbor and was brought back to the ship in a shaking stupor by MPs. The captain fined Bob sixty dollars, but three months later, after no further trouble, the captain canceled the offense from Bob's military record.

It was during this time that Bob pursued his interest in forced sexual contact with preadolescent girls; he could only have sex successfully with preadolescent girls and only after terrorizing and hurting them, leaving some of them unconscious, or possibly, dead. A man could get away with this in Okinawa.

seven

Tyler, age 9, at Chalker Beach

WHEN I AM SEVEN YEARS OLD, my mother starts her job at the Connecticut General Life Insurance Company; she holds a grudge against Aetna and doesn't apply there. She refers to her new employer as C.G. Today the company is called CIGNA. Her job is with the newly introduced housewife shift, three-thirty to ten. This time frame allows housewives to work when their older children come home from school to babysit for their toddler and infant brothers and sisters until the dads get home from work around five and take over. (Day care is an unheard-of concept.) When all the housewives' children come of school age, the mothers are able to segue into nine-to-five jobs all trained and ready to go. Still, no one I know has a mother who takes advantage of the housewife shift besides mine.

From the time I am seven until I go to college, I see my mother once a day for ten seconds (except for weekends) as I run in the door after school while she runs out to catch the city bus.

I am responsible for my brother from five after three until five-fifteen when my father comes home. After-school activities have to be eliminated.

Why? asks the teacher in front of the whole class when I say I won't be at choir practice.

My friend rings in, Because she has to babysit her brother. And he's *twelve!*

I look at my shoes.

Another kid explains, Her brother is *crazy!*

In an attempt to comfort me, a shy girl in my class named Irene says to me, apropos of nothing, My brother is twelve, too.

Irene doesn't say anything about having to babysit for him; I can tell she's just trying to be nice.

I feel myself choke up but I don't cry as I am used to not crying. I crush down the whimpering that tries to come out of my throat. Even whimpering now causes my brother to bite his wrist.

One day, actually, I press Tyler.

Tyler, what happens when you hear crying?

He ignores me.

Or sneezing?

Nothing. I persist: Or laughing?

I keep at him because he is only biting his wrist a little bit. Nibbling.

Finally he says, A cloud of needles flies into my face and it takes me a long time to pull them out because they have barbs at the end.

Oh.

I go to the kitchen and make chocolate chip cookies. I let him eat half the batter instead of merely giving him the bowl to lick.

Mickey at Charter Oak Terrace

• • •

IN THE HOUSING PROJECT, we have our own little school, the Charter Oak Terrace Extension School, grades K through 2, and a nice playground. For grades three through six, we cross Chandler Street, the eastern border of Charter Oak Terrace and go to the Mary M. Hooker Elementary School. Our sweatshirts, which read HOOKER SCHOOL, elicit many a chuckle, but we students don't know why.

Charter Oak Terrace is six acres of row upon row of two-story, whitewashed, cement block buildings. This grid is divided into four sections, the A, B, C, and D sections. The A and B sections are on the west side of the Hog River, a tributary of the Connecticut River, and the C and D sections are on the east side. We are assigned D and my mother is happy because that's the closest section to our church, St.

Lawrence O'Tooles, which means she can walk to High Mass after my father takes me to the children's Mass at nine. She has yet to rise to the monumental challenge of learning to drive, something especially difficult for a woman on the verge of a nervous breakdown.

Hundreds of children live in Charter Oak Terrace. We are instructed time and time again by parents and teachers not to go to the Hog River. Still, some go and they drown.

The real name of the Hog River is the Park River, which once meandered prettily through the city of Hartford. But in the mid-1800s, the residents began calling it the Hog because of its stench. Hartford's garbage and all the waste from dozens of factories lining the Hog are dumped into the river. A century later, a plan is put into effect whereby the Hog River is diverted underground, confined by large culverts until it empties into the Connecticut River. This diversion of the dangerous river begins just *beyond* Charter Oak Terrace. Since only Working Stiffs live there, fuck them. In the sixties, a neighborhood activist, Ned Coll, renames the Park River yet again. He names it the River of Tears as part of his proposal to see that the rest of the river is piped underground. No dice. Ned Coll runs for the presidency, is a candidate in the 1972 Democratic primary. At a debate where he is sitting at the end of a table with George McGovern, Gene McCarthy, George Wallace, Hubert Humphrey, and Scoop Jackson, he holds up a dead rat and tells the TV audience that there are many, many poor children who have to live with rats.

George McGovern wins the primary and Ned goes back to trying to save children's lives in Hartford.

Today you can canoe the Hog River with a conservation group, an adventure with perhaps not quite the cachet of the Sewers of Paris Tour.

We have conservationists when I am a girl but they are called "bird-watchers." They are degraded because they are Republicans as Hartford is a Democratic city.

When I am growing up the bird-watchers try, to no avail, to stop the demolition of Hartford Public High School, the second-oldest secondary school in the country, after Boston Latin. Hartford High is to be demolished to make way for a cloverleaf-patterned exit-entrance ramp for the new Interstate 84. Alas, no dice. So under the bulldozer go terrazzo floors; two hundred twelve-foot-high solid cherry doors; carved stone balustrades; and authentic Palladian windows, each pane cut into shape by hand. The only things saved are the telescope, which is used by the honors science class—no girls allowed in the honors science class—and a marble sculpture of an owl, our mascot, which sat over the main entrance for over a hundred years. I figure the "bird-watchers" don't want the school demolished because of the owl over the door.

My father takes me to the Hog River when I am four. It is a hot summer night. My parents and I, and my Uncle Guido and Auntie Palma are sitting outside on beach chairs in our six-by-six-foot front yard in Charter Oak Terrace.

My father is saying, If we'd had a plan to knock out the krauts' ball bearing factories we'd have won the war within a year of Pearl.

Uncle Guido says, You're goddamn right about that, Yutch.

My cousin Paul, a year younger than I am, has fallen asleep in his mother's arms. I listen to the adults talk while we all try to ignore my brother's solitary conversations, which are emanating from his bedroom's open window above our heads, conversations based on what my parents and aunt and uncle are saying while he eavesdrops.

Tyler begins shouting—bellowing, actually—into his Red Phone connected directly to the Oval Office in Washington, D.C. Tyler's Red Phone is an old Campbell's Chicken Noodle Soup can. The reason Tyler is shouting is his need to hammer home the gravity of the calamitous Japanese aggression.

He yells into his Campbell's can: *We are severely damaged at Pearl Harbor!*

Then, once Tyler has FDR's attention, he goes on to describe the extent of the attack. The actual president at the time is Harry S. Truman as FDR is already dead.

My mother tried to get Tyler to trade in his chicken noodle can, which was rusting, for a new one. Tyler's response was: Prepare to dodge ack-ack fire from our left flank, men.

That meant no.

While we sit outside on this midsummer night, I watch Fluffy and her litter of kittens lying under a shrub. I beg to have one of the kittens but I can't as Tyler can't abide meowing. A dog comes trotting down the street, seemingly minding his own business. He stops, sniffs the air, and lunges through our little circle and into the shrub where he grabs one of the kittens and rips its throat open, which sets Fluffy to screeching. My brother, inside, begins screeching, too. My father and Uncle Guido chase the dog away while my mother dashes in to Tyler before he can maul his wrist.

When Tyler is settled down again, back to communicating with the White House, my mother comes out and she and my father, my uncle and aunt, continue to chat. The commotion does not wake up Paul, who is a deep sleeper. I watch the fatally injured kitten squirm while its mother licks it even though my own mother says, Mickey, don't look.

When it dies, my father picks it up by the tail, takes me by the hand, and we walk to the bank of the Hog River. He throws the kitten into the black water amid the bedsprings and tires.

My heart is broken. I have nightmares and wake up screaming in my crib: *Stop, stop!* I am not screaming *Stop* to what is going on in my parents' bed, but my father's remedy is the same: He brings me a glass of water and tells me, correctly, that I am having a nightmare. But I keep screaming so my mother runs to my brother and my father takes both my hands and tells me, Mickey, say the Hail Mary.

I have learned the Hail Mary only recently.

My father says, Mary will make the nightmare go away.

And so I pray: Hail Mary, full of grapes, the Lord is with thee . . .

The prayer ends . . . *now and at the hour of our death, amen.* The last line of the prayer tells me that I will die, too. I whisper a prayer of my own: Mary, don't let a dog kill me. Don't let a dog rip open my neck. Don't let my father throw me into the Hog River.

37

Mary answers my prayer so I don't believe what I learn later in catechism—that Mary doesn't answer prayers, but rather she *intercedes*. I don't know what *intercedes* means. I only know that Mary doesn't let cruising dogs kill me.

I am named after her and Jesus's grandmother too. This pronouncement oft-declared by my mother is an attention grabber.

People ask, What grandmother?

My mother smirks and says, St. Anne!

Everyone laughs at the bizarre but true fact that Jesus had a grandmother.

The *Ann* in my name is spelled without the *e*. My mother feels the *e* is one letter too many.

WITH MY FATHER'S PROMOTION to foreman at the Abbott Ball Company and my mother's new job at C.G., my parents now have an income that no longer allows us to qualify for low-income housing. They buy a house and we leave Charter Oak Terrace. I am finally out of the crib, out of my parents' bedroom. I am seven.

We move to a little Cape Cod house on Nilan Street, on the other side of Chandler, parallel and one block from the Mary M. Hooker School. In the year that Terrace residents begin to make the kinds of salaries that force them out, colored people from the South begin moving in, Freddie Ravenel and his family the first. The real estate values around the Terrace plummet, so the house my parents buy on Nilan Street is a bargain, which is why they are able to afford it.

The people who sell us our new house leave their upright piano. My mother is melancholy. She knows how to play, but Tyler forbids the sound of a piano, far more assaultive a noise than crying. She must give up the thought of playing; otherwise Tyler will probably sever his hand. My mother won't have a nervous breakdown over this particular disappointment because she is no longer on the verge. She is at C.G. instead, working at a job she loves. Also, she's moved on from basketball to golf and becomes as adept a golfer as she was a basketball player. At first she plays Hartford's public courses and then joins a country club. She squeezes in a bowling league, too.

People say to my parents about Tyler, You spoil him. But the alternative to spoiling Tyler is to watch him sink his teeth into his wrist and bite it to the bone.

My father enlists Uncle Guido to help him get rid of the piano. Uncle Guido brings Paul so I will have someone to play with and therefore stay out of the way. I am happy because Paul is my best childhood friend even though we fight a lot since he's an only child and I am an only normal child so we aren't accustomed to sibling relationships. Also, I am not allowed to have friends to visit, only cousins.

Because the piano is so heavy and cumbersome, my father must face the fact that he and Uncle Guido will not be able to carry the piano out of the house by themselves. Also, they will need a truck to haul it away and even though my cousin Roger Belch has been recruited in the effort because he owns a truck, they'll need a hydraulic lift to get the piano up and into the truck. A hydraulic lift is an item no one can produce though my cousin Hawk Deslauriers, who has accompanied Roger, says, Hey, I know where I can get ahold of a hydraulic lift. And the guy I have in mind won't even know it's gone.

His voice then lowers to a whisper: So long as we get it back into his garage before he gets home from *The State.*

The State is a place where many people work. I think it is the name of a company, like the Abbott Ball Company, or like C.G. I don't know it is actually any number of jobs offered by the state of Connecticut. My Uncle Ray is at *The State.* He is a toll bridge collector.

My father and Uncle Guido rule against borrowing a hydraulic lift without the owner's acquiescence. Instead, they get a couple of axes and a sledgehammer out of the back of Roger's truck.

I say, Wait!

I tell my father that Paul and I would like to save the ivory strips glued to the piano keys. Can we peel them off, Dad?

The men look at one another thinking, Why the hell would they want to do that? But Paul and I prevail and are allowed to salvage the ivory while my father, uncle, Roger, and Hawk prepare for the demolition by raising a short one. Paul and I divide up the nearly paper-thin ivory bars, and we put them in our Dutch Masters humidors. (My father has managed to secure an anniversary humidor for Paul too.) My *WEA* scab has disintegrated to nothing. One day, when I hear: *Ashes to ashes, dust to dust,* I understand the metaphor exactly.

First, the men rip the top and back off the piano. Paul and I look inside. The insides of the piano make me of think of the insides of a horseshoe crab, an animal I look forward to observing each summer when we go to the beach on Long Island Sound. Unexpected things are under the shell of a horseshoe crab; that shell, Tyler says, is the prototype for the Nazi helmet. Peering into the guts of the piano I spot a *harp*. I beg to keep the harp. My father says, No, Mickey.

Uncle Guido says, Just what Tyler needs . . . you running around strumming a harp.

Paul says, Then can I keep the harp?

I experience jealousy for the first time. I beg Mary to intercede, Please say no, please say no.

Uncle Guido says, We don't have room for a harp.

They don't. They have moved from the Terrace to a four-room ranch near the Luna Club and it isn't all that much bigger than the apartment they had in the A section of the Terrace.

The reason the men feel free to swing and pry with reckless and noisy abandon is because Tyler has been taken out for a ride by my Auntie Margaret to see the dike that was constructed in downtown Hartford in 1938 after the great hurricane, which caused the Connecticut River to overflow its banks submerging Main Street under several feet of water. Tyler is the only one who knows that the cement wall next to I91 in Hartford is a dike. Paul and I are tempted to go along with Auntie Margaret because we know Tyler will demand an ice cream cone along the way and Auntie Margaret will stop at the Lincoln Dairy. But the destruction of the piano is too exciting an event to pass up even for ice cream. (My mother, meanwhile, is on the course. She still works the housewife shift at C.G. so that she can play golf during the day when either Auntie Margaret or Auntie Mary can stay with Tyler.)

My two uncles and two big cousins take up their weapons and smash the piano to smithereens, harp and all.

Paul and I then help out, putting all the large and small chunks and fragments of the piano into Roger Belch's truck. Then we head out through Charter Oak Terrace to the Hog River, where we throw the horseshoe-crab parts into the water to join the bedsprings, tires, and Fluffy's kitten.

In the fifties, there is no such thing as a tag sale and you don't insult someone by offering them something you don't want, even a piano.

I MAKE FRIENDS with the kids on Nilan Street: Judy, whose father is dead (unheard of), Cookie, whose parents are divorced (unheard of), and Joyce, whose father is a bookie (common). One day I am coloring with Joyce at her kitchen table while her father is organizing piles of little slips of paper. There is a knock on the door and the knock becomes a hammering. Joyce's mother grabs her husband's papers and runs to the bathroom where she flushes them down the toilet. She misses a few so Joyce's father eats them. He is chewing and swallowing when the police break the door down. Joyce keeps coloring and so do I. The police race through the whole house but they will not find any of the pieces of paper. They leave. One little piece of paper is under my foot. I pick it up and give it to Joyce's father and he thanks me. I wait, hopeful that he will eat that one too but he doesn't.

The next morning my mother is reading the *Hartford Courant*, puts it down, and stares at me. She says, Did anything happen at Joyce's house yesterday?

I tell her what happened. She doubles over with laughter and then calls everyone she knows and tells them what I told her. That night, a man comes to our door and hands my father a bottle of twenty-five-year-old scotch. When the man leaves, my father says to me, Good work, Mick, and then takes me out for a hot fudge sundae at the Lincoln Dairy. I don't know what I did to deserve my mother's laughter or my father's treat. I don't ask because I don't want to risk losing the trip to the Lincoln Dairy.

I AM A BED WETTER and every day there is a sheet blowing in the breeze from the clothesline. The neighbors deduce that Tyler wets the bed. My mother, always stepping up to defend Tyler, sets them straight whereupon they report this fact to their children and I hear about it every morning on the walk to school with my new playmates. They hold their noses and chant:

Mary-Ann wets the be-ed. Mary-Ann wets the be-ed.

When I am an adult, hired by Mary Warburg of the banking Warburgs to put her personal papers in order, we become fast friends. In her diaries, she has written that she was a bed wetter. I say to her, So was I.

She says, And so was my best friend, Mary Astor.

Wow.

Then she says, I suppose if one's name is Mary, one is a bed wetter. Isn't that too divine?

Then she makes us each a gimlet so we can toast divine bed wetters named Mary everywhere.

eight

On April 3, 1946, Bob Malm was separated from service on the Charles F. Osborne in Charleston, South Carolina, where the ship was mothballed and then decommissioned on April 18. The captain asked Bob what his intentions were—what duty he was considering—and Bob told him he hadn't really thought about it; whatever came up would be fine with him. The captain suggested submarine duty and sent a recommendation to Washington whereupon, in May, Bob was transferred to New London, Connecticut, where he would attend submarine school and then receive a promotion to chief petty officer.

Bob, at that point, was a big and brawny twenty-three-year-old military man.

After ten weeks in New London, Bob realized that the small Connecticut city was not Okinawa—forcing himself on little girls was tricky business. He asked for a transfer, which was not granted.

During the month of July, New London's south end was plagued by what police described as a reign of terror. Homes were broken into late at night and on several occasions girls awoke to the feel of a man's hands around their throats choking them. In every case, other members of the households heard the commotion and the man fled. A special police detachment was put on patrol.

One night, a young girl, visiting from West Hartford, was sleeping in her aunt's house. She saw Bob Malm coming in the window and screamed, and he ran off. A police cruiser nearby was dispatched to search for a tall sailor. Bob was arrested in uniform.

The girl's parents refused to press charges. They didn't want her terrorized further and they wanted her back home right away. But the state's attorney trumped up a charge of robbery, which didn't require the child to testify but rather her uncle, who agreed to do so. The state claimed Bob Malm had stolen money from the house.

Bob was found guilty and sentenced to one year in prison. He was undesirably discharged from the Navy "due to trial and conviction by civil authorities of robbery." (An undesirable discharge, as opposed to a dishonorable discharge, connotes violations that are felonies by civil law.)

Bob's mother and sister, upon hearing of his discharge and jailing, told his lawyer to relay a message to him. They never wanted to hear from him again; he would not be welcome at his home in Los Angeles upon his release from prison.

nine

Tyler and Mickey with cousin Paul

NILAN STREET. My own bedroom. I am overjoyed and the number of nightmares I have goes down. There is wallpaper with pink roses on the wall, the pattern almost as beautiful as the internal red glow of the coal furnace that I will never see again. Now my father turns a little disk on the wall to heat the house instead of shoveling coal. The outside of the house is clapboard, unlike Pippi and Grandpa's houses, which are sided with something called asphalt shingles, rough thin squares with edges that curl up in the hot summer sun. The floor is wood instead of linoleum. I touch the wood with my fingertips taking in the pattern of the oak grain.

We have a new chair, a wingback upholstered in a pattern of grapevines. Its back is velvet, the color of wine from the grapes. I sit behind it and feel the velvet with my fingertips. I feel the cover of my favorite book, *Silver Pennies*, too. *Silver Pennies* is a collection of children's poems, many of them having to do with fairies and several of them written by Yeats. The cover is midnight blue and there is a girl on the cover sitting in the grass reaching up into the night sky. She is reaching for the silver pennies embossed on the cover spilling down upon her. I feel the small silver disks. They are cold and smooth.

Tyler has the other upstairs bedroom under the dormers of our cookie-cutter Cape Cod house. I am not a good sleeper even with fewer nightmares because I am afraid of the dark what with all the previous primal sex I witnessed four feet away from my crib. Night lights are verboten because they are a waste of electricity. In the fifties, you are aware of wasting electricity, wasting food, wasting water. Wasting time is not a negative phenomenon; if you have time to waste, it means you're happy and doing well. Waste all the time you want. Afraid of the dark means I must pull my hands and feet in close to my body because if my foot hangs over the side of the bed, a blade will come down and slice it off. Perhaps Joseph Ignace Guillotin, the French physician who proposed the concept as a method to execute people, was afraid of the dark. (Mary Warburg will tell me she was afraid of the dark so her father gave her a loaded gun to keep by her bedside.)

What soothes me in the night is Tyler's voice, across the hall.

He is always in conversation with his "critter," a mangy, one-eyed stuffed animal, its fur entirely worn off. It might have been a teddy bear once. When I am an adult and I see the critter lying on Tyler's bed, it reminds me of a swarthy five-month fetus.

Sometimes Tyler calls: Sister, come tell a story to the critter.

Autistic people don't like to use real names. He calls our mother Lady and our father Pop-pop.

The stories he prefers are anecdotes that chronicle some trouble he got into when he was little. I am happy to run to his bedroom and get into bed with him and the critter because Tyler is not the least bit afraid of the dark. How could he be when he has far more serious things to be afraid of—like clouds of needles lodging in his face.

His favorite story is the commandeering of the elevator at G. Fox, Hartford's fifteen-floor department store. We call G. Fox, Fox's. Before Fox's is forced to close when malls are invented, you might need a new blouse to pep up your old suit so you'd go to Fox's, get off at the ninth floor, where the entire sprawling space is devoted to rack after rack of blouses organized by color. Bring the suit along, and a sales lady finds the perfect match immediately.

I am with Tyler that day at Fox's, the day the elevator story is born. He is nine and I am four.

My father is shooting the breeze with a friend he meets on the lobby floor by the elevator. (In the days of the big department stores, the buildings are so otherworldly that they have lobbies like the Plaza Hotel, a place that actually no longer has a lobby but rather a shopping mall. Ironic.) My father's friend's name is Abe Lieberman. My father calls out to his friend, Hey, Abe, you Jew bastard!

Abe's face breaks into a grin and he calls back, Yutch Tirone, you sonofabitch no-good wop, how the hell are ya?

They smack each other on the back, shake hands, and then get down to the business of comparing notes as to which horses should have won in the fifth at Narragansett yesterday, as opposed to the one that did, which they didn't have, goddamn it. Abe says, My nag stopped to take a leak at the clubhouse turn.

Tyler and I slip away into one of Fox's elevators. It goes up. Once the last passenger is ushered out at eight—Shoes—the elevator operator always steps across the threshold to hold back the shiny, bronze accordion gate in case it malfunctions and crushes a dawdling customer. Tyler pulls the gate out of the operator's hand and throws it shut. Then he swings back a lever closing the back-up metal door. He presses a special button that means the doors won't open no matter who is outside hammering away at all the floor numbers. Down we go.

We ride up and down pretending we are in a flying boxcar, transporting the troops across enemy lines. Tyler keeps saying to me, You're a fine soldier, Sergeant. Where did you train? Hickham?

I say, Yes sir, I did.

A maintenance worker is called to the scene by the elevator operator, who tells my frantic father there is nothing to be done but to wait us out. My father knows it's an extended combat mission Tyler has planned on so he asks Abe Lieberman to go see if Lukey Welch is working that day. Lukey Welch is our neighbor in Charter Oak Terrace. I call him Daddy Welch and his wife, Mommy Welch. I don't know why but I do. Lukey Welch is Fox's head painter. Abe finds him and brings him to the lobby floor elevators.

My father says, Jesus Christ, Lukey, Tyler's stuck in the elevator.

Lukey Welch says, Where the hell's Mickey?

She's in there with him.

Jesus Christ!

We have landed the flying boxcar back at the first floor so we hear all this. Tyler makes a slashing gesture to his throat which I know is a signal not to speak so I don't. I am a fine soldier trained, after all, at Hickham.

Lukey Welch says to my father, Can Tyler handle a bump on the noggin?

My father says, What choice have we got here, Lukey?

None.

Lukey Welch doesn't concern himself with my noggin as I am the normal one expected to handle any problems with panache never mind that it's not normal for a four-year-old to have that kind of *je ne sais quoi.*

Lukey Welch says to the maintenance worker, What in the Sam Hill are ya doin' standin' there like some kinda fuckin' wooden Indian? Go get a plank and we'll stick it into the shaft between the floors.

The maintenance man says, We'll burn out the motor if we do that.

Lukey Welch says, The only other choice is to shut down the electric power and if we do that, Mrs. Auerbach will take a shit and fire every goddamn one of us. Now go get a fuckin' plank!

Mrs. Auerbach is G. Fox's granddaughter, who now owns the store.

Tyler hits twelve, Men's Furnishings, and up we go. Then down to the main floor again. Then up, and our elevator hits the plank. We come to a jarring stop and our heads bang into the ceiling and we land in a heap. I don't cry, of course.

Tyler and I disentangle and get to our feet, come out, and there is a crowd gathered. Lukey Welch is standing in front of all the people in his paint-covered overalls. As I am rubbing my head, I say, Hi, Daddy Welch.

He picks me up.

The crowd applauds, which sends Tyler running for the hills. Abe catches him and he and my father get him into our Ford parked out on Main Street. My father takes off but Tyler gives an order to reconnoiter because his heroic gunner, who trained at Hickham, is missing in action. My father does a U-turn on Main Street, and Lukey Welch is standing there on the curb in front of Fox's still holding me in his big freckled Irish arms.

All the way home, my father says, Don't tell your mother, either of you.

Tyler says to me, Name, rank, and serial number, Sergeant, that's it. Then he says to my father, But don't forget to stop at the Lincoln Dairy, driver.

We get ice cream, we don't tell our mother, but Daddy Welch tells Mommy Welch, who does tell my mother, and there is hell to pay. Tyler doesn't pay, my father does. And me. My father gets the silent treatment for about a month, and I am deprived of *Big Brother Bill,* my favorite radio show, which I listen to on Saturday morning, while Tyler is still asleep so it won't bother him.

When I finish telling Tyler his favorite bedtime story of the Fox's elevator, he knows the deal is that he has to tell me a story, too. But first he shares a three-month-old chocolate chip cookie he's rationed. He gets it out from under his rug.

I request *Cinderella.* Here is Tyler's version of *Cinderella:* A lady goes to a ball and a prince wants to marry her but she runs away. She loses her shoe, which is made of glass. The prince finds it. Luckily, no break-

Mommy and Daddy Welch

age. Cinderella's wicked stepsister tries it on because the prince says he'll marry whoever the shoe fits. She puts her foot into it and . . . *grunt, grunt: Fail-*ure! Then her other stepsister tries and . . . *grunt, grunt: Fail-*ure! Then Cinderella tries and . . . *grunt, grunt: Suc-*cess!

We giggle. My father yells up the stairs, *Mickey!* Are you in Tyler's bed?!?!

I scuttle back to my room on my hands and knees and call out, No, Daddy.

Tyler also calls out, not to our father but to me: Continue your watch, soldier. No enemy made it through our lines tonight due to your diligence. I'll be seeing to your commendation. Count on it. And remember, first and foremost, we must protect the antiquities.

Aided by Tyler, the critter salutes me.

I hear my father's distant voice a moment later. He is reporting to my mother. He says, They're both in bed, for Christ's sake.

My mother says, All I know I have a member-guest first thing in the morning.

I hear Tyler say, Over and out.

ten

 $\mathbf{B}$ OB MALM began his jail term on August 8, 1946, and was released a year later on August 18, 1947. In the middle of the night of August 18, a New London resident caught him outside the bedroom of his thirteen-year-old daughter. Bob clambered down a fire escape, the father screaming from the window, so the people on the street held Bob down until the police arrived. He was arrested again less than twenty-four hours after his release from prison. He was brought to the New London courts on charges of breaking and entering. Since he hadn't stolen anything or hurt anyone, he was given a suspended sentence and one year's probation for breach of the peace.

eleven

Paul, Mickey, and Auntie Palma at Burgey's Barn

TYLER NOT ONLY has the bigger of the two upstairs bedrooms in the new house he also has a "den," the room downstairs that
is supposed to be the master bedroom. My parents sleep in what
should be the dining room off the kitchen. My brother earns these
privileges because A, he's retarded, and B, he now has twelve hundred
books, which take up a lot of space. It is wise planning. My father
buys him three books a month. My brother reads books twelve hours
a day, listens to polka music on his record player two hours a day, and
plays Crazy Eights, War, and Slapjack with me when I get home from
school. It is difficult for Tyler to get more than four hours sleep per
night because he also has to fit in his daily "rounds."

Rounds are what he must do to negate things that rile the demons in his head. Besides noise, Tyler cannot tolerate the color red—might as well look into the sun at high noon as gaze upon a red sweater. He can't tolerate being touched, either. He cannot look in a northerly direction—my mother has mirrors placed strategically on all south walls so Tyler can see a reflection of what is to the north; his demons allow for that, sports that they are.

Once assaulted, he must go through a series of rituals—rounds—to exorcise the reverberations of a touch, a noise, a glimpse of red, or an accidental glance out the living room window instead of the mirror facing it. He repeats the word *kish* over and over. Hs kishes while sitting in his chair, and then he taps his right foot with his left hand and then his left foot with his right hand, over and over and over, kishing the whole while. Then he goes up and down the hallway, which runs six feet between his den and the kitchen. Up and down, up and down, he goes, a zillion times, kishing and tapping until he is finally finished though sometimes he can barely remain standing from the exertion of it all.

A PRIEST COMES to bless our new house and he arrives while Tyler is on his rounds. We sit in the living room—the only time I remember my mother, father, and me sitting there—while Tyler becomes a flying blur past the doorway every few seconds, kishing wildly. The priest does his best to ignore the performance, which is not unlike trying to ignore a chimpanzee turning somersaults on your coffee table.

He says to my parents, Tyler is a cross to bear. Because of your cross here on earth, you will have two free tickets to heaven. There are chairs in heaven with your names on them.

My parents stare at him.

Tyler, he says, is a blessing in disguise. He has opened a deeper spirituality within your family that people would envy.

They stare.

Tyler's life has a God-given purpose.

Then the priest opens his satchel and takes out a golden ball with a handle sticking out of it. He reaches in again and out comes a Hellmann's Mayonnaise jar of holy water and a golden bowl. He pours the holy water out of the jar into the golden bowl. He dips the golden ball into the water and shakes it on us as well as the house. Since he shakes it on me, I hope I now have a free ticket to heaven, too, where there will be a chair with my name on it. My mother, father, and I will have a room in heaven sort of like the living room of the three bears. Goldilocks will not come in and break up my little chair though I won't be surprised if Tyler does. The priest doesn't shake the golden ball at Tyler. Actually, he aims the ball once toward Tyler's flyby and Tyler shouts out:

Schnell, schnell! Mortar fire!

Sometimes, Tyler is the enemy. Today he is the Desert Fox though his German vocab is limited.

The priest then hightails it out of our house, leaps into his T-Bird, which he has left running in the driveway so as to be sure to make the flight to his vacation home in the Bahamas.

My mother leaves to go shopping for a new purse and my father goes into the kitchen to make himself a pot of coffee, which he drinks constantly since he gets so little sleep. Both my parents are sorely disappointed though they'd never say so. Asking the priest to come and bless the new house was a ruse. They were hoping the priest would do something when he met Tyler—come up with a solution to what is becoming an unmanageable problem, Tyler at twelve. He's big. I have overheard the term *wet dream.* One morning there are two sheets on the clothesline, mine and Tyler's too. He's on the sharply cutting edge of adolescence. But advice from the priest is not forthcoming, and his version of comfort utterly useless. So my parents will continue to raise Tyler without a clue as to what is best for him or for them either. Me, they don't worry about. If I gripe about anything at all, my father says to me, Mickey, you get down on your knees and thank God that he didn't make you like he made Tyler.

I picture God sitting around with his Dutch Masters disciples, angels, and all the saints shooting dice; if snake-eyes comes up, the next baby born is seriously touched in the head. I hate to think God makes these decisions more deliberately than that.

When I grow up and come to fictionalize Tyler in my first novel, a writer from Boston calls me to ask if I will agree to be interviewed for a book about the effects a sibling suffering from a mental illness has on a brother or sister. Her own sibling, a sister, is schizophrenic. The writer says to me, I'd come home from school and my mother would ask me to pitch in with cleaning up the kitchen because my sister had, yet again, slit her wrists. My mother and I would start wiping up all the blood. My mother would say, *Let's have this all cleaned up before dinner.* As if my sister had spilled the sugar bowl.

The writer finds that children who are raised with mental illness in their homes develop a wonderful coping mechanism that will affect them favorably all their lives. The good that comes of being raised in a loony bin is our ability to weather the most awful of crises—remain calm and take care of business. In other words, we do not say a word, just wipe up the blood and move on like nothing ever happened.

TYLER FIXATES on World War II because his early childhood is enmeshed in the news of war. He lives for the delivery of his weekly subscription to *Aviation Week* and his two major Christmas presents: *Jane's Fighting Ships* and *Jane's All the World's Aircraft,* two books published annually in the U.K., each weighing maybe fifty kilos apiece.

The *Jane's* covers are the same navy blue as most women's dresses of the fifties, but their titles are embossed gold. Just as with the silver pennies, I run my fingertips across the cold smoothness of the *J,* the *a,* the *n,* and then the *e,* the apostrophe, and the *s,* and become generally transported. I am always looking for ways to be transported out of the bedlam that is my home. I depend on school, outdoor play from dawn to dusk on weekends with the neighborhood kids, visits to my countless cousins, and summers at Chalker Beach on Long Island Sound. When literal transport isn't available, feeling something tactile is helpful.

Besides the oak floor, the velvet wing chair, and the embossing on books, I also feel my mother's silver mink collar on her black Persian lamb jacket. My mother can't afford a full-length mink, and a stole is a public admission that she can't, so she decides on a Persian lamb jacket with a mink collar, which she purchases with a bonus she receives from C.G. for suggesting a better way to analyze data, saving the company three million dollars a year. (Her jacket is exactly like the one Whoopi Goldberg will wear in the movie *Ghost.*)

When I'm into a really good book or if I'm worried about something, even now I find myself holding the bottom corner of my shirt up against my face the way I did with my mother's fur jacket. My mother notices me doing that once. She tells me I started pressing soft things against my face when she took away my baby bottle on my first birthday, right after we ate the cake—the accepted practice then among no-nonsense mothers.

As a child, I don't read the military books in my brother's library; I read the books my mother bought for him when he was an infant, on layaway from a door-to-door salesman. Even though my parents didn't have a pot to piss in or a window to throw it out of, my mother came up with a dollar a week so that baby Tyler would have two shelves of classic children's literature intended to start him on the road to an eventual and brilliant career as a priest, preferably with the Society of Jesus. Despite my mother's countless novenas, a religious vocation isn't in the cards for Tyler though I believe the Jesuits might have signed him up considering the rare editions in his library. Tyler never reads a one of the books my mother bought him—I do. All of them, a hundred times over.

Included in the collection, in addition to *Silver Pennies,* are a first edition of Felix Salten's *Bambi* (1929), which I read before Disney makes the movie. Also, *The Knights of the Round Table, Robinson Crusoe,* the children's *Odyssey,* and a dozen others. She also pays fifty cents a week for the twelve-volume *Journeys Through Bookland,* which contain every myth, fable, and fairy tale ever conceived, plus full-length works such as *The Swiss Family Robinson,* and *Tom, the Water-Baby,* all illustrated with art nouveau prints and original drawings. In the fable *Why the Sea Is Salt,* the illustration of the ship going down has naked women interwoven with the foam of the giant waves turning the ship over. The women don't have tails. They are not mermaids. When I read the *Odyssey,* I understand they must be sirens, the same ones who tempt Odysseus.

Many of the stories in *Journeys Through Bookland* have antagonists who are evil Jews.

Before Tyler begins demanding military books, my family owned only two books meant for adults: *The Power of Positive Thinking,* by Dr. Norman Vincent Peale (also known as the Reverend Norman Vincent Peale), a best-selling treatise on what is now called denial, and the *Bedside Esquire,* which contained short stories and essays that appeared in *Esquire* magazine over a couple of years in the early thirties. Both books were given to my mother when she was in the maternity ward with Tyler so she'd have something to do.

In the forties, women were hospitalized for two weeks upon giving birth. It took at least two weeks for them to fully come out of the heavy-duty, anesthesia-induced near-coma they were put into. Forceps were a given. Nurses saw to remind doctors to pull their paper booties over their shoes to avoid sepsis when they planted a foot on the edge of the delivery room table inches from their patient's birth canal to give them the leverage necessary to haul the babies out.

Dr. Peale's book doesn't interest me but I read the *Bedside Esquire.* I am eight. The seventy-seven stories and essays include an excerpt from the novel *Christ in Concrete,* by Pietro di Donato, a scene narrated from the point of view of a man trapped in the footing of a building under construction. The concrete mixer is leisurely pouring its contents upon him and the wet cement crushes his lungs, fills up his nostrils, and finally, buries him. The reader gets to know what it's like to suffocate in the worst possible way.

The *Bedside Esquire* also includes William Faulkner's "The Ears of Johnny Bear," Ernest Hemingway's "The Snows of Kilimanjaro," Ben Hecht's "Snowfall in Childhood," Paul Gallico's "Keeping Cool at Conneaut," Ring Lardner's "Greek Tragedy," F. Scott Fitzgerald's "The Night Before Chancellorsville," D. H. Lawrence's "Strike-Pay," John Steinbeck's "The Lonesome Vigilante," Theodore Dreiser's "You, the Phantom," Erskine Caldwell's "August Afternoon," Havelock Ellis's "The Euthanasian Garden," Irwin Shaw's "The Monument," John Dos Passos's "The Villages Are the Heart of Spain," and the ever-famous (and my favorite) "Latins Make Lousy Lovers" by Anonymous, who turns out to be Helen Brown Norden, the only woman included.

All those stories collected from one magazine over just a few years.

No story of John O'Hara's is in the book because I come to understand he called the editor of *Esquire,* in public, "a sucker of cock."

The overleaf of the *Bedside Esquire* is covered with Tyler's art—one B-52 after another just like the line of planes he drew on the doctor's office wall who set my broken arm.

Besides the *Bedside Esquire* and the books my mother buys Tyler when he is a baby, I read two newspapers every day: The *Hartford Courant* and the *Hartford Times,* the latter now defunct. I read the *Courant,* which is the morning paper, when I get home from school as I have no time before school. I read the *Times* when it comes to the door at 5 P.M. Through reading, the vast majority of my unanswered questions get answered even if the knowledge gained is often awry. My mother gives me a book on menstruation when I am ten. The vagina part is so confusing I am left with the impression that the monthly flow will spill out of every pore in my body and I will have to wrap puffy white oblongs called Kotex around my arms and legs and therefore wear long sleeves, slacks, and mittens even in summer. With my trust in Mary and the Lord, I assume the blood will not come out of my face.

To this day, I sometimes mispronounce words because of the dearth of speech in my home; aside from a nightly fairy tale and my prayers, no one really spoke to me much except Tyler, who was the voice of George Patton. Tyler didn't allow the radio or records to be played, except when he was asleep, but when television arrived, my cousin Roger Belch fixed us up with earphones, which produced a lot of static. And the Church carried out the theory that children should be seen and not heard. When I was in college, I mentioned the cartoon character Yosemite Sam to a friend. I pronounced it *Yoze-might* Sam. Also, I thought the park was pronounced that way, too. So first, this friend and I had a laugh, and then she said to me, Why do you have so much trouble talking?

twelve

LIVING AT THE New London, Connecticut, YMCA, Bob Malm managed to last a year supporting himself with odd jobs before he was arrested again. One night, he attacked a seventeen-year-old girl who he seriously injured when she put up a struggle. But she would not press charges. The police, who had had quite enough of Bob Malm, noted that he stole her purse, which he hadn't. Consequently, he was charged with robbery with violence.

He was convicted and sentenced to seven to ten years and sent to the state prison in Wethersfield, a historic town just a few miles from Hartford.

thirteen

Uncle Guido: the Greatest Generation

TYLER'S DEN is lined with sagging creaking shelves, the subject matter of every book, World War II: theaters of operation, battles, weaponry, and what with Mr. Jane, obviously, warships and fighting aircraft. The den is probably ten by ten feet and there is only space for his books, him, a chair, and a table covered with oilcloth where his record player sits. Although the rest of us aren't allowed to play records, Tyler plays two hours of polka music every day. He also has a tiny radio; Sunday afternoons he turns on the radio and listens to the

Polka Hour. (We try to set me up with a radio in an upstairs closet when I enter my teens, but Tyler detects it what with the base sounds of rock and roll.)

With his great aversion to noise and loud sounds, how it is that polka music soothes Tyler, no one can figure. But I guess it's because he hears it from the time he has working ears, in utero, just like everyone else in Hartford, Connecticut.

Hartford in the fifties, just prior to the influx of African-Americans from the South and Latinos from Puerto Rico, is divided into distinct European fiefdoms, each with a ruling church: Italy is represented by St. Augustine's; Ireland by St. Lawrence O'Toole's; French Canada by Our Lady of Sorrows; and Poland by Sts. Cyril and Methodius. My bashful school friend Irene, who still lives in the Terrace, is Polish and her mother has a special dispensation to take her across town on some Sunday mornings to the children's Mass at Sts. Cyril and Methodius though she is not a resident of the Polish parish.

If you live in Hartford, you are a polka fanatic whether you are a Polish parishioner of Sts. Cyril and Methodius like Irene, or not. You eat guinea food, drink in harp bars, ostracize the frogs (since, as the most recent immigrants, they are at the bottom of the pecking order), and you listen to the polka. At all weddings—Polack, Guinea, Harp, or Frog—you dance the polka. (I find today that weddings aren't the wild fun they used to be because no one is racing around the dance floor, polka-ing and shouting *hoop-eye, shoop-eye* at the tops of their lungs.) The best dancers in my family are my Uncle Norbert's wife, Auntie Ida, and Auntie Doris, who specialize in the side by side, arms-around-each-other's-waists polka-style, and when they partner up and take wing across the floor, you know to get the hell out of their way.

Hartford's stars are the polka accordionists Stosh and Yosh Wisczn-nesky, "The Connecticut Twins," and little Jean Marie Kabritsky from a suburb of Hartford, New Britain (a Polish enclave affectionately called New Britsky), who plays tambourine and sings the "Beer Barrel Polka" and Arthur Godfrey's smash hit "She's Too Fat for Me" with a voice not unlike Ethel Merman's. Tyler has an autographed photo of

Jean Marie in her national costume festooned with ribbons matching those flowing from her tambourine.

Tyler calls the radio station so often to request another of Jean Marie's hits that they promise to send him a picture of her if he'll quit. He negotiates, demanding a new, updated picture every year and they comply. (In the last picture of Jean Marie to hang over his table, she looks about forty years old and weighs maybe three hundred and fifty pounds, but still appears very merry.)

There is also a Polish reference in Hartford connected with Saturday night card playing, a diversion enthusiastically enjoyed across ethnic lines. Whether poker or pinochle, gin rummy, or canasta, none of the games hold a candle to the popularity of that native Connecticut game, setback, which is unique in that making points of your own is secondary to forcing your opponent to lose points. In setting your opponent back, the game offers a socially acceptable way to humiliate and denigrate friends. Also, when you play setback, and an opponent makes a careless move, you hiss "New Britsky." In other words, you're announcing the fact that the player is such an asshole he might as well be a dumb Polack from New Britain.

My mother is a champion setback player and is asked to leave her golf club when she accuses an opponent of cheating during a setback tournament. The opponent is the president of the club. There is huge opposition to the request that she resign her membership since the president of the club thinks he's entitled to cheat, which jars all the members, and my mother has the lowest handicap of all the ladies. But she storms out, and then she joins another club.

ONCE MY MOTHER STARTS her job at C.G., my Uncle Guido and my cousin Paul come over every Monday night to keep my father and me company. While Paul and I play Parcheesi or Sorry in the cellar, the two men have coffee with a shot of grappa, which my Italian grandfather makes. Playing in the cellar is fun in the summer when it's hot outside, but my cousin and I freeze in the winter. There is nothing we can do about it; Tyler won't let us play anywhere else since we can't be trusted not to whoop and holler at a fortuitous roll of the dice.

Paul and I look forward to one special Monday night each year during the lowest point of winter in late January. We anticipate it more than we do Christmas and Halloween. It is when Uncle Guido and my father make bagna cauda for the four of us. Bagna cauda is the national dish of northern Italy, where my Italian grandparents emigrated from, that part which used to be a nation unto itself until the early twentieth century. Bagna cauda means *hot bath* in the Piedmontese dialect.

Bagna cauda is the most delicious thing on earth and my Uncle Guido is a great cook besides. He was in the second wave of the invasion forces in Normandy, U.S. Third Army. Patton attached Uncle Guido's outfit, the 188th Combat Engineers Battalion, to the Fourth Armored Division and ordered them all to race across France to Belgium, only to see them stopped temporarily and devastatingly at the Bulge.

One of Uncle Guido's favorite war stories is when his platoon is freezing in the woods outside Bastogne for a month. The men have run out of food so Uncle Guido gathers a bushel of fungi he breaks off dead trees, plus wild onions and shoots of dandelions waiting under the snow for spring. Then he fries his bounty in the back fat of a squirrel another GI manages to shoot. All the soldiers tell him that his guinea food is the best thing they ever tasted. They begin to help him forage. They don't give any of the food to their German prisoners. Instead, they escort the prisoners behind a barn and shoot them. Uncle Guido says there just wasn't enough food to go around so whenever they'd take prisoners they'd have to shoot them to save them from dying of starvation.

I am so wrapped up in the story that a question comes right out of my mouth: Did you ever shoot any prisoners, Uncle Guido?

He doesn't say yes or no. He says, If one of us lost a buddy, he'd get to shoot the prisoners.

At that age, I understand that this *lost* means the buddy is dead. I say, And then he'd feel better?

No, Mick, he'd feel worse.

Did you lose any of your buddies?

My father says, Mickey, find a pot holder for your Uncle Guido before he burns himself.

When you make bagna cauda, you simmer a great load of garlic cloves and a ton of chopped parsley in an aluminum Italian version of a fondue pot filled with bubbling melted butter and olive oil. The parsley is the last of the harvest from Auntie Palma's garden, which she protects with burlap after the frosts arrive. Most of Auntie Palma's parsley has been gathered by Christmas but she has one section of the parsley patch between the asphalt of her driveway and the foundation of her house that faces south. She reserves this particular parsley patch for our yearly bagna cauda. Auntie Palma chops her other parsley harvested earlier very finely and stirs the bright green pile into rendered salt pork, a whole lake of it filling a huge frying pan. Then she shuts off the burner. After the parsley-laden fat becomes firm again, she cuts it into little cubes and freezes the cubes. She does the same thing with her basil. All winter, she grabs a few cubes, fries them, and they become the base for spaghetti sauce or chicken cacciatore or stew. My Auntie Palma has a spotless, white kitchen that smells like any good kitchen in Turin.

The last thing to go into the bagna cauda is a couple of cans of mashed anchovies. Paul and I are allowed to pry the keys off the cans—we've had plenty of practice before, peeling the ivory off the piano keys—and then roll back the tin lids. Actually, we have a race to see who can roll a lid back first. But neither of us is particularly competitive and who cares about winning a race when you're about to eat bagna cauda?

Paul and I are always warned to be careful not to trip over the extension cord leading from the pot on the table to the outlet in the wall. This order is given with such seriousness that we know not to ignore it.

65

When the cloves of garlic are soft, the bagna cauda is ready.

On one side of the bagna cauda is a platter of raw peppers and cauliflower cut in bite-size pieces. On the other side, two big loaves of Italian bread. You take up a fork, spear a piece of raw cauliflower or pepper (though other vegetables I've come to learn are included in a bagna cauda if you prefer), and you dip it into the still-simmering brown liquid laden with anchovy pulp.

Dig in deep, you kids, Uncle Guido says.

That's where the best part of the butter is. Everything but the bottom inch of the hot bath becomes ghee, which is why, I suspect, as an adult I come to love Indian food.

Next, withdraw your forked, dripping vegetable piece from the pot carefully holding it over a chunk of Italian bread—previously ripped off the loaf by my father—so you don't drip onto the table. Then, pop it into your mouth. After about six pieces of vegetables, your chunk of bread is entirely saturated with the bagna cauda so you eat that, too. The most heavenly tasting bread imaginable.

During the feast, Paul and I burn our tongues on the simmering bagna cauda and also our wrists against the edge of the hot pot. We don't care. While we eat our crunchy raw vegetables and besogged bread, Tyler appears to pilfer a little bread himself, and then runs back to his den, giggling. He doesn't really like the bread, he just likes to tease us. When we have pizza, he'll sneak into the kitchen—dramatically on tiptoe—and grab a chunk of sausage from someone's slice and then dash back to his room. He doesn't eat the sausage. His diet is mainly canned food: he loves all Campbell soups—his favorite Scotch Broth; Dinty Moore Beef Stew; Franco-American Spaghetti; Chef Boyardee Ravioli; and Spam.

When the bagna cauda pot is empty, we wipe it out with the last of the bread which we then somehow stuff down our throats though we are filled to overflowing. Then we open the windows and doors and put on fans so that my mother won't get a migraine when she comes home from C.G.

Since the odor of garlic is carried by your bloodstream for twenty-four hours, I go to school in the morning with not only my breath smelling like garlic, but my skin and especially, the roots of my hair. Though severely ostracized by my classmates holding their noses dramatically, I don't care because the bagna cauda is worth it.

Paul doesn't care either.

One Monday, my father decides to expand on this tradition of a yearly feast. We will have a second winter treat. He will make *trippa.*

I say, What's *trippa?* unable to roll the *r* the way he does.

It's the cow's stomach.

I think, Uh-oh.

When my father unwraps it from the butcher paper, it looks exactly the way I imagine a cow's stomach might look, a great white thing which is flat on one side and sort of honey-combed on the other. My father takes the next day off from work so he can watch the *trippa,* which has to be simmered for a long time in the same pot we take every summer to the beach to boil lobsters. He starts simmering the cow's stomach after breakfast.

Uncle Guido arrives just at five-thirty having rushed home from his job on the line at the Fuller Brush to grab Paul. Paul and I watch with anticipation as my father lifts the heavy organ out of the pot and plops it on the platter we use for the Thanksgiving turkey. He cuts a strip for each of us. But Paul and I watch and wait—this surely isn't anything like Bagna Cauda. After a great deal of tearing and hacking with knives and forks, my father and my Uncle Guido each stuff a piece of cow's stomach into their mouths. They look like two men eating the sole of a Converse sneaker, chewing and chewing to no avail.

A few minutes later, my Uncle Guido, his mouth as full as when he first put the *trippa* in says, Yutch! When the hell did you start cooking this goddamn thing?

My father speaks with his mouth full, too. He says, This morning.

Uncle Guido chews some more and then he says, Jesus Christ, Yutchie. You were supposed to start it last night.

My father chews some more, too, while he explains that my

mother won't allow anything to cook all night while they are asleep because she is afraid of a kitchen fire. Actually, she'd said, That thing'll stink up the whole house. Cook it tomorrow. I'll be playing golf all day. I have a nine A.M. tee time.

Uncle Guido doesn't respond to my father's excuse for not cooking the *trippa* all night. He knows you don't cross my mother. So he just looks down at his plate, looks up at my father, and then they both begin laughing as they continue to try diligently to chew until they are finally able to swallow the one bite. Then they throw the whole *trippa* into the garbage can, which is an especially out-of-character thing for them to do having come of age during the Great Depression. No scraps ever make it to a garbage can in my house.

Then my father makes us all salami and provolone sandwiches with roasted peppers. Uncle Guido and Paul refer to them as *sang-wiches.*

Before he leaves, Uncle Guido gives me one of the many brushes, combs, and magnified makeup mirrors that he's picked up at Fuller over the years.

fourteen

Bob Malm's sentence was reduced to five years for good behavior and he was released from the prison in Wethersfield on April 5, 1953. He was given a job as dishwasher in the kitchens at the Cedarcrest Sanatorium, a tuberculosis hospital in Newington, a nearby suburb of Hartford. He lived at the hospital and resided in an on-site dormitory for employees.

His parole officer met with him weekly and his every report described Bob as a diligent worker, and a reformed, upstanding citizen.

After work, in the early evening, Bob prowled residential streets unable to suppress his hungers, knowing he'd have to wait until October when the clocks changed to Eastern Standard, when the streets would be dark at five o'clock.

Fall arrived, and Bob Malm continued his after-dinner strolls around the sanatorium. But a lot of local people worked at Cedarcrest who didn't live in employee dormitories, and many of them walking home from work spotted him and waved hello. He realized he'd have to move on to other neighborhoods, where people didn't know him. So when he could get a ride to the center of Newington, he'd catch the Hartford bus taking it all the way to the end of the route at downtown Main Street. On the ride he noted residential areas, and soon began getting off the bus at different stops in order to scout the quiet streets including my own neighborhood stop at the corner of New Britain Avenue and Hillside Avenue.

One November evening after work, he got his ride to Newington center, and then took the Hartford bus. He didn't get off at my stop this time; he got off at another corner a mile farther down the route at Beaufort Street. He strolled along Beaufort toward Hartford's Little Italy, anchored by St. Augustine's Church, prospecting in the shadows of its elegant soaring double spires.

fifteen

Auntie Coranna, the Belch children, and Mickey

MY MOTHER IS ACCUSED, in whispers, of putting on airs. Her airs consist of having her hair colored, leaving one white streak in a wave above her forehead. Another air is seeing to it that I have dance lessons–tap, ballet, and acrobatics. Acrobatics is the same as the floor event in gymnastics but without mats and performed to tunes such as, "The Sunny Side of the Street." Also the acrobat is not in a leotard but dressed up as a princess in the sultan's harem or as Harlequin. A third air is managing with my father to rent a cottage every summer in Old Saybrook at the beach. The cottage we rent is called Burgey's Barn.

Constable Burgey once built a garage in the middle of a marsh he owned in Old Saybrook, a town on Long Island Sound between New

Haven and New London. (Today the marsh is called wetlands and you can't build on it.) He needed the garage for his two trucks and an abundance of generators, chain saws, other miscellany, and every hand tool ever invented. The building looked like a barn because it had a small window under each end of the peak of the roof and because it had a loft. The loft was actually his house; the loft was closed off and divided into four rooms heated by a woodstove. He lived in the loft with his wife and daughter. He eventually installed several mismatched, lopsided windows all around the loft, but people still called it Burgey's Barn.

Once the job of constable became a paying job rather than a volunteer enterprise, he made enough money to build a real house for his family up the road on dry land, whereupon he got the bright idea to rent out the four rooms above the garage as a summer cottage with the stipulation that he would continue to be in and out downstairs when he needed his tools and junk.

My parents are his first renters. He wants a hundred and twenty-five dollars for the season—Memorial Day to Labor Day—but my father jews him down, as such negotiations are termed, to a hundred. My father asks him for the key, but Constable Burgey laughs and says, There's no key because there's no lock.

Constable Burgey comes to visit us on our first day to see if we are settled in. He notices that I have to sleep on the couch in the living room so he goes to the front door, which is at the top of the two-story exterior flight of stairs, turns, and stands there thinking. Just inside the front door to the left of where he is standing is the bathroom, which contains a toilet and nothing else. The bathroom does have a lock of sorts, a small piece of wood loosely nailed to the inside edge of the door. Turn it to the horizontal position and the door is blocked.

To Constable Burgey's right is the kitchen. Straight ahead is a closet. He says, I'll be right back.

The constable goes down to his garage, gets some tools, returns, and proceeds to take the door off the closet. Off he goes again to put the door down in his first-floor cavern and then comes back up dragging a frame and a mattress behind him. He jams what will be my bed into the closet. He says to me, There you go, little girl, while he dusts off the mattress with a rag. He explains to my father that he won't put the door back on because if it accidentally closes during the night, I will suffocate. Anyone who enters the cottage between 9 P.M. and 7 A.M. first sees me, three feet in front of them, pretending to be asleep.

I brag to everyone I know in Hartford that we spend all summer at a cottage near Katharine Hepburn's house, which is true except for the "near" part. I am putting on airs. The community in Old Saybrook where Katharine Hepburn lives, Fenwick, is three miles away. The houses there are sprawling turn-of-the-century behemoths with wide porches, turrets, and gardens. Our cottage is in Chalker Beach, a community of seasonal shacks. When my father and I are in town buying salami at the butcher's, sometimes we see Katharine and my father says, How ya doin', Kate? And she says, I'm just fine, young fella. She is the same age as my father. She never really looks at him. She chooses not to see me either.

In the summer I am free of my brother's constraints. I swim all day and in the hour between lunch and swimming when I am not allowed to go in the water because digestion will cause stomach cramps and I will drown, I build elaborate sand castles. I also fish and catch blue crabs with my French grandfather. When Pippi visits us, my father drops him and me off at Oyster River, which passes under Route One. It is six in the morning and my father is on his way to work at the Abbott Ball Company. He commutes to Hartford every day, two hours in each direction. Pippi and I climb down the bank of the river, which is actually a wide salt water creek, carrying lines, sinkers, a long-handled crab net, a bucket of bait, and a bushel basket for the crabs. The bait is fish heads from the fish Pippi catches the day before from a charter fishing boat. I am not allowed to fish with Pippi when he goes out on the charter because no women or children are allowed.

Pippi sits on a lawn chair in the shade of the Route One bridge wearing his old three-piece suit plus cap. I strip down to my underpants because it's usually ninety degrees and humid. I ask my mother why Pippi dresses this way at the beach and she says it's because he's French, not American. All day, we use a slow-motion, hand-over-hand technique to pull in a fishhead tied to the end of a hand line with a blue crab tearing at it until the fishhead and the crab are in the net. Then we swoop the net into the air, the crab captured. Sometimes a crab will sense the net and let go of our bait. Pippi never criticizes me for pulling the line too quickly; he knows when we lose a crab it is because the crab is a smart one.

It isn't easy dumping the crab out of the net and into the bushel basket because blue crabs are wildly aggressive. They wave their large menacing claws crazily and entangle their thin legs in the net as they try to get out. Once in the basket, Pippi lays a wide piece of wet brown seaweed onto their backs, which calms them, or otherwise they'll rip each other's claws off.

Once in a while, I go upriver and take a quick swim to cool off. Also, I observe the shenanigans of fiddler crabs skittering in and out of their holes on a sunny bank.

Pippi and I don't talk to each other because of the language barrier.

My father is back to pick us up again at five-thirty. Wade Abbott, who owns the Abbott Ball Company, lets my father leave work an hour early in the summer with pay because he is such a valued employee. Also, the hardening room maintains a temperature of about a hundred and twenty degrees in the summer and Mr. Abbott cuts down production allowing the heat treaters to take breaks outside under a tree so they don't die of heat stroke.

We return to the cottage with our bushel of blue crabs. I am sunburned. I appreciate the pain of sunburn as it means I'm at the beach.

When we arrive back at Burgey's Barn, my mother has the water already boiling and my father dumps the crabs into the pot. Then we sit around the kitchen table cleaning the crabs—rip off the shells, break them in half, and pick out the meat, which we flick into a bowl placed in the middle of the table. Once all the crabs are cleaned, we spoon the meat onto toast. My mother calls this a feast. She speaks colorfully. Every spring she tells people she can't wait to Shangri-la at the beach. She uses Shangri-la as a verb. The beach, along with C.G., the golf course, the bowling alley, Rose her hairdresser, and local card tables are the places that pull her back from the verge of a nervous breakdown.

My mother and father drink ice cold Pabst Blue Ribbon. I get to have my favorite drink as a special treat since we're having a feast—Tom Collins mix—and Pippi drinks the wine he makes. Both my grandfathers have grape arbors and make their own wine. My Italian grandfather always gives his visiting grandchildren wine. We hate it. But he insists. Unlike Pippi, Gramps speaks pretty good English though it's heavily accented. He says: If you kids don't drink wine every day you'll be white like the sink.

So we drink our little glasses of wine because we don't want to look like sinks.

My French grandfather, Pippi, doesn't insist on anything.

While we eat crab, Tyler is in his bedroom listening to Jean Marie Kabritsky belting out her signature hit, "Who Stole the Kiszka," a polka about a missing sausage with the sausage owners shouting for someone to call the cops. Kiszka is a sausage made of internal pig organs. Tyler is also enjoying his can of Chef Boyardee now served in three small bowls with a side of three slices of Spam. His compulsions continue to multiply. Now, everything must come in threes. Along with his dinner, he has three glasses of A&W root beer.

The next day at high tide, Pippi and I go eeling. After the killing of Fluffy's kitten, eeling is my introduction to violence not counting the crucified Christ hanging over all our beds with Christ nearly naked and dying of his wounds: nails through his hands and feet; thorns poking through his head and out one eye; a blood-gushing stab wound to his side. The *pièce de résistance* to Christ's suffering is when he begs for water and the miserable Roman soldiers hold a vinegar-soaked sponge on the end of a spear to his cracked lips. Once when I had a cold sore, I dabbed vinegar on it with a Kleenex and nearly went through the roof. I didn't shout out, though, what with Tyler.

Eeling doesn't affect me as much as the kitten incident plus I actually get to take part in this violence. I am, in fact, expected to do so. First I learn to pierce a struggling sandworm with my hook following the demo by Pippi. Blood spurts out of the worm just the way blood spurts out of Jesus's side. Then Pippi and I take up our sinker-weighted hand lines and spin them in the air before hurling them into the water. We wait till we have a bite and give a sharp yank in order to set the hook into the eel's esophagus. We pull in the line, hand over hand, and the minute the eel is on the beach Pippi grabs him and swings him with all his might into the jetty, fracturing the eel's skull. You have to do this or the twisting, twining eel will get all wound up and tangled in your line. If it's a small eel, I get to smash its head against the jetty.

Then Pippi cleans the eels on the beach, gutting them and slicing each one into three-inch lengths. Back at the cottage he pickles the eels in brine with a few bay leaves floating in it. If we catch a lot of eels, he gives a few to lurking Italian women who run off to toss the eels into their simmering sauce. On the rare crabbing occasions when we catch a soft-shelled blue crab, Pippi gives it to an Italian woman for her sauce and she acts as if she's won the lottery. After a few days, everyone is feasting on pickled eels at Burgey's Barn while drinking cold beer, homemade wine, and I, Tom Collins mix.

When I am an adult, I will decide to carry on the time-honored eeling tradition. Out on the beach, I explain to my two children how we must first hook the sandworms. I hold up a black hook. The children look from the hook to the white box from the bait store with the sandworms all snoozing quietly amid the pile of shredded seaweed. My son seizes the box and he and his sister run down to the water's edge and set the worms free.

What the hell am I thinking?

MANY OF MY AUNTS and uncles and cousins visit us at the beach. My favorite visitors are Auntie Coranna and Uncle John Belch. He is always called John Belch to differentiate him from my Uncle John

Tirone, who is married to my Auntie Kekkie. There are five children in the Belch family, three of them have names starting with R: Roger, Ruthie, and Richard. The sixth child, Rita, won't be born until my Auntie Coranna is forty-seven. The other two are Jackie, who is named after Uncle John Belch, and Billy, named William because my Auntie Coranna so loves the name.

Jackie is the first person I ever know who dies.

Jackie is a mongoloid. We don't have the expression, Down syndrome. Until I am eighteen years old, I think Jackie was adopted from the wastelands of China.

Jackie especially loves to come to the beach because he enjoys doing his imitation of a foghorn, which is right on. He tries to teach Tyler how to do it, and Tyler tries but can't get the hang of it. Tyler has an affinity for Jackie; it's as if Tyler understands that they are both crazy as loons. And Tyler tolerates the foghorn sound because, like the polka, it brings him back to that nice time in utero before his brain synapses derailed. The minute Jackie hits the sand, he runs off along the beach, squats behind the jetty, cups his hands over his mouth, and does his foghorn imitation in an extraordinarily deep voice. The second syllable of *Beeeee-yawww* is just the right number of decibels deeper than the first. Because he is able to throw his voice as well, his imitation is so effective that everyone on the beach looks out across the sound and comments on the approaching fog bank, which never materializes.

When Jackie is twenty-one, he is looking out the kitchen window of his house and he sees his little brother Richard fall out of their maple tree. Jackie collapses with a massive heart attack.

I ask, What's a heart attack?

My mother says to me, Richard scared Jackie to death. Jackie got such a fright, his heart stopped beating.

Henceforth, I am perpetually terrified that I will have a heart attack. So far, though, Mary remains hard at work interceding.

My father says, That poor Jackie! Dead before he even hit the floor. But at least he didn't suffer.

In those days, there is no surgery perfected that can mend all the physical anomalies of a child with Down syndrome so those children die at a young age. Twenty-one years is considered nothing short of miraculous.

Richard is fine. He is four years old. He falls out of the maple tree all the time.

I am five. My mother buys me a navy blue coat to wear to Jackie's funeral. I am so impressed that I now have something to wear that is the color of the *Jane's* covers just like all the adult ladies.

My mother decides I should go to the wake, too, not just the funeral. I can see my father is very nervous about that development. But I am not—I don't know what a funeral is and I don't know what a wake is either. I don't really know what *dead* is for that matter, not for another year when Pippi allows me to go eeling with him. I am looking forward to a new adventure.

My father does his best to prepare me. He tells me that even though Jackie is dead and in heaven, his body is still at Fisette's Funeral Home. How that can be, I don't ask, since there is no other part of Jackie that I can comprehend besides his body. I can't figure out which part of him is in heaven. This is precatechism classes so I don't know what souls are either, though I hear them mentioned during Mass when we pray for the repose of the souls in purgatory. What is repose? What is purgatory? I don't know. I believe we are praying for our shoes when they are at the shoemaker's to get new soles.

My father says, Now, Mickey, I'm going to take you up to the coffin and Jackie's body will be lying inside of it. He'll look like he's asleep.

What a coffin is, I don't ask either.

We'll kneel down in front of the coffin and say a prayer for Jackie's soul.

Ah-hah. It is Jackie's shoes that are in heaven. But then why pray for Jackie's shoes? Why not pray for his body so it has a place to go, too?

Are you listening to me, Mickey?

I sure am. I say, Does Jackie get to go to purgatory?

Of course not. He's a Mongoloid. He goes straight to heaven. He didn't know the difference between right and wrong. Just like Tyler.

I do not refute this fantasy. Tyler knows right from wrong, he just doesn't care one way or the other. I ask, How will Jackie get to heaven?

My father says, The angels will carry him. Now, once we say our prayer . . . Try to say it to yourself, Mickey . . . we'll go over to Uncle John Belch and Auntie Coranna and give them a little hug.

Uncle John Belch and Auntie Coranna will be there?

He sighs, Yes.

And Roger and Billy and Ruthie and Richard?

Yes.

Now I am feeling less anxious. I'm going to see my cousins, who are so much fun.

My father says, After you give them a little hug, you must tell them you're sorry.

Tell who?

Uncle John Belch and Auntie Coranna.

What for?

For Jackie's death.

I can't believe my ears.

Then my father says, All right?

I think, All right? But I haven't done anything. Why do I have to apologize?

All right, Mickey?

His voice is now stern. I can tell he wants me to do as I'm told.

All right, Daddy.

Then I say, What about Ma?

She'll be staying home with Tyler.

If he isn't working, my father is the one who always stays with Tyler. Many things are amiss. Richard is the one who fell out of the tree, not me. Surely my father is mistaken to think that I had anything to do with Jackie's heart attack and being dead before he hit the floor.

At least now though, I know where Jackie's going. Part of him, anyway. Heaven.

I do not want to go on this adventure, but I understand that I have no choice. Without telling my father, I make a decision; I will not say I'm sorry because I am so sure my father is wrong, that my Uncle John Belch and Auntie Coranna wouldn't dream that I could possibly be responsible for Jackie's heart attack. Much as I hate to think so, maybe my father is actually *lying* because he also says that Jackie is imitating foghorns in heaven and he's got all the angels in stitches. Jackie only imitates foghorns at the beach. Or maybe my father isn't lying; maybe there's a beach in heaven and the angels get to swim and make sand castles when they're not flying around. That would be nice.

My father buttons my new coat but I find I am wishing I had no new coat. I am wishing I didn't have to go to Jackie's wake at Fisette's Funeral Home. A wake is the trail left by a boat at the beach. I cannot figure out what will be trailing along behind Jackie's coffin. Coffin. Did I hear correctly? Maybe my father meant Jackie would be *coughing*. Maybe when you're dead you can still cough.

We arrive at Fisette's and my father and Mr. Fisette glad-hand each other in the parking lot. Mr. Fisette asks my father if he had that long shot in the fifth at Rockingham. My father reaches into his pocket and waves a C-note under Mr. Fisette's nose. Mr. Fisette says, Jesus Christ, Yutch, you're always in on the action.

Then we go inside.

There is a room as dark as church and with church music playing very softly. The room is full of people sitting in one row of chairs up against the wall to our left, and another row against the right wall. The people in the chairs face each other and stare at us as my father and I walk down the empty center of the room to the coffin. The coffin turns out to be a five-foot-high garden. Bushels of flowers climb all the way up the walls. As we come closer, I can see Jackie lying deep within the garden. Only his upper body is visible. Rosary beads are twisted around his hands. He doesn't look like he's sleeping like my father said. Once I saw a dead bird, and at the time, I didn't know that the term for its inert posture was called *dead*. Jackie reminds me of that bird. It's not Jackie, it's a Jackie-bird and it's dead.

My father is right about kneeling down. Someone has put a kneeler like the ones in church in front of the garden/coffin. My father and I kneel down on it and I am overwhelmed by the smell of so many flowers at once. I say the Hail Mary aloud because I can't figure out what it means to say something to myself. Then my father takes me by the hand, we stand, turn, and walk to my Uncle John Belch, who is sitting right up against the edge of the flowers.

I do not have to hug him, he hugs me. Then I just stand there in front of him and do not say I'm sorry, even though my father is nudging me.

Uncle John Belch takes my same hand that my father had been holding, pulls me close, and says, Are you sorry, Mary-Ann?

I say, Yes.

And now I know I really did kill my cousin Jackie. But I also know, when Auntie Coranna hugs me so hard and doesn't let me go for such a long time, that I'm forgiven.

sixteen

P ATRICIA D'ALLESSIO, called Pidgie by family and friends, was a happy, pretty seventeen-year-old just a few months into her junior year of high school. She'd gone to a friend's house on Beaufort Street directly after school to work on a history project due in a week, the last day of school before Thanksgiving break. The girls lived two blocks apart, the friend on Beaufort Street not far from the bus stop, and Pidgie on the corner of Beaufort and Franklin Avenue, the long thoroughfare running though the heart of Little Italy. The friend's mother invited Pidgie to stay to dinner since the girls were so determined to get a good start on the project before completing their other homework assignments.

Pidgie called her mother, who gave her permission and told her to call back when she was about to leave her friend's house so she could watch for her. Neither of the girls' mothers drove and their fathers wouldn't be home from work until later.

The two friends finished their project, had dinner together, and then Pidgie called her mother to say she would be leaving in five minutes. That was when Bob Malm stepped off the bus down the block. Pidgie put on her coat and wrapped her scarf around her neck. Pidgie's father got home from work just as she was skipping down the porch steps of her friend's house carrying her books in her arms and managing a wave good-bye.

The friend shut the door as the phone rang—Pidgie's mother calling to say that her husband had just arrived home and he'd drive over to get Pidgie. But she was told Pidgie had already left. Pidgie's mother hung up and explained to her husband that Pidgie would be home shortly and to keep an eye out for her while she finished cooking their own dinner.

It was 6:45 P.M. and in November that meant it was pitch dark outside. Hartford's streetlights were positioned two hundred feet apart and each gave off just a small arc of light.

Halfway between the two Beaufort Street homes, Bob Malm spotted Pidgie hurrying along. Pidgie didn't think twice about the man approaching from down the sidewalk; there were plenty of cars driving by—fathers, including her own, returning from work. In fact, she was able to make out her father's car in the driveway; she knew he must have just pulled in or he'd have come and gotten her when she called home. All winter he parked up against the sidewalk as it would mean less snow to shovel in case there was a storm in the night.

Bob smiled at Pidgie and she smiled back. He stopped and offered to carry her books for her. She said, No thank you. He walked in step beside her so Pidgie decided to pretend the next house was hers. She would go up the porch and in the front door. She'd babysat many times for the family who lived there; the door was unlocked; all the doors in Hartford were. That is what she was thinking while Bob calculated the halfway mark between two streetlights where it was darkest.

Just as Pidgie was about to turn into the walk leading to the house where she'd babysat, Bob struck.

seventeen

Pippi and Mickey in the "yard" at Burgey's Barn

WITH JACKIE'S PASSING, I am worried that I'll have to go to Fisette's Funeral Home every day to pray alongside his body but that doesn't happen. Jackie will be buried. Buried!

Under the ground? I blurt out.

My mother says, Where else?

I figure Mr. Fisette will dig a hole in his backyard and put Jackie in. If the alternative is to be tossed into the Hog River, so be it.

My parents somehow decide I will not go to the cemetery for the interment. My father is now saying *interment* instead of bury—he perhaps noticed my shock. However, I know that even though it's a different word, Jackie will still be buried in the ground. But I am relieved that Jackie will be buried in a place called a cemetery, not Mr. Fisette's backyard. I picture a cemetery to be a park with more flowers.

Though Jackie is dead and buried, incredibly, things remain the same. When the following summer arrives, we are Shangri-La-ing at the beach, and my mother announces that the Belches will arrive the next day for their annual visit. I wonder if Jackie will be with them. Perhaps my parents were mistaken and he didn't get buried but rather became alive again like Jesus did on the third day.

My Uncle John Belch has a delivery van instead of a car so he can fit his big family in. The van pulls up next to our Ford in front of Burgey's Barn and all the Belches pile out. I check to see if Jackie is with them. He isn't.

We walk to the beach and I run to Jackie's hiding spot in the jetty where he squatted and imitated the foghorn. Then I come back to our blanket and lie down next to my father. I whisper to him so that the Belches don't hear me: I want Jackie to come back now.

My father says, He's in heaven.

I look up into the blue sky and I say, Maybe the angels will bring him back today.

Mickey, he will never come back. The angels don't bring you back from heaven.

It's one way?

He smiles sadly. Yes. But we'll see Jackie again when we go to heaven.

What if we go to hell?

Of course we won't go to hell. Try not to think about it.

I try, but I am thinking God is very mean to take people away and never let them come back. I believe heaven is a lie, just like Santa Claus, the Easter Bunny, and the Tooth Fairy. Then I stop thinking.

I AM SUCCESSFUL at not thinking about dying again until I turn seven when I bump into death number two via Kathy Delaney.

Kathy Delaney is an especially beautiful, round-faced, blue-eyed blonde, her little nose and rosy cheeks sprinkled with pale freckles.

My first memory of Kathy stepping front and center out of the background of my life is in Mrs. Merucci's second-grade classroom at the Charter Oak Terrace Extension School. She leaps out of her seat, lifts her dress, and says, Omigod. I cut my can!

Our chairs at the makeshift school are old and rickety, and breed slivers. A sliver goes right through Kathy's underpants and her can is bleeding. Mrs. Merucci hustles Kathy off to the nurse and then she gives the rest of us a lecture on the appropriate vocabulary we need in order to refer to our private parts. She has us all stand, puts both hands on her ass, and has us repeat the word *buttocks* aloud.

Buttocks, we all call out.

Then she touches her chest and says, *Breasts!* Repeat!

We all call out, *Breasts!*

Then she puts her hands in front of her crotch and says, *Privates!* Repeat!

Privates! most of us shout, and the others, *Pirates!*

I have never heard any of these words before. My Auntie Mary calls her breasts, stars. Once she said to my mother, My stars are itchy, and my mother said, So scratch them, and Auntie Mary reached into her bodice and scratched. But I thought Auntie Mary said *jars* not stars, just as some kids in Mrs. Merucci's class now think their genitals are to be called *pirates.*

My mother doesn't use the word *can.* She calls a rear end, derriere, which I associate with the Lincoln Dairy. There is only one counter stool at the Lincoln Dairy where Tyler will sit. One day we go in and another child is sitting on Tyler's stool so Tyler pushes him off. The child cries hysterically and Tyler goes running out into the traffic, my father in hot pursuit. I say to the child's distraught mother, My brother's retarded and he doesn't know what he's doing.

However, I am aware that Tyler knows exactly what he's doing. The man who runs the Lincoln Dairy backs me up, tells the mother he won't charge her for her son's new ice cream cone—the old one is on the floor—and then he makes me my hot fudge sundae while we wait for my father to come back. A few minutes later he does, Tyler in tow. My father apologizes to the woman and offers to pay for her ice cream as well as her son's. He makes Tyler apologize. Tyler says, Sorry, and then he says to the sniffling child, That's my stool, *dummkopf.* The woman easily diagnoses my brother as not retarded but rather a sociopath and grabs her child and makes for the door.

I think of the word derriere again during rehearsals for graduation from Hartford Public High School when we are told that our school song, "O Hartford High, beloved school, all hail to thee . . ." is, like "Danny Boy," sung to the tune of "Londonderry Air," and was written centuries before the lyrics to "Danny Boy," hit the air waves. This is yet another reminder of the pride we should feel that Hartford Public High School is the second oldest high school in the country after Boston Latin. I figure the original lyrics must have been some Shakespearean bawd sort of song referring to London's can. (Excuse me, Mrs. Merucci, London's buttocks. Excuse me, Ma, derriere.)

The night that Kathy cuts what had been her can but is now her buttocks, I test my new vocab at home, singing about breasts and buttocks. Consternation breaks out. After I explain Mrs. Merucci's lesson, my mother says to me, Kathy has a lot of older brothers and a mother who is sick in bed, and that is why she is so vulgar.

I hear my father say a little later to my mother, Buttocks is a lot worse than can, if you ask me.

She says, No one asked you.

I think, If you ask me, jars makes more sense than breasts, which are chicken pieces that you eat.

No one asked me.

That same year, Kathy is in my catechism class, the prelude to making our First Holy Communion. Our classmate Irene is in our catechism class too, although Sister Mary Bernadette announces Irene has a special dispensation from the bishop to receive her First Holy Communion at the Polish church, Sts. Cyril and Methodius because she's Polish and that's where she goes to Mass. However, she will receive instruction with us because there isn't any way to get her to the other side of Hartford for her church's after-school cathechism class. At the same time, Irene will not be given a partner for our procession rehearsals. Irene is mortified to be singled out by Sister, and on top of it, has to parade down the aisle of the church alone.

After a cathechism class where we practice asking forgiveness of the priest hearing our confession—*Bless me, Father, for I have sinned*—Sister Mary Bernadette announces that poor Kathy Delaney might be missing the first few procession rehearsals because her mother has been very sick, bedridden for months, and now the family has lost her. We all figure that mothers who get very sick and live in their beds will then get lost and have to be found and put back to bed again. But then Sister Mary Bernadette asks us all to say a prayer for Kathy's mother in Purgatory so she can get to heaven ahead of schedule. I learn that *lost* can also mean you are dead.

All adults, even nuns, adhere to the Reverend Dr. Norman Vincent Peale's supposition of Positive Thinking. When you're both a man of the cloth and a doctor besides, people will believe anything you advise, for example, the use of euphemisms. Or maybe people have just been waiting and waiting for permission from the right person to tell them to believe whatever the hell they want to believe instead of the truth as long as it makes them feel better for the short term.

Although Kathy Delaney's mother is the second official person whose death I am connected to following my cousin Jackie's, I have, by now, been made aware of other deaths. My mother says things like: That poor Carl Luzzi. They opened him up? Loaded with cancer! *Loaded!* Sewed him right back together again. Damned shame. One of the best bowlers at the Washington Lanes.

I picture cancer inside someone as oatmeal and the person suffering from it in danger of bursting.

AFTER THE DEATH of Kathy's mother, all the nuns act maternally toward her, but she will have none of it. She isn't used to mothering.

She prefers the camaraderie of her older brothers. Kathy and I are the same height so we are partnered in the First Communion procession. My cousin Tommy, who is married to Auntie Doris, is a professional photographer. He manages to get a perfect shot of me at the Communion rail just as Father Kelly puts the host gently upon my tongue. When my mother sees the picture she says, That Kathy Delaney has spoiled this picture.

I look at it. Kathy's horrified face is turned toward me. She is next. All of us are in a panic because if the host touches your teeth it is a mortal sin, which means if you get hit by a Mack truck that week before you have a chance to go to confession the next Saturday you'll go straight to hell. Kathy figures if that happens she'll never see her mother again.

Tommy also gets a picture of me walking back down the aisle to my pew. My eyes are downcast and my face has an especially concentrated expression which everyone says is angelic. But Tommy takes the shot just after I leave the Communion rail. In the picture, the host has by now leapt to the roof of my mouth, where it has attached itself by its moist gluten. I suck at the host all the way back to the pew, desperately trying to keep it away from my teeth in case I'm to be hit by a Mack truck. Once again, Mary intercedes, answers my prayer, and sees to it that the pasty host slides on down my throat.

My mother scrutinizes the picture. She says, She looks like she's seen a ghost. And my God, that Kathy Delaney!

Kathy is clearly crying. The host has unquestionably touched her teeth.

There is another picture of Kathy Delaney sitting next to me at our First Communion breakfast and she is staring into space. Kathy Delaney never speaks directly to me until death number three, when we are in the fifth grade.

eighteen

Bob malm grabbed Pidgie's scarf and twisted it until it was tight around her neck. He grabbed her books from her. While she struggled to breathe, he dragged her through backyards and then threw her to the ground next to a garage under some thick shrubs.

He put the books down, and with his free hand unzipped his pants and then reached under Pidgie's skirt and yanked down her underpants, twisting the scarf around her neck tighter to keep her from fighting him. Pidgie continued to gasp and struggle for breath. He kissed her, felt her genitals, and pressed his penis against her and then ejaculated within seconds.

He was finished satisfying himself, which had required that he tighten the scarf enough to produce terrible sounds from Pidgie's throat so that, during his ejaculation, he could enjoy the thrill of hearing a female in ecstasy over his performance. Now he kept it twisted long enough to order her not to squeal or he would come back and kill her. He loosened the scarf and she nodded. Then he helped her get dressed, walked her home, even holding her hand, and once they were in front of her house, made her promise again, *Don't tell anyone!* She managed to mouth the words, I won't. Then he apologized and kissed her good night. His idea of a date.

Pidgie managed to control herself, but as soon as she was safe inside her home, she became hysterical. Her parents hadn't been worried about her yet. The time it took the man to snatch and assault her took no more than five minutes. Pidgie's mother tried to get her to drink a glass of water. She kept gagging on it, her throat was so swollen. Finally she was able to tell her parents what happened. Her father immediately called the police. A cruiser pulled up and when the police officer came into the house, Mr. D'Allessio told him his daughter had been attacked, pointing out the flaming red marks around Pidgie's neck. Pidgie gave the officer a clear-eyed description of the man and then he asked her to tell him specifically what the man did to her. She did while holding tightly to her mother's hand. The police officer took some notes and then asked Pidgie if there were any witnesses to what happened to her; asked what she was doing out-side after dark; asked if she had a boyfriend.

Back in the cruiser, he radioed in to say that he didn't have a rape case on his hands after all. He apparently believed that the marks on the girl's neck could have been hickies.

nineteen

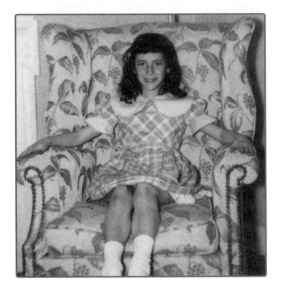

Mickey on first day of fifth grade

THE FIFTH GRADE starts out like any other year, but all that has been normal, routine, rote, habitual, *usual* comes to a wrenching halt just fifteen days before Christmas. From that Christmas season on everything will be masked from me by a Norman Vincent Peale–inspired blindfold, which doesn't remove itself until the end of seventh grade when I put into writing, into an assigned essay, the name *Irene.*

At the time of fifth grade, Tyler is now fourteen years old. Life takes an abrupt turn for him as well as me because he is in the throes of that most awful of all times, adolescence. When a mentally disabled child reaches puberty, hell is loosed and all positive thinking falls by the wayside. There is no luring a priest to the house under false pretenses. There is no invitation to come bless anything. Tyler, our free ticket to heaven, is now having sex with the coffee table. He is humping anything he comes in contact with and he's masturbating in the kitchen at noon. Tyler has to have his bath wearing a bathing suit to keep his hands away from himself, a remedy developed by my stricken father.

Interestingly, this is at the same time Ambassador Joseph Kennedy is having similar problems with his daughter, Rosemary. Except Rosemary is managing to sneak out of the house to make friends with the local neighborhood boys. Any boys. Any and all boys. Big boys. Their dads. The ambassador, like my father, knows he must protect his vulnerable child. So he has her lobotomized. Sadly, she loses her personality in addition to her sex drive. Still, if my father had known of such an option, he'd have done the same thing.

Instead, he becomes Tyler's jailer, training him to sleep during the day and be awake at night so he will be able watch him. My father crushes sleeping pills into Tyler's food to help attain the new schedule. The phone stays off the hook all day long so he won't be awakened. My mother can only call out. My father sleeps during his lunch hour at the Abbott Ball, and catnaps when Tyler is listening to his polka records at 2 A.M. I am now forbidden from getting into Tyler's bed and when I pass his door, his critter looks so much more forlorn, lying on Tyler's shoulder gazing out the door at me with his one shiny black button eye.

AT NINE YEARS OLD, when I am starting the fifth grade, my father calls up the stairs each morning to wake me up, and then he goes off to work. I don't stand in the kitchen waving any longer. Instead I call out, I'm up, Dad. Then I listen for the back door to close and the engine of his car to start, our latest Ford. When I can no longer hear the sound of the car heading down the street, I get out of bed. My mother, still on the housewife's shift at C.G., doesn't get up till long after I've left the house.

Miss Bowie is my fifth grade teacher. Within days of the start of school she will become the teacher I deem my favorite because she never yells, never so much as raises her voice one little note. She does sing lustily, however; her rendition of "Red River Valley" is right up there with Dolly Parton's. My mother's yelling sends my brother into paroxysms of anguish and terrorizes me. When I come to have children of my own, I take them along with my mother to New York to see *Peter Pan.* The theater is full of children, not the kind of people my mother enjoys being with. A couple of little girls in front leap up now and again in utter enchantment. Their parents have to tug at their dresses to get them back into their seats. Once, they don't tug hard enough. My mother bellows, *Sit down in front!* All the actors onstage freeze and poor Sandy Duncan can't come up with her next line.

Although the calm and collected Miss Bowie is a descendant of the man of knife fame, she pronounces the first syllable of *Bowie* to rhyme with *how,* not *hoe.* I believe the reason she mispronounces her name is because half her right index finger is gone. I think she hopes that with the mispronunciation people won't ask her if she chopped it off with her giant knife. She writes on the board with her thumb and half-finger gripping the chalk. Until mid-December I can't concentrate on learning because I am so mesmerized by her half-finger, after which I can't concentrate on anything except the practice of positive thinking.

In the fifties, girls wear cotton dresses that button down the back. One morning I button my dress wrong. When I come into the classroom, Miss Bowie notices right away.

Mary-Ann, isn't there anyone home to see you're *dressed* properly? Everyone's eyes travel to me.

Utilizing the justification which allowed for Kathy Delaney's rough edges, I say, My mother is sick in bed this morning.

I can tell Miss Bowie knows I'm lying because she rebuttons the dress very gently and then pats my shoulder, sorry that her irritation at my mother sounds as though she is upset with me. As I sit down at my desk, the boy behind me says, I saw your *undershirt.*

I am an adept liar by the time I reach fifth grade to offset such embarrassments caused by things like dress-buttoning mortification to say nothing of having a brother who sneaks out of his bedroom at two in the afternoon and hangs out the front door wielding a View-Master, directing passing children to pose and say *cheese* before my mother drags him back inside. Her first tack, hiding his Brownie camera, had proven ineffective; after all, what's the difference between a Brownie with no film in it and a View-Master? At any moment someone might say to me, Do you live in the house with the crackpot?

No, I lie, he lives next door. (I am clearly in training to be a fiction writer, i.e., a professional liar.)

Every year in elementary school, as part of our health curriculum, we begin our lessons on the basic food groups with a survey of what all of us ate for breakfast that morning. In Miss Bowie's fifth grade, the kids call out in answer to her question, What did you have for breakfast?

She points to James with her half finger.

He says, *Scrambled eggs!*

To Gail.

Cocoa and cinnamon toast!

To Susan.

Pancakes!

To Judy.

Wheaties!

To me.

Eggs Benedict! I add some color: *With Canadian bacon inside!*

What I actually have for breakfast is a swig of Hershey's Syrup, which I suck out of the triangular hole in the top of the can before running out the back door, improperly buttoned.

Miss Bowie raises an eyebrow at my Eggs Benedict, but lets it go.

My classmate Irene, the girl who goes to Sts. Cyril and Methodius, has no idea how to lie. Miss Bowie is determined to draw her into the group as Irene is so bashful.

What did you have this morning, Irene?

Irene's quiet little answer is, Leftover *golabkis.*

Golabkis, a Polish version of potato pancakes, is pronounced, *gawumpkees,* an especially comical word. We all scream with laughter, even me, who Irene once comforted.

FIFTH GRADE is the first year we will have a subject called Composition. We will learn to write themes. We are issued small notebooks with blue covers called *Theme Books.*

Miss Bowie says, in order to encourage us to be creative, The themes won't be graded.

We are simply expected to bring in our theme books every Monday morning and each of us must stand and read the themes we wrote over the weekend. Miss Bowie gives us our first assignment. Our theme will be: The Greatest Living American.

Come Monday, all the children in the class have written the minimum number of sentences called for—five—on Dwight David Eisenhower, our new president. I have written three and a half pages on Ted Williams.

Miss Bowie is pretty much slumped across her desk in boredom when my turn comes to read since we do everything alphabetically and my last name begins with T. I read my theme and when I am finished I see that Miss Bowie is sitting up straight, gazing at me thoughtfully. There are only two kids after me, Donna Walsh and a colored kid named Stonewall Jackson Werry. When Donna and Stonewall finish their testimonials to the president, Miss Bowie says, I would like Mary-Ann and James to go down to the principal's office. You will read your essays to Mr. Friedman.

Albert I. Friedman is our principal.

James is the skinniest kid in the class and the opening sentence of his theme is: *The price of grapes went down when President Eisenhower was elected.*

As James and I head out the door gripping our theme books, I hear Miss Bowie on the intercom saying to Mr. Friedman: Listen, Al, as a Democrat and a Sox fan, you are going to love this performance.

She pauses then she says, Trust me.

Out in the corridor, James is sweating bullets. He says to me in a voice that hints of dried-up saliva, My father wrote my essay.

The school secretary ushers us into the office of Albert I. Friedman. He is short, bald, and wears horn-rimmed glasses and a bow tie. He says, Ladies first.

I read.

While I read, James's hands are shaking so hard I don't know how he's holding onto his theme book.

When we are both finished, it is the only time I see Mr. Friedman smile. When he smiles, he looks exactly like Sergeant Bilko. The rest of the time he looks like a mug shot.

Back in class, Miss Bowie asks me how I know so much about Ted Williams. I tell her. My father takes me on two yearly excursions; one is a trip to Fenway Park. My father informs me on a regular basis that Ted Williams is the greatest hitter in baseball. He refers to Ted as the Splendid Splinter. Being Italian, my father feels free to refer to Joe DiMaggio as the Dumb Wop. When Joe later marries Marilyn, my father says, Now there's a wop's wop.

Today, of course, the Splendid Splinter is dead and decapitated, his splintered head hanging in a meat locker. Marvelous.

The other yearly excursion is to New York where we don't go to Yankee Stadium. The trip to New York is on my birthday. My father tells my mother that since I can't have parties because of Tyler, he will take me to New York to see the sights instead. Once Tyler attains adolescence, he is no longer allowed to accompany us on my birthday trip to New York; my mother must stay home with him and so she sulks for a week. She doesn't complain though, because she can't tolerate child-oriented activities and is glad not to have to participate.

We go to New York on the train. (There is no such train anymore. You want to go to New York from Hartford, you drive or go Greyhound or you fly from Bradley Field to LaGuardia which, all told, takes at least two days.)

Each year, I get to choose three New York venues. By the time I am nine I have visited the Hayden Planetarium; the Museum of Natural History; Coney Island, where we take a ride on the parachute; the Empire State Building; a television studio where we watch *The Lucky Strike Hit Parade* rehearsals with Dorothy Collins, Snooky Lanson, and Gisele MacKenzie; the UN; the Statue of Liberty; the Bronx Zoo. Every attraction a child could dream of. We don't go to see the Rockettes because my father says, That's for tourists. His feeling is that tourists are dumbbells, not us.

How do you tell a dumbbell, Mick?

Yankee fan.

That's right.

My favorite New York City site is in Times Square, where we watch the man in the Camel's billboard blow smoke rings just like my father does. I decide when I grow up, I will smoke Camels, not Luckies. But I come of age in the sixties when I will smoke Marlboros just like everyone else. Also in Times Square is a movie house that shows nothing but Laurel and Hardy, Abbott and Costello, and the Three Stooges. We duck in at the end of our days in New York for a few yucks before we have to run for the train ride back home to Hartford.

When Tyler comes to New York City, before he enters puberty, my father has to be far more vigilant than he is with just me. One time we go to the Statue of Liberty and there are several Japanese businessmen at Battery Park waiting in line with us for the ferry. Tyler picks up a long stick, gets down on his belly, aims the stick at them, and says, *The only good Jap is a dead Jap,* which is a quote from a Marine lieutenant who led his troops through the bullets and surf onto a Pacific atoll.

Then Tyler fires. He shouts, Take this for Kwajalein, you yellowbellies. He fires again. And this one's for Corregidor, you . . .

My father disarms him and throws his stick into the Hudson River. Tyler says, Men, your weapons have been confiscated and consigned to the ammo dump due to . . .

•   •   •

MY BEST FRIENDS in fifth grade are Gail and Susan, who I know from religious instructions at St. Lawrence O'Toole's Church, where we are preparing for Confirmation. We are overjoyed to be in the same class. Also, our parents deem it acceptable for the three of us to walk by ourselves to the library across the street from the church after the Confirmation classes. Gail and Susan sneak off to the five and ten up past the library, but I stay and carefully select the three books I will take home. There is a children's section and an adult section; children cannot go into the adult section until they are twelve. Sometimes I sneak over there and slip an adult book between my two children's books but the librarian never fails to catch it when she checks me out.

Where did you get this? she asks, holding up the offending book.

Over there, I lie, pointing to the children's section.

It was misshelved, she says, and puts it under the counter.

I stay at the library long after Gail and Susan have gone home. I don't tell my father that I walk home alone.

At Mary M. Hooker School, Miss Bowie assigns Gail, Susan, and me a new friend, Magdalena Rodriguez, from Puerto Rico, who is a member of the first Puerto Rican family to move to Charter Oak Terrace. Today, Hartford, Connecticut, is home to the largest Latino population per capita in the United States including New York, Los Angeles, and Miami.

Gail, Susan, and I are to help Magdalena learn English. We get the job as we are smart and finish our work before the other kids do. Miss Bowie has us sit at a corner table with Magdalena, and we are instructed to begin Magdalena's lessons with her colors.

We hold up a red crayon and we speak, loudly and clearly, as Miss Bowie has demonstrated:*Red!*

Magdalena puts her hand over her mouth and her head down.

So we say louder and even more clearly, *Red,* Magdalena! Say, *red!*

She starts chuckling and then we chuckle too, and all we ever end up doing is giggling together so Miss Bowie tells us she is seeing no progress and if she doesn't see progress in another week, she will have to abandon the experiment and try something else. Maybe she will ask Mr. Friedman if Miss Collins, a teacher who knows some Spanish, can tutor Magdalena with her lessons after school in her own language until she learns enough English to manage and therefore not fall behind in her studies. (Miss Bowie's logic, based on experience, is the practical, educationally sound philosophy behind bilingual education before it became a political football.)

Gail, Susan, and I huddle with Magdalena and tell her with a lot of sign language and props that our English lessons with her get us out of extra workbook assignments. Therefore, we must make progress. Magdalena nods. She *understands*. We clamor up to Miss Bowie and tell her Magdalena can't talk English yet but she *understands* English. Miss Bowie is skeptical. I turn toward Magdalena, scrunched down in her seat.

I say, Magdalena, stand up.

Magdalena senses in my voice that I really need her to do this. She stands.

Gail is so enthusiastic she doesn't really think before she commands: Magdalena, lie down!

Magdalena collapses and sprawls on the floor.

Miss Bowie says, Susan, do not tell Magdalena to roll over. Then Miss Bowie says, Magdalena dear, please get up.

Magdalena gets back in her chair.

The class cheers except for three die-hard bullies who laugh at us, and try out the new word they've picked up: *Spic.*

Miss Bowie sends them to Mr. Friedman, which is exactly what she does on the first day of school when they say, regarding Stonewall, I ain't sittin' next to no nigger.

Out on the playground after lunch, Gail, Susan, and I play jump rope with Magdalena. One day, Susan is absent so we need a fourth but no one will play with the spic. It hasn't taken long for the majority of the Mary M. Hooker students to learn to hate, which is the theme of a song from the Broadway hit musical *South Pacific*—Miss

Bowie makes a point to play "You've Got to Be Carefully Taught" from the original cast recording on our classroom record player.

Gail asks Irene to jump rope with us. Irene is so shy no one ever asks her to play with them. She protests, not because Magdalena is a spic, but because she is shy. Gail does not give up and Irene finally agrees.

Magdalena can't speak English but she sure can jump rope. She is an expert at ducking in, taking the transfer of the rope hand-to-hand without missing a beat, and then easing the other person out. We assume kids who live in Puerto Rico must jump rope all day long. We already know Irene can jump rope because, often, she brings a jump rope to school and jumps way over in the corner of the playground by herself. Once Magdalena has proven herself, I—as leader of this particular pack—suggest we go on to Double Dutch. We tie Gail's rope together with Irene's, and then take a minute to practice. Once we're in tune, we take up a classic jump-roping chant while Gail and Magdalena are first to man the ropes, and I the first to jump. We chant:

Pom, pom, pom the girls are marching,
Calling Irene to my door,
Irene is the one who is gonna have the fun
So we don't need Mary-Ann anymore.

I skip out and Irene skips in and we chant some more:

Pom, pom, pom the girls are marching,
Calling Magdalena to my door,
Magdalena is the one who is gonna have the fun
And we don't need Irene anymore.

Magdalena passes the ropes to me, jumps in, Irene skips out, and on we go chanting and jumping until the bell rings. As we coil up our ropes, it dawns on us that Magdalena has been singing the Double

Dutch chant. We dash back into the classroom and announce joyously, Miss Bowie! Magdalena can speak English!

We shove Magdalena in front of us and Gail, Irene, and I start chanting, *Pom, pom, pom, the girls are marching* . . . But up goes Magdalena's hand to cover her mouth and down goes her head. *Giggle, giggle, giggle.*

We finish the song without her and Miss Bowie can see how disappointed Gail and I are so she says, Well, at least you girls got *Irene* to singing. Irene smiles shyly.

The next day everything changes. The world will be tampered with and won't ever be the same again.

twenty

ON DECEMBER 9, an overcast day in the mid-forties with evening rain predicted, Bob Malm left Cedarcrest Sanatorium to head into downtown Hartford for the premier of *Gun Belt*, starring George Montgomery and Tab Hunter. Bob had seen to getting Wednesdays off because Wednesday was the day Hartford movie theaters changed shows.

As he walked to the bus stop in the center of Newington, he was picked up by a pair of fellow workers. He told them he was going to Hartford to catch a movie after attending to a little business downtown. They dropped him at the bus stop, where he only had to wait a few minutes. His bus left Newington and traveled to Hartford via New Britain Avenue, past Hillside Avenue, my neighborhood stop, past the Beaufort Street neighborhood, where Bob had gotten off two weeks earlier, and on to Main Street, Hartford.

Bob stepped off in front of Fox's, and went to the credit department to settle a bill, which he claimed he had already paid. The credit department agreed there'd been a mistake, apologized to Bob, and he went on his way. He needed white undershirts, the uniform of dishwashers. Rather than buy them at Fox's, he hunted out places along Main Street that sold the cheaper brands, the five-and-ten's. Woolworth's, Grant's, and Kresge's. But he couldn't get the price he'd counted on and decided to wait for a sale. Besides, his movie would start in fifteen minutes.

Walking south on Main Street he took a right one block from Fox's, onto Allyn Street, where he went into the Allyn Theater. He didn't catch the first movie on the bill but was just in time for the main feature, *Gun Belt*.

twenty-one

Mickey in navy blue coat, Easter Sunday, 1954

ON December 9, Miss Bowie's fifth grade concludes the study of electricity with a field trip to the Hartford Electric Light Company. Hartford was the first city in the United States to have electricity for all the residents. I don't learn this in the fifth grade but rather in high school while touring Mark Twain's house on Farmington Avenue. Hartford is a very chi-chi place at the time electricity becomes a practical way to bring light to homes, and Hartford's influential, elite citizens—not only Mark and his next-door neighbor, Harriet Beecher Stowe, but others like Samuel Colt, the inventor of the repeating handgun, and Oliver Winchester, whose company, the

New Haven Arms, outproduces Colt when it comes to rifles. They see to it that their city is first to be wired up. Hartford is electrically illuminated while Manhattan still depends on gas, and Connecticut produces more guns than any other place in the world. (This latter is still true although the manufacturing end of the business is outsourced.)

All the kids in Miss Bowie's class look forward to the field trip because it marks the end of studying not only science but everything else, since the trip also signals the beginning of daily rehearsals for the school Christmas pageant. And every afternoon we will build sets and paint posters. Our principal, Albert I. Friedman, is Jewish, so our school's Christmas pageants always feature a dusty cardboard menorah stuck off to the side of the living crèche.

Except for Mary, only boys are in the living crèche. The boys get to be Joseph; they get to be the wise men; they get to be about five dozen shepherds. The most beautiful girl in the sixth grade plays Mary. I am always chosen to be one of the narrators, standing in the dark in front of a microphone reading from Matthew about how there is no room at the inn. None of us know what an inn is aside from the fact that there is never any room in it. I imagine it to be a restaurant with a long line at the door because once a year at Chalker Beach we go to Luigi's Restaurant in the center of Old Saybrook. One year, Luigi says he doesn't have any room so we go to the docks at Old Saybrook Point, stare at Katharine Hepburn's house in case she comes out, and then go back to Luigi's where Luigi has now made room for us.

We also don't know a stable is a barn—imagine it more of a zoo—otherwise we would not be so enamored of Joseph.

I do my narration job thinking the whole time that I am not even pretty enough to be included in the one other role for girls—the Heavenly Host. Before I come to learn the many meanings and grammatical permutations of the word *host,* I think host is short for hostess. There is no room in the inn for Mary and Joseph, and there is no room for all the hostesses on the stage, so they face the audience in a long line on the floor in front of the stage. In front of me. They each hold flashlights inside of toilet paper rolls painted red to look like Christmas candles. Illuminated from below, their faces are ghoul-like, their nostrils appearing as black walnuts. This means that many of the kindergarteners sitting up front on the floor have to be taken out, traumatized.

On an overcast morning, Miss Bowie's class sets off on the field trip, piles into the chartered bus, and zips through Hartford passing through neighborhoods we've never seen before.

Once inside the vast electric plant, we fifth-graders are led to a dingy corner where a man sits at a desk, his space cordoned off by two sheets of plywood braced to the floor. This is the vice president. When we first hear our guide will be the vice president, we are thinking along the lines of the new vice president of the United States. But instead of Richard Nixon, we get a fat, pockmarked guy in overalls. Clean overalls, though, so as to differentiate him from the scores of other men wandering around outside the plywood purportedly bringing electricity to our homes.

All thirty of us fifth-graders, plus Miss Bowie, crowd into the vice president's cordoned-off corner within the plywood. He winks at Miss Bowie a lot while he explains things about electricity to us, but we pay no attention because our eyes are riveted on a girlie calendar nailed up on one of the pieces of plywood behind him. We fidget and snicker and elbow each other. The vice president thinks we are laughing at his jokes and he keeps snickering, too, besides winking at Miss Bowie. I guess the calendar is a fixture to him so its existence probably doesn't register except when he turns to a new month.

The pinup girl for December is wearing a Santa hat and is in profile, one knee up on a chair, her hands stretched out holding the back of it. She is naked except for a filmy nightgown with white fur around the cuffs and hem. Her huge jars are shaped like torpedoes, a piece of ammunition featured prominently in *Jane's Fighting Ships*. I can't take my eyes off them, wondering how a flat human chest can, over a short period of time, develop such incredible appendages.

The vice president and Miss Bowie lead us through the plant. We are bored out of our minds, biding our time till lunch. Shy Irene will be my lunch partner; we will sit across from each other. Miss Bowie has paired everyone up in hopes that no one will get lost when we are turned loose for half an hour at noon to eat and then play cards. Lunch will be undertaken in a dingy room on a long wooden table that is gouged and stained. We climb onto benches on either side of the table across from our partners and take out our lunch bags. The Hartford Electric Light Company provides the milk, which is warm. There is extended talk of puking.

Except when she is sitting, Irene looms over all of us. She is tall for her age and a year older than everybody else besides. I have come to understand that Irene and I have something in common—we both shouldn't be in fifth grade. I am nine though everyone else is ten. This is because my mother took me to the principal of the Charter Oak Terrace Extension School when I was four and had me recite the names of all the states and their capitals. This was to show that I should go to school a year early. The principal agreed to the plan. Irene, on the other hand, repeats first grade, the dreaded result of not keeping up. Which means she is eleven instead of ten. And when you stay back, you're not only shy, you're humiliated and probably de-pressed, the latter a word no one knows in the fifties. Instead we say, blue. I remember my Auntie Yvonne saying to my mother, I've been feeling blue lately. I'm eavesdropping and wishing Auntie Yvonne were feeling blue right then so I could watch her skin become a bril-liant aquamarine.

Irene's big dark eyes are exactly like Loretta Young's, except Loretta's sparkle with merriment and Irene's are lackluster. I under-stand completely that the embarrassment I often feel about such things as improperly buttoned dresses and having a crazy brother even doesn't hold a candle to Irene's shame.

I finagle my way into sitting between my two best friends, Gail and Susan. Magdalena Rodriguez from Puerto Rico isn't on the field trip because she doesn't have the two dollars we are required to bring in to Miss Bowie to pay for our chartered bus. On the day the money is due and Magdalena doesn't have it, Miss Bowie goes to the intercom and calls Miss Collins, a second grade teacher.

Think you can translate a note into Spanish for me? she asks. We hear Miss Collins's scratchy voice: I'll give it a whirl. Then Miss Bowie scribbles a note and selects me to bring it to Miss Collins. At the end of the day a new note comes back. Miss Bowie gives it to Magdalena and says to her, For your *madre*.

The next day Miss Bowie goes over to Magdalena and asks quietly, Did you give your *madre* the note? Magdalena nods. What did she say?

She say no.

Miss Bowie pats her shoulder and says, Magdalena, I think your madre will let you go on next year's field trip when you are a bigger girl.

Miss Bowie does not correct Magdalena's grammar; her feeling being one step at a time.

IRENE AND I both have bananas in our lunch bag. We have a race to see which of us can eat our bananas the fastest. Gail, who wears a Bulova wristwatch, times us. Irene beats me by three seconds but Susan protests.

Susan says, Irene swallowed after Mary-Ann's last swallow.

I haven't a competitive bone in my body so I say, It doesn't matter who won.

One of the boys informs me that I'm actually a sore sport.

I say, Okay, Irene won. Then I say to the boy, Mind your own business, Bozo.

Gail says, Yeah.

Susan says to him, So just shut up.

Irene doesn't say anything. Instead she takes out a bag of Oreos and shares them with us, even the Bozo.

Irene's cookies are the part of our field trip we enjoy most.

The bus arrives back at Mary M. Hooker School after the final bell. Mr. Friedman has to call everyone's parents to tell them we will be arriving home late. My mother decides not to wait for me, to leave Tyler alone since he's sleeping anyway, so no one picks up the phone at my house. She has put a pillow over the phone to muffle the ring; taking the phone off the hook is no longer the solution to risking Tyler's being awakened from his daytime sleep because in the primitive telephone system of the fifties, this screws up a lot of lines in addition to ours and we get a call from the phone company telling us not to do that.

I say to Mr. Friedman, My mother works.

No one picks up the phone at Irene's either. Irene says softly, My mother works, too.

I meet Irene's Loretta Young eyes.

Mr. Friedman says, Who watches you girls after school?

Irene says, My brother.

Your brother?

Irene speaks more softly yet: Fred. He's in high school. He's probably outside.

Mr. Friedman looks to me. Mary-Ann?

My brother.

Is your brother in high school?

He's fourteen.

Mr. Friedman doesn't know my brother is crazy and not allowed to go to high school or any other school. This is before we become a litigious society so no one has ever thought to sue the Hartford Board of Education for denying Tyler his constitutional right to a free education. In the fifties, no one goes around applying the Constitution to life.

Mr. Friedman lets Irene and me walk home by ourselves. Irene heads down the hill to Charter Oak Terrace and I head up toward Nilan Street.

That night, when I am getting ready for bed, a dog down the street won't stop barking. Tyler is upstairs in his bed. Soon he will wake up for the night. Just as my father gets into his jacket in order to go out and find the appropriate neighbor and tell him to stifle his dog, the dog stops barking. Good. Now Tyler won't wake up biting his wrist before he's even had breakfast.

twenty-two

O<small>N</small> D<small>ECEMBER</small> 9, Bob Malm left the Allyn at six forty-five and had dinner at the White Tower restaurant, a burger joint. Bob finished his meal, walked south on Main Street, then took a right on Asylum Street. Crossing streets to the west and heading south between them, he was aimed in the general direction of Newington though he could have chosen a more direct route, staying on Main until he reached New Britain Avenue. But he preferred residential areas, streets packed with quiet little homes on eighth-acre city lots, full of children.

He walked across the Trinity College campus, along Fraternity Row, until he reached Zion Street, bordering Trinity on the west. He strolled along Zion until he saw a lighted storefront just down Ward Street. It was the Lincoln Dairy.

He went in. There were no children there, no young girls. He had a cup of coffee. Maybe he sat on Tyler's stool.

He paid for the coffee, left the dairy, and continued down Ward until he came out at Hillside Avenue, the street he'd been looking for. He took a left on Hillside and headed south knowing he would eventually come to New Britain Avenue, his bus route. He knew there was a bus stop at the corner of Hillside and New Britain Avenue, my neighborhood stop, two and a half blocks from where I lived on Nilan Street.

Directly across New Britain Avenue from the stop itself on the northeast corner was a drugstore where, as a teenager, my friends and I would order a soapsuds, a concoction made of milk, syrup, and soda water, known as an egg cream in New York City.

Across Hillside and kitty-corner to the bus stop was a small grocery store called Jack's. Its real name was the United Food Store, but no one knew that. The owner's name was Jack and so the store was called Jack's. Every year Jack strung a clothesline from his ceiling. Hanging from the clothesline were the pictures of the Miss Rheingold contestants. This was a promotion for Rheingold Beer and you had to be eighteen to vote for Miss Rheingold but Jack lets us kids vote anyway.

Jack's was where we'd go when we had to grab a loaf of bread, or a quart of milk if our supply didn't last through the weekly milk delivery. One time my father sent me there to pick up one hot dog for my dinner as I didn't like what he was making for himself and Tyler—boiled kielbasa. Even though he tried to convince me that kielbasa was just a fancy hotdog, I didn't agree. I hated the way the kielbasa skin burst while it was boiling forcing a disgusting lump of its stuffing to stick out. When I was living in Charter Oak Terrace I saw a little dog get run over by a truck. Its skin burst and a lump of its stuffing sprung out. And the doctor who opened up Carl Luzzi's stomach probably released the oatmeal cancer in the same way.

I walked to Jack's and I asked for my one hotdog. Jack said, What're ya havin'? A party? I was mortified.

Next to Jack's on Hillside was the five-and-ten where I bought my mother a beautiful pin for Mother's Day. The pin turned out to be a curtain tieback. My mother opened her present and laughed hysterically. This was much better than the time my second grade class made candleholders for Mother's Day out of empty Wisk bottles. My mother opened her gift and said, Dear God, what the hell are those teachers thinking? Then she threw it in the wastebasket.

While Bob Malm had been drinking his coffee at the Lincoln Dairy, my friend Irene was having dinner with her mother and her brother, Fred, who rushed through the meal and at five forty-five went off to a nearby elementary school to watch a basketball game. Irene's mother told him to be home by eight. After he left, she wanted to cook potatoes for a cold salad for dinner the next night. Since she worked all day, she had to get this chore taken care of right then. She worked as a cleaning woman at a warehouse that stored sheaves of tobacco, floor to ceiling. It was the same job my father first gave Freddie Ravenel at the Abbott Ball Company. Irene's mother, like Freddie Ravenel, did not expect a promotion, but Freddie got one though he was a colored man. Irene's mother wouldn't because she was a woman.

But there weren't enough potatoes so she sent Irene to a neighbor's to borrow a few. But the neighbor didn't have potatoes to spare. Irene stayed at the neighbor's for a while and watched the *Camel News Caravan* with John Cameron Swayze. When she returned home, her mother was going to let it go but Irene had come back from her field trip with her cookie bag empty and now she was wishing she'd saved a few.

Irene's mother looked out the window; several children were playing under the streetlight. One of them was Kathy Delaney. Irene was told she could run out to Jack's to pick up a new box of cookies and also two pounds of potatoes. She told her to hurry right back because it was going to rain. Maybe some of the kids outside were going to the store, too, and she could join them.

Irene put on the same jacket she wore on the field trip, red with a fake fur collar. Around her neck was a square silk scarf—if it rained, she could put it over her head babushka-style. The temperature was not quite cold enough for her angora hat. We all wore silk scarves in those days. My mother even had a couple by Vera, who was the marquee scarf designer—the Hermès of the fifties—but at a hundredth of the price.

Irene left her house at D-10, Charter Oak Terrace, which was on Dart Street, the southern border of the D section of the Terrace. Her mother watched her cross the courtyard out back, and then Chandler Street, the east border of the Terrace and up Dart Street until she couldn't see her any longer. It was six forty-five.

The children playing under the streetlight were gone now.

Irene walked up Dart Street to the end and took a left on Broadview Terrace, a ridge fifty feet higher than Chandler down below, a lovely street where a mayor named Nilan had built the first house in the neighborhood at the corner of what would become my street.

One block from Dart, on the corner of Sequin Street, Irene ran into Kathy Delaney and the other children. She asked them if they were going to the store so she could walk with them. They said no, they were just out playing and had to go home soon. She joined them in a game of climbing onto the big steel mailbox on the corner of Sequin and Broadview and jumping off. Then Irene had to get going. It was seven-ten.

Irene walked one block past the rear of St. Lawrence O'Toole's Church and took a right on the next street, Coolidge, which ran along the side of the church. St. Lawrence O'Toole's was having a new church built on top of the old one. The old church's roof had been raised and replaced with a concrete slab so that, even with the new church, there would be a spare one downstairs for Midnight Mass overflow. The new St. Lawrence O'Toole's was one of the very few big Catholic churches built in the fifties anywhere. Just like fifties furniture, the whole church was blond. It was blond inside and out; the bricks were blond and the walls inside were painted blond. The statues were carved from pale oak and blended right in.

When the church was consecrated, the parishioners asked Father Kelly when the artist intended to paint the statues. My mother hissed, Damn fools.

The crucified Christ, forty feet long, hanging above the altar was also carved oak. He was not looking up to God saying, Father, Father, why hast thou forsaken me? which is the typical pose. This artist chose instead to show a dead Christ and so Jesus's head was slumped down onto his chest. Mommy Welch said to me, It's very sad but at least his suffering is over.

After Irene passed the church, she crossed Coolidge Street before it merged with New Britain Avenue, which veered off to her right. On the other side of Coolidge was our little branch library, a dark, squat Gothic building in stark contrast to the blond church growing across

114

the street. The library marked the spot where Coolidge Street ended at New Britain Avenue.

On the library side of New Britain Avenue, Irene walked along the sidewalk over a tiny brook, one of the hundreds of offshoots of the Hog River, past the Brookside Tavern on her left and then into Jack's store. In just one square mile, my neighborhood had a school, a church, a library, a five-and-ten, a drugstore, a tavern, and a grocery store. Small-town America, really. Downtown Hartford was another planet, a place where your mother took you to buy your Easter outfit.

Jack saw Irene come in. His clerk weighed the potatoes. Irene bought her two items with a dollar bill and put the change, sixty-one cents, in her little change purse. Maybe Jack asked her, What're ya havin'? A party?

Across the street, Bob stood in front of the drugstore and watched a teenage couple come out of the grocery store, Brenda and Charlie, who lived in Charter Oak Terrace and were both seventeen years old. They headed west toward home. A few minutes later, a little girl came out. A little girl holding a grocery bag. A little girl who was clearly alone. Irene. It was seven twenty-five.

Bob followed Irene from New Britain Avenue to Coolidge Street and left on Broadview Terrace until she reached Sequin Street. Normally, Irene didn't walk home down Sequin Street, but that night she did, probably because a soldier had passed her when she crossed Coolidge—perhaps he'd made her nervous. There were houses on both sides of Sequin; safety in numbers is perhaps what Irene instinctively felt.

Dart Street had houses only on one side; on the other, undeveloped wooded lots. Besides, Irene probably saw that the teenage couple—Brenda and Charlie—had turned down Sequin. She probably couldn't see Kathy and the other kids in the light mist just forming. They were now playing a game of leap-off-the-wall behind the St. Lawrence O'Toole rectory down Broadview Terrace. It was a retaining wall, the property leveled off below to create a parking lot. If she had, she might have joined them again.

From behind her, Bob Malm said, Hello.

He approached her and she said hello back even though she knew not to speak to strangers. It is difficult to reconcile that rule with the rule to be polite. It was seven thirty-five.

Bob grabbed both ends of her scarf, twisted them, and pulled her to him. She pulled away and he yanked her back.

Kathy Delaney and her pals had left their jump-off-the-wall game when they'd spotted a couple turning into Sequin Street who they assumed to be Brenda and Charlie. It was even darker now, drizzling, and they couldn't see too well. They decided to have one more game before they went home; they would play a game they called Detective and follow the couple walking down Sequin Street.

Kathy saw the girl she thought was Brenda twirl away from the boy she thought was Charlie, and then twirl back. The couple was too far away for Kathy to recognize that Brenda was actually Irene and Charlie was a stranger.

Halfway down Sequin Street there was an empty lot. The family that lived in the house next to the lot had bought the double-size property in the thirties planning to expand the house into the spare lot. They never expanded the house and they never sold the lot either. Instead, they kept their small boat on it. As Bob dragged Irene alongside the lot on Sequin Street, he spotted the rowboat up on blocks. He pushed and pulled at her, dragged her along until he had her under the boat with him.

He'd hidden himself and Irene under the boat because he was aware of Kathy Delaney and her friends a block away. He twisted the scarf tighter so that Irene couldn't cry out. He would conceal himself and Irene under the boat until the children left the area.

The "detectives" meanwhile—once they reached the corner of Sequin Street—had lost sight of the couple they thought were Brenda and Charlie. They decided to go home via Sequin Street since they were there. Halfway down the street, the overturned boat beckoned to them. Children love to throw stones. They throw them at each other, into water, at the sky, and at their greatest preference, windows. A boat up on blocks would do. Kathy and her friends picked up stones from the gravel driveway and fired them, pelting the boat. Then they heard a harsh, deep voice shout, *Beat it!*

They dropped their stones and ran. When they were out of breath, they slowed down, laughed and laughed, thrilled. When children are spotted throwing stones, the most fun part is fleeing without getting caught. It was seven forty-five.

Kathy decided it was time to get home. The drizzle had become a light rain. The children ran off.

But Irene could not run away from Bob Malm.

Bob saw a boy with a dog come out of the house next to the lot. He knew he was not in a good spot to do what he intended to do to Irene. The boat was barely big enough to hide them. Once the boy and the dog went back inside, he dragged Irene out from under the boat by her scarf and pulled her to the back of the empty lot, somehow got her over a chain-link fence, and then dragged her across the adjoining backyard on Coolidge Street. She was crying and struggling so he twisted the scarf more. He looked up and down the rows of backyards but didn't see what he wanted.

He ran Irene across Coolidge Street in the dark interval between two streetlights. He headed down a driveway separating two houses and saw a picket fence in the rear of the backyard to his right. Behind the fence he could just make out a shed. Perfect. My own yard on Nilan Street, which backed up to another Coolidge Street yard, also had a shed where my father kept the lawn mower and snow shovels. But Bob had found one to suit. The yard he chose belonged to a police officer, Michael Proccacino, and his wife. The couple had no children.

The door in the shed was locked but Bob was, by then, so sexually aroused he'd take his chances in the darkness between the fence and the shed. He'd have to hurry; he heard a dog barking. Inside the house, Officer Proccacino and his wife argued about their dog. Mrs. Proccacino went to the kitchen window. It was pitch black outside and raining. She said, Probably a skunk. The couple gave the dog pork chop bones.

Bob Malm threw Irene to the ground and unzipped his pants. Then he yanked down her slacks. Her panties came with them and one shoe. He kissed her face, he felt her genitals, he took out his penis, he rubbed against her, he ejaculated. He did not penetrate her. Bob Malm had never been able to keep from having an ejaculation long enough to complete intercourse.

During the assault he let the scarf tighten and loosen so he could hear Irene gasping and choking for air.

He stood up. He pulled Irene to her feet. He got her dressed and then he told her not to tell anyone. But she managed a courageous act. She said, I will tell. I'm going to tell my mother.

So Bob grabbed the two ends of the scarf again and this time tied a knot as tight as he could. Then he made a square knot just to make sure the scarf wouldn't loosen. It was the simple square knot the seamen of the U.S. Navy used to secure equipment on the deck of their ships. Irene stopped struggling to breathe and fell to the ground.

Bob heard someone yelling at the barking dog. He took Irene's shoe, which had come off with her slacks, and tried to put it on her foot. But he didn't bother to untie the laces and couldn't get it on properly. He noticed her panties lying in the grass. He stuffed the panties under the corner of the shed. Then he went down on one knee, looked at Irene one last time, her arms were thrown up over her head, a final physical effort to escape Bob Malm as she fell dying.

Fifty minutes had gone by from the time Bob dragged Irene under the boat with him to hide from Kathy Delaney and the other children. It was eight twenty-five.

Bob hustled back to the corner of Hillside and New Britain Avenue to grab the first bus that came along. The bus picked him up at eight forty. It was the Hillside Avenue bus, not the bus to Newington, but Bob didn't care.

The rain was coming down heavily.

• • •

IRENE'S BROTHER FRED arrived home at eight to find his mother frantic. Irene hadn't returned home from the store and she'd phoned everyone in the neighborhood. No one had seen Irene. She sent Fred out to look for her. He went out into the rain all the way to Jack's store taking Sequin Street. When he passed 80 Sequin shouting his sister's name, he was parallel with 80 Coolidge Street, where Bob Malm was murdering his sister. Maybe Irene heard him calling her name.

When Fred reached Jack's, it was closed. The store had closed at eight. Fred ran all the way back home again and never passed a soul. He just missed crossing paths with Bob Malm rushing to the bus stop.

Fred returned home without Irene. His mother got her coat and insisted the two of them go out again. First, they went directly to their neighbors, including the Delaneys. Mr. Delaney had Kathy come into the kitchen and asked her if she'd seen Irene. Kathy said to Irene's mother, Yes. She and some kids had seen Irene on her way to the store. No, they never saw her after that.

Irene's mother and Fred went up and down the streets all the way to Jack's store and back. They had one last hope; they stopped at a home on Sequin Street two doors from the empty lot with the boat. They were friendly with the family—the people used to live in Charter Oak Terrace. Maybe Irene wanted to get out of the rain and stopped there. Once inside, she saw that one of her favorite shows, *Arthur Godfrey's Amateur Hour,* was on TV and stayed awhile, meaning to call home but forgetting because of the distraction. Irene loved television. But no member of the Sequin Street family had seen Irene that night. They looked at Irene's mother and brother oddly. Such a friendly visit from Irene was entirely out of character. Irene was just too bashful to do such a thing. Irene's mother and her brother Fred were surviving on wishful thinking.

When they arrived home at D-10, they were soaking wet and they called the police. It was nine twenty-five.

Soon, the cop on cruiser patrol in the southwest corner of Hartford was crawling the streets looking for Irene. He didn't stop though, didn't knock on any doors, didn't search any backyards—just cruised before returning to D-10. He made suggestions to Irene's mother: Maybe your daughter took the bus downtown; maybe she went to a friend's; maybe she ran away from home. Irene's mother insisted Irene was a timid girl with no really close friends and that she would never run away from home. The police officer wondered aloud to Irene's mother as to why the girl was allowed to be out after dark. Her mother said all the neighborhood kids walked to the store; they all knew they had to be home by eight o'clock. In fact, she'd seen several children outside playing that evening.

But my friends and I—just one block away from the increasingly poverty-stricken residents of Charter Oak Terrace—were not allowed outside after dark. When the streetlights came on, we came in. My parents both drove; no need to send me off to the store for potatoes. Irene's father had deserted his family five years earlier. The trip home from the tobacco warehouse was a long one for Irene's mother; it required a bus ride from the warehouse to Main Street and then a transfer to the New Britain Avenue bus, and then a mile walk home from the corner of Hillside. She was a single mother. She depended on her children to do things like run out to the store for her. Even after dark. After all, there was no crime in our neighborhood. It was the last days of nobody-locks-their-doors-in-Hartford.

BOB SAW A BAR from the window of the Hillside Avenue bus. He got off at the next stop, walked back to the bar, went in, and asked the bartender if he could call a taxi. The bartender took the phone from under the counter and put it on the bar in front of Bob, who called a yellow cab and then ordered a beer. The cab was there in a couple of minutes and Bob left his half-finished beer behind.

He was back at the sanatorium fifteen minutes later. He changed his clothes and went down to the recreation room. Everyone was talking about the contestant on *Strike It Rich* who had won over a thou-

sand dollars. That show had just ended. Now Bob joined them to watch, incredibly, *Dragnet,* which had come on at nine thirty. A few stayed on with him for the ten o'clock fights. At eleven he went to bed but couldn't sleep because he began to quiver and shake uncontrollably. A shaking stupor like at Pearl Harbor.

Officer Michael Proccacino left for work at 11:30 P.M. after dozing on and off through the fights on television. His wife was in bed. It had been three hours since a little girl was strangled in his backyard and her body left lying in the rain next to his toolshed.

He changed, got in his car, turned on the ignition and the windshield wipers and lights, and immediately looked over his shoulder in order to back out of the driveway. If he had looked at his backyard illuminated by his headlights, he might have seen Irene's body just on the other side of the white picket fence in front of his toolshed. But then again, he might not have because the rain was falling heavily as midnight approached. No one had called him about the child who had gone missing right there in his neighborhood. When he arrived at police headquarters a few minutes before twelve, he took off his rain gear, shook out the coat, hung it up, and went to his office.

At 12:03 A.M., he received the first radio dispatch of the evening concerning a missing child. He passed it back to the radio dispatcher to transmit to all cruisers on patrol. Cops walking their midnight beats were not sent the dispatch. Missing children always turned up. Sometimes in their own beds. In addition, this particular child lived in Charter Oak Terrace. The cops weren't feeling the pressure they'd have had placed upon them if it had been a little rich girl from West Hartford.

It was a quiet night. There were no updates on the missing child throughout Officer Proccacino's shift.

At seven the next morning, his shift ended and he called his wife to wake her, which was his habit, and went out to his car. The rain had stopped.

Over the next half hour, Mrs. Proccacino got dressed and cooked

121

breakfast. She was just finishing when she heard her husband's car pull into the driveway at seven-thirty. Officer Proccacino's headlights lit up his yard for the instant prior to his turning them off. The light bounced off the white picket fence, something the officer was vaguely aware of. He came through the back door just as his wife went to the kitchen sink, where she happened to glance out the window. The sky was overcast and the feeble light of a winter morning was even dimmer than usual but she noticed what seemed to be a pile of clothes between the picket fence and the toolshed. Mrs. Proccacino thought laundry had blown off the clothesline next door in the previous night's rainstorm.

When the police officer walked into the kitchen, he was about to tell his wife of the child gone missing from Charter Oak Terrace—the D section just down the street—when she said to him, What's that outside, Mike? The laundry from next door?

Officer Proccacino peered through the window and knew instantly what he was seeing between the fence and the shed. His brain registered the color red and then it registered *body*. He knew the missing child had been wearing a red jacket. As he raced outside, he remembered how his dog had been barking the night before. His stomach turned over.

He stood beside Irene and then bent down. Her face was swollen and blue. A trickle of blood was coming from her nose and a few drops had spilled onto her jacket. Around her neck was a silk scarf tied so tightly that it was sunk deep into her neck. He noted the bulky knot. Officer Proccacino knew Irene was dead but he followed procedure. Without moving her outflung arm, he felt Irene's wrist for a pulse.

Then he stood and ran back to the house. As he dialed headquarters, he said to his wife, We had a report of a missing child last night. She's out behind our fence and she's dead.

Mrs. Proccacino grabbed a kitchen chair and put it behind her husband's knees and he sank into it. Within minutes, the yard at 80 Coolidge Street was overrun with police officers, the first, Policewoman Ellen Brown, one of Hartford's two policewomen, who was

on foot patrol nearest to the address. The Hartford Police Department was the first in the country to hire female police officers for jobs other than taking dictation. They could not be placed in line for promotion though. Policewoman Brown couldn't believe that no one had told her about a child who was missing from her own neighborhood beat.

There was no crime lab in Hartford. The state had a coroner's office and the coroner had a medical examiner available to him. But the coroner could not be reached and neither could his assistant, so the backup from West Hartford, Dr. Harry Allen, was called up on the Proccacinos' kitchen phone. He arrived fifteen minutes later. He examined the scarf around Irene's neck. Dr. Allen asked, We got a Navy man here?

One of the cops stepped forward. He had survived the attack on Pearl Harbor. He looked down at Irene, scrutinized the scarf around her neck and said, That's your basic square knot. We do it neater than civilians. We do it like that.

Captain Jimmy Egan, head of the Vice Squad arrived. Egan looked down at Irene and remembered the station house talk two weeks earlier of a possible assault that took place on Beaufort Street. He feared he might have a rapist on his hands, one who had turned to murder. (This was a time when the word *serial* meant a short film played before the main feature and was not applied to rapists or killers.) At that point, Egan decided to wait before telling the chief his suspicions. He would first check out the report filed on the Beaufort Street attack. Egan knew he'd somehow have to find a few minutes at headquarters to hunt up the report and read it right away. Every police officer in Hartford would soon be on the streets, including him. Especially him.

While the crowd of cops on the scene expressed relief that Irene was fully clothed, obviously hadn't been sexually assaulted, Egan scanned the ground where she lay. He noted her shoe half off and then he saw a sliver of pink silk under the corner of the toolshed.

Just then, Hartford's Chief of Police, Michael J. Godfrey, came running into the yard. He looked down at Irene and then followed Jimmy Egan's gaze to the corner of the shed and what lay beneath.

twenty-three

WHEN WE COME to school the next day, all of us in Miss Bowie's class talking about the high point of our field trip to the Hartford Electric Light Company—the girlie calendar—some sixth-graders arrive all excited. We are drawn to their elite circle.

Irene is *missing!* they say.

Missing? We look around. Irene isn't in the playground.

She was *kidnapped!*

We look around again. No Irene.

One of the boys says, She's probably out sick.

I say, Yeah!

I tell Gail and Susan and Magdalena that the warm milk at the Hartford Electric Light Company probably made Irene sick.

We don't wait for the bell to line up to go in. We are already at the door pushing and shoving as soon as we hear its grating *bbbrrring.* We pour down the halls. Gail, Susan, Magdalena and I lead the crush into Miss Bowie's classroom. Miss Bowie is standing behind her desk facing the door, waiting for us. Normally, she is flitting around the room, pinning stuff up on the bulletin board, or storing new packages of manila paper on the shelves under the windows. My friends and I stop, and the rest of our classmates behind crash into us.

The days are at their shortest in December. The electric lights are on in the early morning dimness. They make the room a sickly yellow. I notice for the first time that the electric light from the Hartford Electric Light Company is not the color of real light.

Miss Bowie doesn't move a muscle. She says, Go to the cloakroom, hang up your coats, and then please sit down at your desks.

We follow her orders, stuff our mittens into our pockets, put our hats up on the shelf over the hooks, and hang up our coats. Miss Bowie does not have to call out or stick her head in the cloakroom door to shush us, to hurry us along as she normally does. We are not speaking and we are not dawdling.

We sit at our desks gazing up at Miss Bowie with our huge need to know whether or not it is true—whether or not Irene has been kidnapped.

She says, There will be no speaking of Irene.

Of Irene. Not *about*. The difference in the two words is big to me.

We are appalled, not that we shouldn't speak *of* Irene, whatever that means, but because the sixth-graders' rumor is true. Gail leans over and whispers to me, They must have found a ransom note!

Miss Bowie assigns two boys to take Irene's desk out from her row and carry it to the door for the janitor to put in storage. Gail raises her hand.

Miss Bowie says, We are not to talk of it.

Gail says, I know, Miss Bowie, but shouldn't we get her things out?

Miss Bowie says, I have emptied the desk.

The removal of Irene's empty desk from our classroom is very solemn. The janitor doesn't make eye contact with us as he lifts it up and takes it away.

We are stricken that Miss Bowie won't wait out Irene's kidnapping before removing her desk from the classroom. Or maybe she thinks Irene won't be back until next year. Or maybe it is a signal to us that no matter when Irene is returned, even if it's next year, she won't stay back yet again, won't have to repeat fifth grade.

Miss Bowie has us all move up one place, and Irene's space is filled in with the desk of the boy who sits behind her. I look at him. His name is Danny. What is *Danny* doing in Irene's place? The change means I have to go from the front of my row to the back of the next. But Miss Bowie puts me in front again because I have trouble seeing the board and need to be up close. I won't get glasses for two years because my mother thinks I am faking the school eye exams. I sort of do; I say—*E!*—when the school nurse points to the top of the eye chart because I know there is an *E* there, not because I can see it.

A sound finally breaks the dead silence in our classroom. Magdalena is crying. Miss Bowie comes down the rows and puts her arm around Magdalena's shoulders. Magdalena is the only one who intuits that Irene is dead.

When Miss Bowie looks up she says, Line up at the door for the Christmas pageant rehearsal.

Susan, Gail, and I make a plan to tutor Irene on the work she'll miss, just like we tutor Magdalena.

THE HARTFORD TIMES arrives every evening just minutes before my father gets home from work at five-fifteen. Each night, once Tyler and I have finished playing Crazy Eights and a game of Monopoly, I bring it in and read the funnies. I especially love Dondi, the World War II orphan adopted and raised by the most loving and caring parents a child could hope for. Dondi is six when I start reading him. I am six, too. When I am nine and in the fifth grade, Dondi is still six. I am about to realize that despite his trials as an orphan, he is not only a lucky boy to have been adopted by perfect parents, he is also lucky in that he will never have to be nine years old.

When my father comes home from work that is how he usually finds me—reading Dondi and the other comic strips. Then I go on to the rest of the paper while my father cooks dinner. On this night, I listen for the paper boy and open the door when I hear his footsteps on the back porch. He hands me the paper. He isn't smiling the way he usually is and he doesn't say, Hi, kid. I take the paper, bring it inside the house, and unfold it. Irene stares up at me from the front page with her big Loretta Young eyes, Irene at seven years old, in her First Communion dress and veil, a big grin on her face. Irene clearly *did* giggle, only at home, rarely at school, where she felt humiliated.

I read the headlines—big, black, bold, block letters—stretching from one side of the front page to the other.

126

GIRL, 11, STRANGLED WITH HER OWN SCARF FOUND BY POLICEMAN IN COOLIDGE ST. YARD

Every article on the front page is about Irene and what happened to her. I sit down at the kitchen table and begin to read.

At seven-thirty that morning, the morning after our trip to the Hartford Electric Light Company, just at the time my father calls me to get up for school, Irene's body was found. It was found in a backyard on Coolidge Street in a yard behind Nilan. Eighty Coolidge Street. An even number. My house is at 75 Nilan Street. That means Irene's body was lying in the backyard of a house just down from my yard right next to a boy named Barry's yard. Barry lives on Coolidge Street next door to a cop. Good thing, my mother said once, he's a ticking time bomb. Barry will later go on to become a juvenile delinquent.

When the school bell rings, nobody knows about Irene's death except the police, Irene's family, and our principal, Albert I. Friedman, who tells Miss Bowie. The media is informed but the police ask that the news be held back until after school begins so that the children won't know about it till they're safe in their classrooms. Best the news is broken to the children by their teacher.

And it is.

There will be no speaking of Irene.

That is how the news is broken.

The local television and radio stations agree to hold off on the story of Irene until after the school bells ring.

I read every one of the articles. When I am reading them for the third or fourth time, I hear my father's car flying into the driveway, the gravel clattering into the side of the house. He always tells people to drive slowly into the driveway because the sound of the gravel hitting our new aluminum siding disturbs Tyler. Tonight he doesn't put Tyler first, ahead of all other things. That's never happened before and it will never happen again.

I hear his running steps. He throws open the back door and,

127

breathless, stares at me in my chair at the kitchen table, the *Hartford Times* spread out in front of me. I am looking up at him.

I ask, What's rape?

He grabs up the newspaper. He rasps: Go to your room!

I don't question why I have to go to my room because of my catechism lesson: The worst sin you can commit against an adult, particularly against your mother and father, is to ask *Why?* when they tell you to do something. Honor Thy Father and Thy Mother.

From upstairs, I hear the sounds of my father cooking. Half an hour later he calls me for dinner. First, I bring Tyler his three eggs and three slices of spam, and place them on the table next to his latest *Jane's All the World's Aircraft* which engrosses him. In the kitchen, I have one pork chop on my own plate, my father, two. We have fried potatoes and applesauce. We have pineapple upside-down cake for dessert. My mother bakes on Saturday and brings her cakes and pies to her Saturday night card game. If there are any leftovers, she brings them back home as is the case this week.

We eat. There is no sign of the *Hartford Times*.

Then my father watches *I Remember Mama* with me, tells me to get ready for bed, hears my prayers, lets me read for half an hour, comes back to my room, and instead of telling me a story, which is his habit, he recites a poem:

"My name is Ozymandias, King of Kings.
Look upon my works, ye Mighty, and despair!"

The poem is apropos of nothing. It is the equivalent of Miss Bowie's saying: *There will be no speaking of Irene.*

twenty-four

PIDGIE D'ALLESSIO'S FATHER picked up the *Hartford Times* after work. Like my own father, he sped home; his wife had already heard. Pidgie had, too. He found her in her bedroom holding a pillow to her chest, his wife sitting in a chair by the bed. Pidgie's friend from around the corner was sitting on the floor. All three looked up at Mr. D'Allessio standing in the doorway. He said, It had to be him.

He walked back to the kitchen and they heard him call police headquarters. He demanded to speak to the officer who had come to their house the night Pidgie was attacked. The family had heard nothing from the police since that night. In the fifties, charging a man with a sexual offense against a teenager was rare—too difficult to prove that the teenager didn't victimize her rapist with her wiles.

When the officer got the message, Pidgie's story came back to him. Before that, he hadn't put together what Pidgie said happened to her and the murder of the little girl. He was under the impression that the little girl was not sexually assaulted. But he'd been ordered, as had all the Hartford cops, that if they came upon the slimmest shred of information, the smallest glimmer of possibility, they were to call the chief's office. That is what the officer did. He spoke to a detective and the detective put him on the line with Chief Michael J. Godfrey, who listened and then proceeded to blow up.

The chief called Captain Egan. Jimmy Egan explained to his chief that the D'Allessio girl hadn't been raped or injured, though there were a couple of marks on the neck that may have been hickies. He told Chief Godfrey that the officer who took the call had also noted that the girl was quite attractive and her father subject to histrionics.

The officer had taken a cursory ride around the neighborhood and concluded there were no signs of a pervert.

Chief Godfrey blew up again. When he was finished raving, Egan told him they were working with the state police, had cast a wide net, and were dragging in all known perverts in Connecticut.

Chief Godfrey himself called the D'Allessios and told Pidgie's father he needed to speak with his daughter. Mr. D'Allessio put Pidgie on the phone. The chief said to her: Young lady, could you identify the man who attacked you?

Pidgie said, Yes.

And would you be willing to come into headquarters to identify him directly once we've caught him?

Yes.

Good girl. And, Pidgie, when the man attacked you, did he speak to you?

Yes.

Would you agree to come into the same room with the man, listen to him speak so you could be sure he was the one?

There was a pause. Then Pidgie said, Yes.

The chief spoke to Pidgie's father and told him what his brave daughter had agreed to do.

Mr. D'Allessio said, Listen, when you know who the sonofabitch is who did it, just tell me where to find him. I'll take care of the bastard for you.

After the chief hung up, he and Egan looked at Pidgie's file. It wasn't especially detailed. The girl claimed she was choked with her scarf and then assaulted but not raped. All the chief said to Egan was: Jesus Christ, Jimmy.

The chief read Pidgie's description of her assailant—a tall, dark man. Then he called Mr. D'Allessio back to tell him that he and a couple of officers were coming to the house to have Pidgie describe the man again. He apologized for having to put Pidgie through this.

Mr. D'Allessio said, My daughter's a tough cookie. Tougher than me.

130

The chief could tell the man had been crying. Not surprising since Pidgie's father must have come to understand what a miracle it was that his daughter was alive.

Chief Godfrey and Captain Egan drove the few blocks to Beaufort and Franklin Avenue accompanied by the other Hartford police-woman, Vera Conroy, who had been the first hired and had gone beyond walking the beat to detective duties though receiving no promotion in rank or pay in accordance with policy.

Mr. D'Allessio answered the door and led the three into his living room. Pidgie and her mother sat on the sofa. Pidgie's father sat down on her other side and the cops took the chairs facing them. Again, Pidgie described the man as tall, and dark-haired, but with prompting from Policewoman Conroy, she said he had a normal voice.

The chief said, I need you to think hard here, Pidgie. Is there anything else about the man who attacked you that you can tell us about. Other than his being tall and dark.

Pidgie said, He had black hair.

What else?

Pidgie looked up into the chief's eyes and then she said, His cigarettes fell out of his pocket.

She shuddered but she went on: He picked them up and put them back . . . back in his pocket.

The chief said, Pidgie, but do you remember what kind of cigarettes they were?

Yes.

Everyone waited. Pidgie took a deep breath. Old Golds.

The chief said, That will be very helpful to us. Thank you. Now I know how hard this must be for you, but was there anything else? Anything at all?

Another deep breath. Pidgie said, He had a pin on his coat.

Pidgie began to shiver. Mrs. D'Allessio took off her own sweater and draped it over her daughter's shoulders. Everyone in the room waited.

Chief Godfrey said, What do you remember about the pin?

It said, *Blood Donor.*

The chief said, Very good.

He would press his luck: Is that all then?

Pidgie said, I remember something else . . .

Pidgie was now staring down at her feet. The cops and the D'Allessios could barely hear her when she whispered: I think something was wrong with his eyes.

Her father leapt up; the questioning was getting to him. He shouted, His eyes? What the hell is that supposed to mean? What was wrong with them?

Then Mr. D'Allessio launched into a tirade about how hard he'd worked to give his family a good home in a nice neighborhood and then this happens.

Policewoman Conroy asked Pidgie gently, What was wrong with his eyes, honey?

She answered, They weren't normal. I mean, not like his voice was normal. His eyes . . . They were . . . they were always in the dark.

With his hand gripping Mr. D'Allessio's shoulder, Chief Godfrey remained silent when Policewoman Conroy asked Pidgie, Do you mean his eyes were deep-set?

Yes.

Her father pressed against the chief's hand and the chief restrained him. The chief asked, Would you say they were hooded, Pidgie?

Pidgie burst into tears.

Egan nodded to his chief. The nod meant such a detail was important. It meant he might know who did it. He'd been studying photographs of perverts all day. His men were now looking into the records of every one of them.

The chief said to Pidgie, I want you to try to calm yourself. And then I have to ask you for one more thing. We are all going to leave the room and I want you to tell Policewoman Conroy here what the man did to you.

The room was silent. Mr. D'Allessio raised both his fists in the air and a noise came from his throat.

Mrs. D'Allessio said, Might I stay, sir?
The chief said, Of course.

ONCE THE COPS were outside the house again, Policewoman Vera
Conroy said to Chief Godfrey, It's the same friggin' guy.

Egan said, And this girl survived because she didn't resist. Would
you say that, Vera?

The policewoman stopped before ducking into the chief's car and
faced her two superiors, eyed them gravely. Here's what I would say:
The D'Allessio girl had no chance to resist. The first thing he did was
to grab her scarf and twist it tight around her neck. Then he brought
her face right up to his and he threatened her. Warned her that if she
cried out he would break it. Her neck. And our little Irene never had
a chance to resist either. He killed her for some other reason.

twenty-five

IT IS DECIDED that Irene's classmates will attend her funeral, but her mother feels it is inappropriate for her friends to be at the wake. I am so deliriously thankful that I will not be expected to kneel in front of Irene's dead body and then have to apologize to her father, who walked out on her when she was seven.

My second funeral, another navy blue coat. A winter coat, but gabardine instead of heavier wool so my mother figures I can still wear it the following Easter. She says, It's always so damn cold on Easter Sunday anyway.

Gail's mother picks me up. Susan, too. Our fathers have to go to work. Gail's mother not only drives, she has her own car. Gail is mortified at this. My mother is now driving too because C.G. becomes the first corporation in the country to move its headquarters from the city to the suburbs. There is no bus to Bloomfield, Connecticut. At first, my mother rides to work with Freddie Ravenel's wife, who is a cleaning woman at C.G. (my mother gets her the job), but Mrs. Ravenel's twelve-year-old Ford station wagon keeps breaking down. A plan is made; my mother should get her license so that she and Mrs. Ravenel can take turns driving one another to work. My father will teach my mother to drive.

My mother, quoting Ann Landers to my father says, I need you to teach me to drive like a moose needs a hat rack.

She recalls the driving lesson he gave her twenty years earlier: They got in the first of the black Ford coupes they owned and he said, Throw it in neutral and let's go.

Throw it in neutral! My mother got out of the car, slammed the door

as hard as she could, stormed back into the house, and her driving lesson was never mentioned again.

My Auntie Margaret will be the one to give her driving lessons.

Once Auntie Margaret deems her ready for the motor vehicle test, my mother goes to the MVD, gets in the car with the inspector, and does fine until he tells her to make a Y-turn.

She says, What's a Y-turn?

She fails her driver's test. When she returns home, she says to my father, What's a Y-turn?

He explains and she says, But I know how to do that. Margaret never told me it had a name.

My mother starts to cry. Tyler goes berserk. I run up to my room and I sit on my bed until the bedlam ends.

My father gives a call to a friend who is with DOT and tells him the situation. The friend appears at our door that night with a license for my mother.

The next day, my father buys our first car without a standard shift. Cars now come in colors. My mother picks a two-tone Ford, powder blue and white.

Though she has a license and a new car, my mother can't drive Gail, Susan, and me to Irene's funeral because she has to be with Tyler, of course. We do not speak of Irene to Tyler.

Gail's mother parks in the Sts. Cyril and Methodius parking lot in a row reserved for cars carrying Irene's school chums. We all climb out and trudge up the steps into the church. Inside, several rows of pews are also reserved for us. The bas-relief Station of the Cross by our pew is "Jesus Falls for the First Time." He is being scourged. His bare back is shredded and globs of blood are flying in all directions.

Miss Bowie sits in front of us next to Albert I. Friedman. Magdalena's entire extended family and then some are already there taking up two pews but in the back. They have walked all the way from Charter Oak Terrace, which is several miles away.

The church is dark even with all the candles lit, which is a signal that this will be High Mass. From a child's point of view, the difference between a High Mass and a Low Mass is that the former is longer—much longer. My mother says to me before I leave with Gail's mother, There'll be three priests on the altar for sure.

She makes the prediction even though such a formation is normally reserved for a bigwig or someone who has donated a lot of money to the church.

Banks of flowers are everywhere and all of them are white. The organ plays very quietly as if, like me, it doesn't want to be there. My mother proves correct; when the church bell chimes, two lines of altar boys followed by three priests glide onto the altar, the priest in the center very old and very tall. With their appearance, the organist does what he is paid to do—create a deafening crescendo. The priests and altar boys find their positions and stare up the aisle. We all turn and crane our necks.

The head seminarian from St. Thomas's Seminary comes down the aisle carrying a long brass pole with a crucifix attached to the top. Then two more seminarians follow carrying thick, lit candles. Then comes Irene.

She is in a white coffin with more white flowers on top. The coffin is carried by teenaged boys, Fred's friends and his and Irene's cousin. Two are crying. Magdalena and her family all start to cry too. Then so does everyone else except for Irene's classmates as we cannot begin to believe that Irene is in the white box. Miss Bowie is holding a Kleenex to her nose. Albert I. Friedman holds her elbow against his side.

Irene's mother comes down the aisle next, with Fred on one side of her and her sister's husband on the other. She is dressed all in black and has a sheer black veil covering her face. I think she is so beautiful. I can't imagine my mother with a black veil in front of her face. Irene's mother keeps stumbling. Everyone is staring at her and at Fred and at Irene's uncle, who keep having to lift her back up.

The priest begins: *Confiteor Deo omnipotenti* . . .

All my classmates, everyone but Stonewall, who isn't Catholic, take Communion. Irene will never take Communion again. The host settles against my teeth. If I die before Saturday when I can go to confession again, I will go to hell. Irene is in heaven. Everyone says that over and over. The old priest says so when he speaks from the pulpit, that she has entered paradise. If I die, I won't see Irene. I'll go to hell even though my father will probably tell everyone that Irene and I are jumping rope with the angels.

I feel dizzy because of the smell of the flowers and because I am so hungry. My father had my Uncle Guido bring me a butterscotch sundae from the Lincoln Dairy at bedtime the night before the funeral and then let me stay up an extra hour besides. Hopefully, the late-night sundae will carry me through to the funeral; I must fast for twelve hours, will not be able to eat my usual breakfast since I'm going to receive Communion at the funeral. What usual breakfast? My father thinks I have Wheaties before I go to school but I never have time to manage anything but my long draft of Hershey's Syrup.

The Mass is a spectacle of priests and altar boys do-si-doing all across the altar, a soprano singing Polish hymns, and all of us kneeling, standing, sitting, kneeling, standing, sitting, kneeling, standing, sitting. Gail's mother wears a big diamond ring. Every time she stands, a light through a stained-glass window hits it, and sends a prism of colors against my navy blue coat. Then the funeral ends and Irene is carried back down the aisle in a reverse of the procession that began the Mass. Her mother's eyes are closed; Fred and his uncle are basically carrying her. We all file out.

In the car, Gail's mother sees to it that we break our fast as soon as we shut the doors. She has a box of crullers for us.

We sit in the car eating the crullers while we watch people pouring out of the church. We watch the teenage pallbearers slide Irene and her coffin and blanket of flowers into the hearse. The schoolchildren will not go to the cemetery as the temperature has taken a winter drop. Irene's mother doesn't want us to catch colds. So Gail's mother drives us to school, all dressed up in our navy blue coats, freezing.

We have a substitute teacher that day who smiles and smiles and lets us color and paint and play with clay like kindergarteners. Then she takes us out to the field next to the Mary M. Hooker School playground and we collect dead weeds, which she refers to as weather-dried wildflowers. She identifies them for us, holds up a few stalks, and says, Wood asters, pointing out that some of the petals still have color to them. Purple. She holds up other stalks. Fleabane. She says to us, Animals roll in these flowers and then fleas jump out of their fur. Then she gives us a big smile of inclusion, letting us in on a wondrous detail: They're also known as daisies!

I am enthralled that there can be so many kinds of wildflowers even if they've turned into dead weeds. Irene is dead now, too.

When we get back to the classroom, we girls squat down to pull prickers out of our socks and the hems of our navy blue coats, and the boys from the bottom of their pant legs. The substitute teacher explains that most of the prickers are a certain kind of seed, square flat brown seeds with sharp prongs on two of the corners so that they can cling to the fur of field mice and rabbits. Or *fox*. And then the seeds are carried to a new place where they will propagate next spring. We examine the seeds, feel the prongs. She says, Beggar's-lice. She tells us what beggars are, how they sleep in fields, how the lice cling to them.

I love the word *propagate*. Also, I know about lice, which stick themselves to the base of individual hair shafts, lay eggs, and propagate so that your head has to be washed with a foul-smelling shampoo or if you're impoverished, shaved.

Our substitute teacher doesn't speak of Irene either but at least she makes an extensive effort to keep our minds occupied. She succeeds.

twenty-six

J<small>UST HOURS</small> after officiating at the funeral Mass for Irene, the tall old priest who was the leader of the three on the altar and the pastor of Sts. Cyril and Methodius Church had something else he needed to do. Monsignor Stanislaus Musiel (same name as the ball player's only spelled differently) wrote down his feelings about the killer. The next morning, he asked the *Hartford Courant* to print what he'd written. He explained his hope that the killer would read his words. The *Hartford Courant* published an extra edition in order to comply with the monsignor's request. Monsignor Musiel wrote:

> *The best thing this person can do—for himself and for the community—is to come forward and reveal the awful burden of conscience which must weigh upon him. It would be far better for him to reveal himself now than to live in the dread of the hunted, and to live with the guilt of his crime.*
>
> *He must realize, too, if he possesses his reason, that the terror this crime has brought to the parents and children in the community is an evil which only he can end immediately. He cannot change what has happened to this child, and he cannot expect leniency for giving himself up. But he can put an end to the evils of fear and suspicion which afflict the community as a result of his deed. Thus, by surrendering, he would be doing the only good he has in his power to perform.*
>
> *If this crime is the result of emotional or mental sickness, it is only by coming forward that this person can hope to receive the help he needs.*
>
> *If he is of sound mind, he cannot help but realize that he cannot escape the penalty of his crime by keeping his silence—he can gain nothing*

that way but to prolong the dread of that day when punishment finally befalls him.

And then the priest spoke directly to the killer:

You have but one course that is right. Give yourself up.

It was a homily, a plea based on orderly reason. It was not a sermon. His words did not contain sentimentality, bathos, spiritual illogic, pomposity, scripture, hellfire, or mention of God. No talk of forgiveness or redemption. (No mention, of course, of closure.) Only emotion for the miserable human condition; Monsignor Musiel felt so much compassion centered in humanism that he suggested Irene's killer possessed the capability to do good even though there was only one good available for him to perform.

I did not experience the fear Monsignor Musiel spoke of when he described the community in his plea to the killer to give himself up. A child's inability to comprehend how an adult can murder her friend preserves her from experiencing fear related to the event. Instead, the fear is related to the irrational—terror of the guillotine lopping off my feet, for example.

twenty-seven

Nobody ever says aloud that Irene is dead—not my parents, not Miss Bowie, not the priest at my church, and not the kids at school. Nobody except for one girl, Kathy Delaney. In all our lives, I don't remember Kathy ever speaking to me, not even when we sit next to each other at our First Holy Communion breakfast.

Kathy Delaney is also absent the day after our field trip to the Hartford Electric Light Company. We figure she hasn't been kidnapped because her desk remains in place. She must be out sick.

I suppose Kathy remembers how we received Communion side by side when we were seven and that's why she speaks to me. She figures maybe I can count as a girlfriend. So in the corridor on the way to gym, the day after the funeral, she says to me with the same terror on her face as in the photo just before Father Kelly gives her the host, When they catch him, I have to *go to court*.

Go to court fills her with the same anxiety she experiences when she is about to receive the host not knowing exactly how difficult it might be to keep it from touching her teeth and going to hell. Her mother has died so, after all, she could die, too, and if she goes to hell she won't see her mother, who the nuns tell her is in heaven.

Now she has no mother to explain to her what *go to court* means, not that she would have understood what her mother was talking about. Who knows what her brothers tell her?

Kathy has one more thing to say to me: I have to go to court because I'm the one who threw stones at the boat.

I run away from Kathy and into the gym because we're told, again and again, not to speak of what happened to Irene. And Kathy is speaking of it. She has to speak of it because she is one of the children who threw stones at the boat and now she must go to court and she is terrified. The reason she was absent the day after Irene was murdered was because she was being questioned by the police.

My guess now is that Kathy thought *go to court* meant she was responsible for the death of Irene, just as I had once thought I was responsible for the death of my cousin Jackie.

MID-DECEMBER DAYS grow dark within an hour and a half of our coming home from school. Now that Tyler sleeps until dinner time, I go outside and play a game of hide-and-seek with my friends, or we get out our roller skates and fly recklessly down the Nilan Street sidewalk leaping over the cracks until we reach Chandler. If there is—Oh happy day—snow, then we make a snowman, or have a snowball fight, or if there's more than six inches, sled down the backyards of Nilan Street, starting between the lilac bushes in my yard, across Eddie's backyard, across the Nelsons', across my friend Joyce's, and into Bobby Turner's. Bobby is skinny and a victim of bullies; they call him T-bone Turner on an oil burner. We sledders must stop because of the hedge between the Turners' and the next house down.

Beginning the day Miss Bowie gives us to understand that Irene is dead, the children in the neighborhood aren't allowed to play outside except in their own yards, which means we aren't allowed to play with each other.

The winter the body of my friend Irene is found in the Proccacinos' yard, there will be no snow throughout December and it's a good thing since we children are all trapped indoors.

On the day Irene's body is found, I walk home with my Nilan Street friends from school and go in my door as my mother flies out to her car to drive to C.G. But on that day she speaks to me: Stay in the house, Mickey, and don't go out.

My mother only knows the rumor that Irene is missing. The doors are not locked though, rumors being what they are. The power of positive thinking. The door will be locked tonight, however, when everyone will learn that Irene has been murdered.

I do not feel comfortable in my house. What is going on?

In the collective plan to pretend everything will be normal if we all act normal, parents refrain from walking us home from school, and mine even leave me alone in my house with my brother until my father arrives home from work.

I do not feel safe or unsafe in my house. What I feel is confused: What happened to Irene?

Today, of course, I would be counseled. In the fifties, revealing one's thoughts and emotions is a sign of weakness and lack of maturity. And of course, complaining is verboten. Yet, the news of Irene's murder is held until the children can get to their classrooms in order to hear that information from their teacher rather than each other. We are protected from the scandal of talking to each other about rumors while at the same time a killer is out there somewhere who can kill any one of us on the way to school.

Poor Kathy Delaney tried to kibitz with me, but beyond the ban on discussion of Irene, I am well trained in silence. Denial is my family's religion, my brother Tyler our god, and the Reverend Dr. Peale our pastor.

IN AN IRONIC TWIST, an ordinance voted into law in 1945 by the Hartford city council that prohibits unaccompanied children from loitering on the streets is put into effect by the council called into emergency session. But there are no children loitering in the streets. Only a murderer is loitering in the streets.

I find that out when the *Hartford Times* arrives just beating out my father's hurried arrival home from work.

I am the only member of my family prepared for the police to come to our door. I know the police will come because they came to our door once before. When Tyler was nine and I four, he decided it would be a splendid idea to rouse his lazy troops by pulling the fire

143

alarm at the box on Chandler Street. My mother uses the term "false alarm" to describe any expected event that doesn't come about. Like if she goes out with her umbrella and it doesn't rain, she comes home, jams it into the closet, and says, False alarm. I think the poetic lilt to the two words strung together as one—*falsalarm*—enchants Tyler. I think this because when I am in college, my American Literature professor tells us that Edgar Allen Poe's favorite words were *cellar door* and so he gave his female characters names with that same lilting assonance: Lenore, Annabel Lee, Eulalie, and Ulalume.

After Tyler pulled the false alarm, when the fire trucks arrived, we were all outside scanning the sky for the smoke. It must have been a weekend because my father was home. Tyler said to my parents, Whoops, false alarm!

They asked him how he knew that and he giggled and confessed to breaking the glass and pulling the handle in the alarm box. My father hustled him into the house and made him promise never to do it again or he wouldn't see another book for the rest of his life. Tyler could tell my father was genuinely angry. He said, I promise never to pull a false alarm again.

But he didn't understand the point in promising to behave. If it felt good, why not do it? Tyler had no morals, had no idea why he should be punished for something that was fun.

After the fire trucks left, a police officer came to our door surrounded by a dozen kids—sort of like the Pied Piper only the kids were leading him rather than vice versa—leading him to the culprit, singing out gaily when they reached D-106: Here's Tyler's house!

I ran into the living room and hid behind the sofa because I thought we'd all have to go to jail where we would have nothing to eat but bread and water and have to go to the bathroom in front of everyone on a toilet with no seat. My Uncle Chick worked at the Hartford County Jail and his description of the facilities stayed with me.

I heard Tyler promise the police officer he'd never do it again. But my father said to the cop, Those kids out there put him up to it.

My mother said, They *encouraged* him.

Maybe they encouraged him but I knew it was Tyler's idea. I knew by the way he'd always eye the alarm box when we'd walk by it, how tempted he was.

The policeman said, A child like this shouldn't be out wandering the streets.

My father said, I thought he was playing.

I was thinking, He was.

The policeman offered no mercy: Keep him inside so he's not a menace.

That is what he said instead of advising my father to supervise Tyler more carefully. This was a turning point in Tyler's life. My father decided the policeman was right so Tyler was no longer allowed outside except with my father who, when Tyler reached puberty, decided it would simply be best if Tyler didn't go out at all, supervised or otherwise. No more commandeering the elevator at G. Fox, for sure.

Two days after Irene is murdered, children direct the police to my house, but this time they aren't allowed to accompany the two officers who come knocking at the door. I peek out the window and see the cruiser, its engine running.

It's near to suppertime. My mother is at C.G. My father is in the kitchen frying chicken wings. He turns the burner off and dries his hands. I run up to the top of the stairs. The stairway is just inside the front door. I don't hide behind the couch because I know I won't go to jail. The upstairs landing will make a good listening post.

Tyler has recently developed an antagonism toward the number four. If the phone rings four times, he bites his wrist until my father reaches Uncle Guido and has him call back so Tyler will hear a fifth ring, which allows for the erasure of the fourth. Sometimes Tyler says he didn't hear the phone's fifth ring and my father and my Uncle Guido repeat the routine. We all come to realize that when people knock on the door, they invariably knock four times: knock-knock-knock-knock. My father puts a sign out on our door: *Please Don't Knock. Use the Bell.*

145

The police choose to knock. Consequently, the first thing my father does before he opens the door is give it a good solid knock number five. I imagine that proves disconcerting to the police but they don't mention it.

They say to my father, You have a son?

Yes.

How old is he?

Fourteen. He's retarded.

So we've heard. Where is he?

There is a pause because my father finds that to be such an utterly stupid question. He says, He's right here.

Where?

In his den. He never goes out.

He doesn't?

No.

Why not?

This cop is clearly not the same guy who gave my father advice on what you do with a retarded kid who pulls fire alarms.

My father says, I told you. He's retarded. It's better that he doesn't go out.

Does he attend school?

No.

Why not?

They won't let him come.

Why not?

They said he was too disruptive.

Pause, number two. Then: We'd like to speak to him.

Yet another pause. My father can't imagine this is actually happening so now it is his turn to ask, Why?

One of the cops says, Routine questions concerning the murder of the little girl. We're talking to all the neighborhood boys.

My father begins to say something, but doesn't. He says something else. He says, I'll get my son.

I'm thinking, this should be interesting.

I hear my father go to Tyler's den and then he and Tyler come out. My father is saying to Tyler that there are gentlemen from the police department who are talking to everyone on the street and they have to talk to him too.

Tyler immediately announces to the police officers, I promise I'll never do it again.

The policemen listen to my father's explanation as to what it is Tyler will never do again.

Then one of the cops asks Tyler, Where were you on Wednesday evening between six and eight o'clock?

In my den.

What were you doing?

Playing my new Jean Marie Kabritsky record, an *oberek*.

An *oberek* is the Polish version of a waltz to be played when polka dancers are in danger of keeling over from exhaustion.

Before the cop can ask another question, Tyler says, Which branch of the service did you serve in?

First, the cop answers, Army, as Tyler's voice can be very authoritative. Then there is a nonplussed silence before one of them says to my father, Where is your wife?

She's at work.

At *work?*

Yes.

Where?

C.G. She's on the housewife shift.

After further conversation that goes nowhere, the last thing the cops say is, We'll be back.

They won't. My father says to Tyler: You were a very good boy to the policemen.

Tyler, never a slouch, asks, When will my extra book come?

Tomorrow.

My father has a stash of bribery books in the cellar.

That night, my father doesn't recite a poem or sing one of our favorite songs: "My Blue Heaven," "I'm Looking Over a Four-Leaf

Clover," "Oh, the Music Goes Round and Round," "C'è la Luna," or "The Sidewalks of New York." Instead he tells me a bedtime story, an adventure of Odysseus, the one with the Cyclops. My father would like to do to Irene's killer what Odysseus did to the Cyclops. Then we say the Our Father and the Hail Mary, and then he says, I called Uncle Guido. Tomorrow night, we're going to have a bagna cauda.

He will celebrate staving off yet another threat to Tyler.

During the bagna cauda, which I don't enjoy for the first time, he says to my Uncle Guido, Good thing that poor kid wasn't killed on Thursday or Tyler would be in the hoosegow.

What he means by that is Tyler's newly developed aversion to the word *Thursday* as well as the number four. If he overhears you say *Thursday,* he comes running out of his den, squealing frantically for us to relieve his torture: Say *Friday,* say *Friday!* Therefore, if the cops had asked Tyler, Where were you Thursday night? They would have had Tyler in their faces, jabbing his finger at them, commanding they say Friday.

My Uncle Guido says, And thank God she wasn't you-know-what. Raped.

AFTER MY MOTHER comes home from C.G at ten-thirty, my Auntie Margaret arrives to pick her up so they can go off to their weekly midnight bowling league. I eavesdrop while my mother changes into her bowling shirt, which has the name *Frank's Restaurant* embroidered across her back, and *Florence* on the chest pocket. (Frank's Restaurant is the best Italian restaurant in town and my family will take me there following high school graduation ceremonies.) My mother's duck pin bowling team won the national championship between the time Tyler and I were born. The tournament was held in Baltimore. Baltimore is the farthest my mother has ever been or will ever be from Hartford. She kept a scrapbook and included in it was a Western Union telegram from my father: *Bring 'em to their knees, Flo.* The Frank's Restaurant team wins and is noted in the *Guinness Book of World*

Records for their record-breaking combined team score in one of the tournament games.

Margaret, my mother says, I can understand the need for foot patrols, but now the D section is demanding lights in their backyards. And they want them on all night! *Oy gevalt.*

Oy gevalt is a popular expression in the fifties because everyone watches Molly Goldberg on TV.

Auntie Margaret says, But I heard a woman at church say her son was approached by a pervert in their backyard so she couldn't let him out after dark anymore.

Margaret, do *we* have lights in *our* backyards? No. I blame the government.

You're right, Florence.

Besides, she says, children should be inside their houses after dark . . . I have to say I blame the mother there.

Auntie Margaret doesn't concur on that one. My mother expands, What was that woman thinking letting her daughter go to the store at eight o'clock at night? Why didn't she call the police when the girl didn't come home? What possessed her to wait until nine-thirty?

Even though my mother feels free to criticize Irene's mother, there is no mention of Irene's father, who deserted the family.

While my mother is going on and on about maternal negligence, the mothers quoted in the newspaper defend Irene's mother.

She's a good woman.

Hardworking.

She took care of her children as best she could.

And one explains, Her husband left her. She worked as a cleaning woman. She needed her kids to run to the store to pick up a few things now and again.

By the time Irene's mother and brother are looking for her in the pouring-down rain, worried senseless that she hadn't returned home from the store, Irene is already dead. I think of my cousin Jackie, dead before he hit the floor. When Bob Malm strangles Irene with her scarf she falls, dead before she hits the ground.

I blame the government. No, I don't. That just comes to me because my mother would say it all the time.

I remember almost nothing else of the two-and-one-half years to follow. And my mother, though seemingly heartless, stops taking photographs, something she did all the time to mark holidays, special occasions, snowstorms, and summer beach get-togethers. There are dozens of pictures of my extended family before Irene is murdered, and there are next to none afterwards—with the exception of my cousin Cleasse's wedding the following spring plus one of me a few days later on Easter Sunday in my navy blue coat.

Part II

Brain Jog

Cleasse's wedding

twenty-eight

KURT VONNEGUT ONCE SAID: *A writer lives for twenty-five years and then spends the rest of his life writing about it.*

Today I see my brain as a card catalog, the old-fashioned kind now replaced by Google. My brain is a mahogany cabinet with twenty-five little drawers, each with a shiny brass pull. Every drawer is stored with a year's worth of events, anecdotes, experiences, and details comprising a range from the celebrated to the obscure that work to go into making a novel toothsome instead of oily. But in drawers nine through twelve, two and a half years' worth of blank cards beginning with Christmastime in fifth grade went missing.

Just as I know the eye chart has an E on top, I also know that sixth grade existed. My teacher's name was Mrs. Driscoll, but that is all I remember. I know, too, that I went to a new school after completing the sixth grade at Mary M. Hooker Elementary School. I don't remember leaving Mary M. Hooker Elementary School, nor do I remember entering Cornelius J. Moylan Junior High. There is a word for such a phenomenon—repression. I repressed life without Irene for two and a half years. I have pictures of my sixth-grade promotion ceremony though I don't recall the actual event. In the pictures, Gail is wearing a beautiful junior high–style dress, Cuban heels, and nylon stockings. And, of course, her Bulova watch. There are points sticking out the front of her dress; she is also wearing a bra. I am wearing an elementary school dress that buttons down the back, fold-over socks, and Mary Jane's. Also, an undershirt. But the next thing I remember after Kathy Delaney said to me, *I have to go to court,* is a day in the month of

May, two and a half years later, seventh grade, at Moylan Junior High School.

My seventh-grade English teacher is Mr. Boyle, my first male teacher ever. He favors girls with developed breasts over those without. He smiles and flirts with them. We, the flat-chested, are invisible entities.

Our May assignment is to finish one of a list of topic sentences Mr. Boyle copies onto the board from his teacher's handbook, and then we are to elaborate upon it for three pages. There is a great deal of grumbling since this will be a weekend homework assignment. The handful of us trained by Miss Bowie are prepared for the necessary thought and attempt at clarity required. Mr. Boyle hands out three pages of lined composition paper. On the way home from school, the paper airplanes shooting across the sidewalks that day have lines.

On Monday morning, we come in with our compositions jammed into our notebooks. Most of the students utilize unusually large script. Some write on every other line.

It's neater that way, one girl says. She is a girl with developed breasts so Mr. Boyle stares at her chest and nods his acquiescence at them.

He orders the kid in the first seat, first row, who happens to be my friend Gail, to begin. Gail starts reading. Mr. Boyle, all disgusted, says, Stand up!

Gail is a beanpole. Her bra is filled with foam. When she turns left or right, her bra remains aimed straight ahead. She unfolds herself from her desk, bumping her knees and elbows. Gail begins: *I have a pet named . . .*

Up and down the rows we go: *On my birthday . . . The day I entered Moylan . . . I would like to attend college because . . .*

Then it is my turn. I stand up in the aisle next to my desk. The topic sentence I picked to complete is one no one else has chosen: *It was a bad day when . . .* I don't remember making that choice. I don't remember writing the composition either. I remember standing up in Mr. Boyle's class and I remember reading it.

I complete the sentence—*It was a bad day when my fifth grade class went to the Hartford Electric Light Company for our field trip.* I catch a glimpse of Mr. Boyle rolling his eyes. I go on to read all I have managed to jam into the three pages. I describe every minute of the trip from the time Gail, Susan, and I meet up in the street walking to school, going into the classroom, taking off our coats. I mention the Pledge of Allegiance, and how some of us forgot to add in the new phrase, *Under God.* I tell how we sang "My Country, 'Tis of Thee" before getting our coats back on, standing in back of the bus, smelling the fumes, getting on the bus, arriving at the electric plant, the vice president's plywood divider, lunch, bananas . . . I describe every single detail except the girlie calendar in the vice president's "office." Then I read the last line: *That night while I watched the* Arthur Godfrey Amateur Hour *with my father, my lunch partner, Irene, was murdered.*

I sit down.

The room is silent. Mr. Boyle cranes his neck to see past the kids in front of me. I do my best to stay within the bulk of Stonewall's back. If any part of me sticks out, that part will be guillotined. My English teacher speaks to me for the first time. He says, Mary, how you *shocked* us with that last line.

I am feeling shock too. Not at being called by only half my name, which I'm used to, but because he didn't remember that Irene went on a field trip to the Hartford Electric Light Company the day she died. He never recognized my *foreboding.* My teacher didn't recall the murder of a schoolgirl two years earlier, a girl who should have been sitting in his classroom, until I jog his brain as my own has been jogged over the weekend while deciding on a topic sentence.

The bell rings. Out in the corridor, I walk to my next class alone. Even Gail and Susan hang back. And then Helen strides by. I don't know her because she was funneled to junior high from another elementary school, not Mary M. Hooker. She comes very close as she passes.

She whispers, Irene was my cousin.

Helen's father is Irene's uncle, the man who supported Irene's mother's weight during the funeral when her own buckling knees were unable to bear such a crushing burden of grief.

Helen just keeps on walking. So do I.

REPRESSING IRENE had been an unconscious endeavor but it would take work for me to *suppress* her, which is a feat I accomplish until I am a commuting student at Central Connecticut State College, where no one calls me Mickey. I am taking a course called Psychology of Self, a requirement for psychology majors and minors. The course demands a one-hundred-page autobiography, which is the reason so few students are in the program. At the end of the course, the professor will discuss each student's autobiography individually. My scheduled appointment arrives.

Dr. Reginald Swann, my professor, sits across his desk from me. He gestures to my manuscript lying in front of him and says, Now *this* is a page-turner.

Thank you.

There's one thing, though. The child Irene?

His eyes are big through his Coke-bottle lenses. I don't say anything.

You gave the child Irene a *single* paragraph?

I'm thinking, I guess I did. I nod.

What were you? Ten, right?

I lie, Yes. It's too complicated to explain my mother getting me into school a year early, one of the zillions of details of my life I was forced to leave out of the autobiography if I had any chance of finishing it before the end of the semester.

Your fifth-grade classmate was *murdered* and all she got was *one* paragraph? *One?*

Dr. Swann, I say, we weren't supposed to talk about it.

Then you suppressed the incident.

Well . . . I didn't think about it.

Exactly. Then he smiled. Would you like to talk about it now?

No.

But at some point, you'll explore the tragedy, won't you?

I lie again, a lie that will stand for a long time. Yes, I will.

All right then . . . Let's leave the murdered girl. About your older brother—he glanced down at my autobiography—Tyler, is it?

Yes.

You say you love him?

Yes.

He was a manipulative lunatic.

I can't imagine a psychology professor using the term *lunatic*.

I say, Well, when you're retarded, you can't help—

Retarded?

Yes.

Your brother is not retarded.

I don't respond. That's because I'm so surprised to hear such a thing.

He leans back in his swivel rocker. He says, Mary-Ann, the man has a library of two thousand military books and he reads prodigiously almost all of his waking hours. Since when is that retarded?

I do not respond quickly enough.

Mary-Ann, can people who suffer mental retardation read?

Not too well.

He smiled again. Then he said, Your brother is an idiot savant. You remember what that is, don't you?

Yes. I recite: It's a form of autism except the person has pools of brilliance.

Very good. Then he sighs and says, The poor, poor fellow. Mary-Ann, did you never consider your brother as suffering from autism?

No.

You never associated that disorder with . . . Tyler's egregious behavior?

No.

He says, You have survived life in a rigid, narrow grid constructed by your brother, who forced you and your parents to run yourselves ragged catering to his every obsession and compulsion, every urge and impulse. He needed the grid, of course, to protect himself from unbearable anxiety.

Oh. I wonder if perhaps my description of the demographics of Charter Oak Terrace put Dr. Swann in mind of a grid.

And do you know why you survived life as a pawn intact?

No.

Then I'll tell you why. You are a *gifted* writer.

Oh.

My professor says, Freud's definition of success is the ability to work and love. You are a cheerful, life-loving young woman and you have successfully written something quite remarkable. So considering the dreadful circumstances of your childhood . . . how is it you've thrived?

I say to him, I never thought of my circumstances as dreadful.

Ah, but they were. Face up to that and explore what allowed you to escape and soar.

Time for another lie. All right, Professor Swann, I will.

The professor can't get rid of another itch that still needs more scratching. He says, The dead girl. Irene. She was a friend?

Yes. But not a close one.

More than just a classmate, though.

I guess she was.

You played with her?

Sometimes. I'd have played with her more but she was bashful.

She lived near you?

Yes.

How was she murdered?

She was strangled.

Raped?

I think sexually abused.

Raped. I'm sorry.

Thank you.

I am overcome that he thinks to express his condolences to me. No one has ever consoled me over the loss of Irene before.

Was her killer caught?

I think so.

You think so? You don't know?

He must have been.

He studies my face. Then he says, I have an assignment for you and I will trust you to do it even though I'm not asking that you do it today, or tomorrow, or in a year's time.

I study his face.

He says, Find out the name of her killer.

I continue to gape at him.

And too, another assignment, Mary-Ann.

What?

Keep writing.

All right.

I'm serious, he says. Then he smiles at me as though I am a little dying dog, just run over by the ice cream truck. He doesn't believe me. His students are blue-collar commuters. We lack any ambition beyond the hope of graduating and becoming teachers. He pushes my autobiography across the desk to me. He's given me an *A*.

Good luck to you, dear girl. I'll be here if you want to talk.

I thank him, leave his office, head over to the local pizza place, and drink a pitcher of beer with my friends. I don't want to know who killed my little childhood pal. Between the beer and the chatter I am able to begin anew to suppress Irene, which I continue to do for decades until I get a telephone call one morning from the book editor at the *Hartford Courant*.

twenty-nine

THE PHONE RINGS and when I pick it up it is Carole Goldberg.

Hi. I'm the new book editor at the *Hartford Courant*. We met once.

She tells me that she introduced me when I was the keynote speaker at a writing seminar a few years back. I recall that and we catch up on things. Then she says, I have big plans here.

Her first plan is to have the *Courant* produce a quarterly literary supplement. She wants the initial quarterly to include profiles of Hartford writers from the Puritans through the most contemporary including the city's mainstays, Mark Twain and Harriet Beecher Stowe. She's hoping to tack on an essay from me on how Hartford impacted my life as a writer. She says, Or *something* like that.

I must have paused because she quickly added, Or anything you feel like writing.

Then she immediately follows that up with, I can't pay you.

Carole's been told she can go right ahead and produce her literary quarterlies with the understanding that her budget will be zero. Since she can't exactly ask the Dunne brothers to write for nothing—Dominic, the international gadfly who is a minor character in my fifth novel, or John Gregory who has just died at huge loss to contemporary literature—she is relying on me, not on the glitterati.

My Auntie Mary was the Dunne *père*'s secretary.

The editor says, The whole operation will end with your essay, Mary-Ann. You'll be my anchor.

So I say, Sure, why not?

I have no trouble reviving the Hartford lore as it's filed away in my brain's card catalog. I start with my family's first public crisis, which happened before I was born when my Uncle John Belch shoots himself in the arm working the line at Colt. The Colts say he brought his own firearm to work, was cleaning it, and accidentally shot himself. Years later, my mother is talking with my Auntie Margaret about the Uncle John Belch debacle, and I am eavesdropping as always and my mother says to Auntie Margaret, As if John *owned* a gun.

Auntie Margaret says, God forbid.

My mother says, This is Hartford, not *Yuma.* I'm telling you, Margaret, he wouldn't have been fired today, he'd have sued! I blame the government.

In addition to the Uncle John Belch shooting incident, my essay includes several Hartford events I remember clearly, some of them occurring before I was born as with the Colt shooting, and some when I am too young to possibly have a recall, like the very biggest: the Great Hartford Circus Fire. The fire is a tragedy that changes the character of the city. I am five months old. The circus comes to town one month after the D-Day invasion; consequently, women and children are the vast majority of the matinee audience.

The mayor is quoted in the *Hartford Courant: New England has lost more lives today than we did on the beaches of Normandy a month ago.*

My mother tells me that on the day of the circus, fire sirens blasted throughout the city and everyone ran outside to shade their eyes and look upward to see if they could spot the Luftwaffe in the skies. Some years before my essay for the *Hartford Courant,* I wrote a novel centered on the circus fire: was it arson and if it was, who set the fire?

I think how my third novel had a scene, set in 1943, with the Tommy Dorsey orchestra playing while Frank Sinatra sang. Writing the scene, I remembered their hit in 1943 was "I'll Never Smile Again." I could see Frank crooning. But I wasn't born yet. My memories of what I've seen and heard are sometimes true, or sometimes they're not. This is a human phenomenon especially difficult for law enforcers who depend on witnesses whose memories are not accurate though they swear on their grandmothers' graves they are. I understand, particularly since, when I'd finished a draft of that third novel, I did some fact checking and found that Frank's 1943 hit was "I'll Never Smile Again," with the Tommy Dorsey orchestra.

When I am finished writing my contribution to the *Hartford Courant Literary Quarterly*, quite pleased with it, I dig up an old photo, which the editor has also requested. It's me at six years old sitting in the back of a goat cart. When I was six, a man with a goat and a cart came to Charter Oak Terrace. He took a big camera out of his suitcase, and then unfolded a tripod. He let the children feed the goat while he set up. The goat feed came in a box that read *Donkey Feed*. The mothers paid fifty cents for the five-by-seven photo, which they received in the mail in two weeks time.

Now I look at the photo and remember my mother's anger when the postman delivered it. She said to my Auntie Margaret, Will she *ever* learn to smile for a camera?

My smile isn't genuine. I don't know how to fake a smile. I look like I have Bell's Palsy in the picture. The goat, a trained professional, has a lovely smile.

I end my essay with a conclusion that makes me a little uneasy but there really isn't time to dwell on uneasiness if I want to make the *Courant*'s deadline. My conclusion: *My writing is driven by such fragments of a Hartford childhood: recollections, images of neighborhood faces, my family's reminiscences. I recover previously unsurfaced memories on a daily basis. Some events occurred before I was born, and some, perhaps never occurred at all. But still, I remember them, and I place the emotions they stir into the consciousness of my characters.*

When I am stuffing the essay and photograph into a priority mail envelope, without any warning the face of my fifth grade classmate, Irene, parks itself right in front of me, her large dark Loretta Young eyes skewering me. She wants something. She wants me to do what Dr. Swann at Central Connecticut assigned—to be released from my brain. She wants me to see to her recognition, see to my remembering what happened to her. In one big flood the two-year gap in my brain—the empty card catalog drawers—fill up with the terrible days and weeks and months that followed Irene's murder. So I throw up a dike. The dike holds. But still I have to take my essay out of the mailer and at least add something—some little thing—which I insert just before the concluding paragraph:

A fifth grade classmate of mine at Mary M. Hooker school, Irene, was raped and strangled in the yard behind mine, down a few. In school we knew not to speak of it. We took Irene's desk out of the row, and everyone moved up. The night after she died, the Hartford Times *arrived with Irene's picture on the front page in her First Communion dress and veil.*

I read it and said to my father, What's rape?

He ripped the newspaper out of my hand and sent me to my room. I asked if I could go out and play instead. He said no. I couldn't go out to play until the murderer was caught. But Irene would never go out to play again.

Now, remembering Irene's eyes, my brain shuts down.

But my brain didn't really shut down; I just couldn't write any more. Suddenly, I can remember reading in the *Hartford Times* on December 10, 1953, that Irene was not raped, hence, the question I'd asked my father. But she must have been. I found myself wanting to understand.

THE FIRST *HARTFORD COURANT LITERARY QUARTERLY* comes out as a supplement to the Sunday edition. It looks quite nice and is acclaimed. On the cover is a close-up of a vintage Royal typewriter. I wonder if Pippi installed the keys. There are articles saluting the oral histories of Native Americans; the terrible sermons of Thomas Hooker (Mary M. was a descendant, but my school was named for her because she was the first woman to serve in the Connecticut State Legislature the year women got the vote); the serene writings of Horace Bushnell; the diaries of the slave Jupiter Hammond; the children's stories of Samuel C. Goodrich; then on to Samuel L. Clemens; Harriet Beecher Stowe, and her sisters Catharine Beecher and Isabella Beecher Hooker (Hookers galore in Hartford); Ann Plato, the first black woman to publish a book of essays; Anne Petry, who wrote the biography of Harriet Tubman, someone no one ever heard of until Ms. Petry wrote her book; Lydia Huntley Sigourney, who published sixty-four books and no one's ever heard of her to this day and no one will unless someone writes her biography; the *Hartford Courant* editor Charles Dudley Warner; Wallace Stevens; Brendan Gill; the Dunne brothers; and the transient Jack Kerouac, who touched down in Hartford for just a few years. With his mom, of course.

The next day, the phone rings. It's Carole Goldberg at the *Courant*.

I say to her, Congratulations. The supplement is beautiful.

She says, Mary-Ann . . .

I wait. What?

I've got a message for you on my voice mail.

Oh good. Some famous editor has seen the essay and wants me to expand it into a book for which he will pay a million dollars and then some movie producer will option the book for another million and I'll be rich.

She says, The message is from the girl's brother. The murdered girl . . . Irene. He'd like you to call him.

I immediately hear Miss Bowie's stern admonition not to speak of Irene, which I complied with being a good little Catholic girl who will not ask adults why.

I write down the phone number on a cardboard coaster, lying on my kitchen counter.

thirty

IRENE'S BROTHER, Fred. Fred is fifteen when Irene dies, so much older than us, another era. All I can think is how I deliberately kept my lines about Irene in the *Courant* essay devoid of sentiment. I am kicking myself. The problem is, though, that I hadn't wanted to be consoling. After all, no one consoled me at Irene's death; I was ordered not to speak of it. I had to wait a dozen years for Professor Swann at Central Connecticut State College to offer me sympathy. If he were still alive he'd be happy to know that when I was finishing my essay I needed to share Irene with the *Courant*'s readers; he was always so patient.

After I hang up, I hold the coaster in my hands staring at it. I'd taken the coaster home from a bar the night before because I liked it so much; the coaster advertises Lillet Aperitif and is illustrated with a rip-off of an 1890s poster, a blonde dancing in a grape arbor holding an oversized bottle of Lillet in one hand and waving a glass in the air with the other. I collect vintage posters.

I walk around the kitchen wanting to get to the phone some other day, maybe copy the phone number off the coaster and onto a piece of paper when I have a minute, maybe lay it back down and pick it up again after a nice short one. Maybe I can just stick the coaster in my *Pending File*, where I am guaranteed never to see it again. Instead, I pick up the phone and dial. The area code is 860–Fred still lives in the Hartford area.

Someone picks up. A voice says, *Fred's Auto Mart.*

I say, This is Irene's friend, Mary-Ann Tirone Smith.

There is a gulp at the other end and the voice says, Please hold on. I'll get him.

It is an employee primed to be ready for a possible call from me. I hold the phone and I hold myself together, I don't know how. I hear, Hello?

I crush the receiver to my ear to keep from passing out. I mumble, Fred?

Yes, he says.

And again, I say that I am Irene's friend and I say my name, and I say the *Courant* has given me his number. And then I wait.

Thank you for returning my call, he says.

I say, I'm sorry.

That's what my father taught me to say to someone who loses a loved one. It is only long afterward that I come to understand one expresses one's sorrow that the loss occurred, not for causing it.

Fred has a soft, calm voice same as Irene. He says, Not a week goes by that I don't think about her. I've thought about her really a lot lately what with the child snatchings going on. Amber Alert. All that.

He pauses. I wait because I am incapable of getting out anything beyond, *I'm sorry.*

He says, I've been hoping there is someone somewhere who remembers Irene besides me. I never dreamed anyone *thinks* about her. I read what you wrote. I feel good knowing there is someone else who thinks about my sister besides me.

I am still holding the coaster. I press it against my mouth without knowing it. Then Fred says, You mentioned her eyes. We always teased her, told her she had eyes like Loretta Young.

Oh, God. Why oh why didn't I say that in the essay? That her eyes were like Loretta Young's?

I speak through the coaster. Yes, she did have eyes like Loretta Young.

I struggle and struggle not to cry.

He says, It was fun growing up in Charter Oak Terrace, wasn't it? Charter Oak Terrace.

I struggle some more, Yes.

Do you remember the name of the bread man?

I stop struggling. I bring the coaster down from my mouth. It is sogged with saliva. Fred has consoled me with a trivia question. I think back on the bread truck, the merry bread man.

I say, I can see his face, Fred, but I can't remember his name. (And besides his truck, I can hear his accent, see his smile, and also his tattoo: numbers on the inside of his forearm.)

Fred says, Remember when he'd try to get our mothers to buy sweet buns? With frosting? And they couldn't afford it so he'd put it on their tabs?

I say, There were no tabs.

That's right. The buns were free.

Fred, I can't remember the man's name. I was younger than you.

He says, It starts with an *S.*

I say, I give up.

Mr. Schustermann!

Omigod. *Yes! Mr. Schustermann!*

Fred and I go on from there, reminiscing, saved by the long ago, saved by the past, the past which came prior to his sister's murder.

I ask if he remembers the glazier, Whitey, an albino who'd come around every spring with a pickup truck loaded with great tubs of putty to repair our loose window panes. Fred remembers. Whitey gives the children fist-size blobs of putty to play with. We roll the putty, squeeze it, shape it into long skinny snakes, try to make something—a cup—cherishing the results of our efforts. I don't tell Fred that one time I snuck back in line to get a second helping of putty. Whitey tells me if I ever do that again he'll cut off my ears. He waves his chisel at me. I believe him.

Fred, I say, Did you have your picture taken in the goat cart?

Yeah, I think so.

I don't ask him if Irene had her picture taken too because she must have. I want to keep reminiscing.

But Fred says, I'm for the death penalty.

With the sudden skip in subject, it is as if I am forgetting who I'm talking to, who we are talking about. So I say, But I think violent acts can only beget more violent acts.

The words are out of my mouth and I can't take them back. He isn't talking about the death penalty, he's talking about whoever it was who killed his sister. But Fred ignores me, has other things to say too, isn't interested in discussing the death penalty so he goes right on talking past me.

He says, A couple of years ago, I had this customer . . . an elderly man. I looked at his name on the credit card. It was the guy who found her. He lived in the house on Coolidge Street. I asked him why he didn't go outside that night to see why his dog was barking.

Up pops a memory. Oh no. The dog barking in the night. The dog was barking at the time Irene was being attacked. Tyler couldn't tolerate a dog barking. Is that the night I'm remembering? The night of the field trip to the Hartford Electric Light Company? Tyler carried on with a vengeance. *Stop that dog. Stop that dog.*

Tyler was running up and down the eight feet of hallway between the kitchen and his den, hands over his ears. When his wrist came up to his mouth, my father said, Tyler, look. I'm going out. I'm going to stop the dog from barking.

But the dog stopped barking while my father was putting on his jacket, the one with a hood—the jacket he wore when it rained. He hung it back up. Tyler calmed down.

Fred says, I mean . . . The guy was a *cop.*

I press the small, rolled-up sog that was once a coaster back to my mouth. I remember. Now I think that maybe my father could have saved Irene if only Tyler had threatened to bite his arm a little sooner or if the dog's barking had persisted.

Don't faint, don't faint, I tell myself, as the piece of memory fits into place.

What an extraordinary coincidence that Irene is killed in the backyard of a Hartford police officer, who is the dispatcher on duty that night—the very cop who sends out the call that a child is missing.

While Irene is being murdered a few hours before the cop leaves for work, his dog is barking and barking. The cop and his wife bring him in and he keeps barking until they give him some table scraps and then he is quiet. That is the night my father sighs and says to me, I better get my jacket.

Fred is going on: The cop told me he just didn't know. The dog barked at everything. Anything.

What has that cop suffered? I think. How many times has he asked himself why he didn't go outside and see what was bothering his dog? And my father. He must have asked himself why he waited until Tyler was about to bite his wrist before getting his jacket. Why didn't he go out right away? And how many other neighbors heard the dog? How many of them were about to call that cop, or in fact, did call him to tell him to quiet his dog? But then he was a cop; who would have dared to complain to him?

Fred is still talking. He says, The police came to our house. They said they needed to talk to me. Two cops got me outside and I thought they were going to offer condolences. They took me to their cruiser and put me in the backseat, locked the doors. One cop said, We all have fights with our brothers and sisters, don't we? So I said that we did. They talked to me some more and then they told me they knew I'd killed Irene and that I might as well admit it. I told them I hadn't. They said I must have blacked out and didn't remember killing her, but that I did. They said they were pretty sure they had someone who saw me do it.

I don't know if Fred hears my voice, muffled, when I say, Oh God.

He goes on: My mother came out to find me. She pounded on the window of the police car. She sent me into the house while she spoke to them. The cops never bothered me again.

Then he sighs.

After the sigh, he asks me about myself, about being a writer—what's it like?—and I answer with some stupid damn thing, I don't know what, and soldier on; my turn to ask about him.

How are you doing, Fred?

He says, Business is good. Oh, and by the way . . .

Fred tells me he is married to a wonderful woman, his second wife. He says, She's very smart and she reads all the time, and she can write . . .

He pauses. Then: But she's very quiet about it. I wish I could encourage her.

I think of a writer I know who is quiet about her work. The two of us had travel pieces included in a collection of essays. She told me she's kept almost all of what she's written hidden away . . . Protected, she said, from agents and editors.

I ask Fred, Do you have children?

I want him to say yes, a half-dozen, all girls.

He says, I have a daughter, but we're estranged. I don't see her.

Jesus Christ. Another little girl in his life, his daughter, only to be gone from him, too. But it is not my business.

We chat a little bit more and then I give him my phone number, tell him to call back anytime. Or his wife can call me if she likes. We'll talk about writing.

After I put the phone down, after my conversation with Fred, I start gagging but I will away throwing up. I believe I am gagging because I have so little experience with crying what with Tyler, who wouldn't allow it. I wonder which hurt Tyler worse. The sound of crying or the barking of a dog?

thirty-one

I THINK ABOUT IT—crying or the barking of a dog? The one that affects my life most, even as an adult, is crying.

When I am married and then have a baby, I am banished by my parents. I cannot enter my Nilan Street home or the cottage at Chalker Beach unless I'm alone, which I never am it seems, not anymore. The new baby will, at some point do what new babies do: Cry.

I accept this. I have been trained to obey the demands of Tyler. I give no thought to complicating my parents' life pointing out the injustice in my banishment. And too, my father arranges for a sitter for Tyler—usually Auntie Palma—so he can visit us once a week. Sometimes, when he doesn't have much time (I now live seventy-five miles from Hartford), we meet halfway for lunch.

When the baby is two as we are getting into the car, she tells the postman that we are going to visit Grandpa. The postman asks, Where does Grandpa live?

In a restaurant, she says.

I have to laugh to myself. Why should a two-year-old question why her grandfather lives in a restaurant when her mother doesn't question his decision to banish her?

My father takes early retirement to devote himself to Tyler's care. He becomes a living tool, a combination hammer and screwdriver, in order to fix the world so that Tyler can be kept in an agitation-free state. A real challenge, that. I don't say anything.

In the summer, we stay at a motel on the corner of Chalker Beach Road and Route 1. My father visits us poolside or we go to the beach;

Tyler is still sleeping during the day. My father's friendly next door neighbor who built our cottage has rigged up a line between the cottage and his house so that if Tyler wakes to find my father gone, he buzzes the neighbor who comes and gets him.

My mother takes early retirement so she can play uninterrupted golf and cards. Also, she and Auntie Margaret take the church bus on outings to the new Pequot bingo parlors.

On occasion, my mother, along with her sister, visits me. She sits stiffly in my living room chair. Overtime she comes to have a great affection for her grandchildren, bringing them gadgets and toys and sweaters she knits. She gets out of the chair to teach them songs from her childhood. Auntie Margaret and I fall all over ourselves laughing at one song in particular, which requires the children to follow her lead in touching their various body parts:

I touch meinself here,
Vat is it, mein dear?
Das is my browsweater here, yah-yah,
And dat's what I learn in my school, yah-yah.

I touch meinself here,
Vat is it, mein dear?
Das is my schnotblower here, yah-yah.
And dat's what I learn in my school, yah-yah.

I touch meinself here,
Vat is it, mein dear?
Das is my bullshooter here, yah-yah.
And dat's what I learn in my school, yah-yah.

I touch meinself here,
Vat is it, mein dear?
Das is my breadbasket here, yah-yah,
And dat's what I learn in my school, yah-yah.

I touch meinself here,
Vat is it, mein dear?
Das is my fartcellar here, yah-yah.
And dat's what I learn in my school, yah-yah.

But my mother doesn't touch the children. Once when she's sitting in the chair, my baby son crawls toward her. She puts her palm up: Don't touch Grandma, sweetheart. Grandma is wearing pantyhose.

So Auntie Margaret scoops him up and the more he slobbers on her, the happier she is.

One day, my father says to me out of the blue, Your mother thinks we can't take care of Tyler anymore. I told her I would take care of him myself.

I'm flabbergasted. He has great fear in his eyes, fear that I will take my mother's side. So I don't. I tell him that's what he's been doing all along.

A shrink would have a swell time analyzing my father's need to spend the rest of his life catering to Tyler instead of attempting to find normalcy in his final years. And Tyler has no advocate who might come up with a solution to his psychopathic anxiety.

I leave it. I have enough of changing diapers, breast-feeding, and getting up at 4 A.M. to write while the house is still. I completely understand Sylvia Plath's sticking her head in an oven.

As the years go by, I miss Tyler terribly.

Part III

The Quest

thirty-two

AFTER I TALK to Irene's brother Fred, I only know one thing: I want to go back and read those newspapers my father didn't let me read. I want to find out what happened to Irene. I want to know who killed her. How dare there be no one who remembers Irene? No one who *thinks* about her? I owe it to her to bring her back. But how stupid is that? She's dead. So maybe I owe it to myself. But who the hell cares about what I owe myself? I guess just Professor Swann at Central Connecticut State College. And Fred cares.

Irene was killed twice, murdered by a horrific man, and then erased by the era that was the fifties—all who needed to talk about her silenced. A memorial is something to preserve the memory of a person. That's what I want to do. Build a memorial to Irene.

I GO SIT in my office and stare into the wall. Thinking is mostly what writers do—stare at walls, out windows, into space. Sometimes, practically drooling. When my son is around seven or eight years old, he comes into the kitchen to find me rooted in front of an open cupboard, seemingly mesmerized by its contents. Being such a soul mate, he calls out to the rest of the family, Don't go in the kitchen—Mom's writing.

Of my eight novels, three are a mystery series. I have felt compelled to create a sleuth who finds out what happened to murder victims, who killed them and why. And then my sleuth brings them to justice. The second in the series is about a serial killer who preys on teenaged girls. When he is killing his last victim, he realizes she's younger than he thought. She's actually only eleven. He stops just short of killing her but abandons her in a place where she will surely die. Then my intrepid sleuth comes to the rescue and saves her life.

I fictionalized Irene's death except that I didn't let her die. But she did die and now it's time to face up to that and allow the memory of her to take hold. A murder wanes, but memory lasts forever. But the murder wanes only when the memory is dealt with.

Taped to my office wall is something JFK once said: *A writer must be true to himself and let the chips fall where they may.* I think about that and what Kurt Vonnegut said too. A little over two of my first twenty-five years are gone missing. Just like my French grandparents having a baby every other year for twenty-four years with that unexplained four-year gap, which I later learn was created by Pippi's service in the Boer War. My gap was created by the death of Irene.

Time to fill in the gap. Sorry, Irene, that it took so long but here we go. Here is what happened to you. Here is who did it. Here is justice. We'll just let the chips fall.

40 POLICEMEN PRESS HUNT FOR STRANGLER OF GIRL, 11

Sitting in front of a microfilm machine, I watch the *Hartford Courant* headline, December 11, 1953, whirl past. I turn the knob the wrong way. More and more headlines flash along. I put the knob in reverse until I find the one I want again. I remember clearly the *Hartford Times* headline of the night before, but not this one in the *Courant*. The photograph I remember from the *Times* is Irene posed in front of a spring-flowering tree, standing straight, wearing her First Communion dress and veil and the big grin on her face. In the *Courant,* a more recent photo fills the page, a close-up, head and shoulders, a fifth-grader with eyes as warm and bright as Loretta Young's.

I read about the killing, the relief that she was not raped is obvious in the reporter's words. No one knew yet about Detective Egan finding the pink underpants. I turn the knob and turn the knob, and read the articles that appeared in the *Hartford Courant* over the next week until I find myself staring into the face of a former sailor from California named Robert Nelson Malm.

He is very very handsome. He is wearing a trench coat and a cigarette hangs jauntily from his bottom lip. He looks like a forties movie version of a private detective, Dashiell Hammett's Sam Spade. I press the print button on the machine and I watch his picture slide out. I pick it up and look at it. He looks sincere; he looks like he'd be able to solve the case of the Maltese Falcon. But I wanted him to look like a ghoul. I hate his guts for being so damnably charming.

WHEN THE ISSUE of the *Hartford Courant* with Monsignor Musiel's plea arrived on everyone's doorsteps, the police had already brought in the man they suspect killed Irene, though he is not charged with that crime. He is, in fact, in police headquarters during Irene's funeral. He'd been picked up because of his record, the incarcerations for sexual assault beginning with the stint in reform school in California when he was twelve and ending with his release from the Connecticut state prison eight months earlier.

Robert Malm is informed that he is a suspect in the attack on Miss Patricia D'Allessio two weeks before on November 22. He is told he will take part in a lineup. He agrees, no doubt relieved that he isn't under suspicion for the murder of Irene.

The courageous Pidgie D'Allessio arrives at police headquarters within an hour after Bob is brought in. (This is a time when newspapers routinely printed the names of victims accusing men of rape.)

Accompanied by her parents, Pidgie first looks at an array of photographs on Chief Godfrey's desk. There are about thirty of them. She scans them, points to two of the photographs and says, These two look like him but they're not him, and with those words, her gaze falls upon the photo of Robert Nelson Malm. The shock of seeing his face causes her to put her own face in her hands.

Policewoman Conroy is in the room, too, and helps Pidgie compose herself. Chief Godfrey is attempting to calm Mr. D'Allessio, who is shouting once again, Where is he? Let me get one shot at him.

Policewoman Conroy makes it clear to Pidgie that she is about to actually see before her own eyes the man who terrorized, humiliated, and choked her almost to death. The man who went on to kill a child named Irene.

Do you understand, Pidgie?

Yes.

Pidgie and her parents are brought into a small room with a large picture window. The chief explains to her, Honey, it's just like *Dragnet*. The other side of the window is mirrored and the nine men you're going to see will not be able to see you. All they'll see is themselves reflected in the mirror.

Pidgie begins to whimper. The chief ignores that. He says, Come, Pidgie, and he takes her inside the room by the hand so that she'll know she is being told the truth. Then the chief brings her back to the other side of the glass.

A line of men led by a uniformed police officer files in. The representative of the department is always uniformed so that the witnesses won't suddenly leap up and mistakenly identify him as the perpetrator of a crime.

The tall, attractive man with black wavy hair and deep-set eyes is seventh in the line. Before he reaches the number painted on the floor, Pidgie moans and doubles over.

Policewoman Conroy knows what to do just as the chief knew what to do. She takes Pidgie's hand in both of hers and says, You have to look up now, dear. After that, you must wait until all the men are standing on their numbers and all you'll have to do is say the number where the man who attacked you is standing. That's all. Just say the number.

The men arrange themselves on their assigned numbers. Pidgie looks up and whispers, Seven.

While she sobs, her father flies to the door, where he is restrained by several officers. Once he gains control of himself, he says to the chief, What's the bastard's name?

Captain Godfrey says to him, Robert Malm.

Mr. D'Allessio repeats the name aloud and does exactly what his daughter did, moans and doubles over.

Before Pidgie will fill out the necessary papers swearing that Bob Malm is the man who attacked her, she has to go into a room with her mother and Policewoman Conroy and listen to Bob Malm speak. The policewoman says, Pidgie, you've seen him. That was the hard part. It's done. This will take just a few more seconds.

Then she squeezes Pidgie's hand. Pidgie squeezes back. The chief tells her father that if he goes in, too, and loses control, they might not be able to get Malm to admit to what he did to Pidgie. Mr. D'Allessio has to agree.

The two women with the teenaged girl between them go into an interrogation room where Bob Malm is sitting between Captain Egan and a uniformed officer. The chief asks Bob Malm, who is cuffed, Did you attack this girl on the evening of November 22?

Bob Malm looks up at Pidgie, gazes at her from beneath his hooded eyes, and says in a bored tone, Never seen her before in my life.

Immediately, Pidgie and her mother are led out of the room. Outside, Pidgie needs no prodding; she says, That was him.

The chief asks, You recognized his voice as well as his face?

Yes.

All present thank Pidgie and her parents and she is told she can go home as soon as she fills out the papers. Policewoman Conroy will help her.

When they've been ushered out, the chief says to Captain Egan: That piece of shit picked the wrong kid when he grabbed Patricia D'Allessio.

Now a second lineup is arranged, and Chief Godfrey and Captain

Egan go back into the interrogation room and sit down at the table with Bob, who is smoking one of his Old Golds. Egan says to him, How ya doin'?

Bob answers, I can't get a break.

Captain Egan asks him, What kind of break do you think you deserve?

I was working that night. The night that girl says I grabbed her.

No, you weren't.

I was filling in for another guy. We're not supposed to do that. But I did him a favor. Our supervisor didn't know about it.

What's his name?

I can't rat out a friend.

The chief and the captain leave the room to see if the taxi driver has been brought in yet, the taxi driver who picked up a fare on the night of December 9 at 9 P.M. at a tavern on Hillside Avenue and took him to Cedarcrest Sanatorium.

He is there, waiting. They inform Bob that they need to reconstruct the lineup. He says, sure.

The taxi driver immediately identifies Bob Malm as his fare on the night of December 9.

Later, a Hartford detective visits the six other men who work as dishwashers at Cedarcrest. All six insist Bob hadn't taken their shifts on November 22.

The next morning, while Bob Malm is processed, arrested, and printed in connection with the assault on Pidgie D'Allessio without any mention of the murder of a little girl two weeks later, Irene is lowered into the ground at St. Benedict's Cemetery on the Hartford/Bloomfield city line very close to the new C.G. international headquarters.

thirty-three

THE POLICE CAREFULLY segue Robert Malm from his attack on Pidgie D'Allessio on November 22, to the murder of Irene committed on December 9. He denies all. He has been denying all since he was twelve years old.

The police know they will need a confession from him. They have no evidence, no witnesses to the crime. They will need a confession because a capital crime, punishable by death, requires two witnesses to that crime or witnesses who will swear they saw the accused and the victim together near the scene of the crime, at the time of the crime.

Connecticut is the only state of the thirty-six with the death penalty on the books that will allow a jury judging a capital crime to determine if the evidence is the equivalent of two eyewitness accounts. Even with that, the death penalty is difficult to achieve without the accused admitting he did it.

Rape requires two eyewitnesses to the crime, period. Equivalent evidence cannot be considered by the jury since rape wasn't a capital crime. What this means is that the police generally don't arrest a rapist unless he's murdered his victim. (Decades later, the feminist movement will be solely responsible for the change to that travesty of law.)

In the initial rounds of the investigation, the police find no one who saw Bob Malm and Irene together. They canvass Charter Oak Terrace and learn that a teenage couple went to Jack's store the evening Irene was killed. The couple saw her enter the store as they were leaving but they don't remember anyone else being in the store at the time. They did spot Kathy Delaney on the way home playing behind the church with other children.

Captain Jimmy Egan visits the Delaney family in Charter Oak Terrace. Kathy Delaney tells him she saw two people she refers to as a boy and girl turning into Sequin Street. She is surprised when Egan asks if the girl was Irene. Since she can't fathom Irene walking with a strange man, she says no. She says it was Brenda and her boyfriend, Charlie. The captain tries to get her to think harder. She insists the girl wasn't Irene even though she was. (Kathy doesn't mention any rock throwing.) Egan finally faces the fact that the children will not make reliable court witnesses when it comes to seeing to it that Malm is condemned to die. He's going to need insurance.

Up at the corner store, Jack initially tells investigators that he never saw Irene in his store the night she was murdered. They show him her photograph. He thinks he knows who she is, but is sure she wasn't in his store that night. His employee pipes up, Yes she was!

He recalls what a pain in the neck it was weighing those potatoes and coming up with exactly two pounds. He says to the cops, If I went over the two pounds her mother would be here the next day complaining.

Jack says, Oh, yeah, *that* kid!

A few days later, Jimmy Egan shows Jack and his employee a photo of Bob Malm and they are in agreement: Never seen him before.

Egan visits each man at his home that night. He explains the police now have the man in the photo in custody. He describes what Malm did to Pidgie a few weeks earlier and tells the men he undoubtedly did the same thing to Irene before he killed her. With that, Jack remembers he did see Irene and Bob Malm in his store at the same time.

Around seven-fifteen? asks the cop.

Yeah. Around seven-fifteen.

Jack's employee remembers, too.

In the Hartford County Jail, Bob Malm, when asked about the grocery store, says, What grocery store?

The police have now got equivalent eyewitness testimony from two people. But the chief tells Egan he doesn't want to use their statements unless he has to because of the risk of having their witnesses swayed under cross-examination by the defense when testifying to the accuracy of what they saw.

But the only evidence the police have is that the killer used a square knot in Irene's scarf to strangle her, a knot taught in basic Navy training, and Bob Malm served in the Navy. But in searching his locker at Cedarcrest, they discover a pair of dirty socks stuck all over with beggar's-lice.

A forensics team dashes to Officer Proccacino's yard, where they are unable to find beggar's-lice. So they walk a few feet to the yard abutting the Proccacinos', Bobby Turner's yard on Nilan Street, where our sledding flights always ended smack up against the Turners' privet hedge. The team finds several patches. Mr. Turner is not such a fanatic about keeping his yard as weed-free as Officer Proccacino. The team next heads over to the Sequin Street lot with the overturned boat. The lot is rife with beggar's-lice just as all overgrown lots are in Hartford, which is something every fifth-grader in Miss Bowie's class now knows.

However, that won't ice anything. The two pieces of evidence are not the equivalent of eyewitness testimony.

And so, Chief Godfrey sets his sights on eliciting a confession from the slick Bob Malm. Beyond questioning, there are only three things he can do to encourage a confession. Beating prisoners has been outlawed since the thirties, but he can withhold sleep, he can keep him from cleaning himself, and he can deprive him of food though the latter guideline doesn't permit starving the prisoner. The chief has learned that if you get a man tired and hungry enough, maybe over a period of three days, he will confess to anything. But then the next day he'll recant. Chief Godfrey doesn't want recanted confessions so orders that Bob Malm be fed and rested. However, Bob is a meticulous fellow, snappily dressed. So the cops directly involved with him will see that he stays in his clothes and not be allowed to shower. They do that out of hatred for him.

The chief will not utilize other acceptable tactics either. He will not threaten the prisoner or lie to him. He could tell Bob Malm that his mother is dying out in California and has asked on her deathbed that he tell the truth; the chief could tell him that they have an eyewitness to his crime; he could tell Bob Malm they found an item of his clothing at the scene of the crime. They could tell him what they told Irene's brother, Fred—that he was in a fog and didn't remember killing her. The police can do this because in *Connecticut v. Palko,* a ten-year-old case, the court ruled: *The object of evidence is to get at the truth and a trick which has no tendency to produce a confession except one in accordance with truth is always admissible.* In other words, call a lie a trick, and it's okay. Tell a grieving young boy he's killed his sister and trick him into an admission. Fine, says the law.

I ask a couple of cops about that. One of them says, As long as lawyers lie, we have to lie too, or we'll have empty prisons.

CHIEF GODFREY has come to get a feel for Bob Malm. He knows Bob has been in police custody too many times not to recognize such a trick. And so, Chief Godfrey will use other methods to soften him up: camaraderie, sympathy, a perceived willingness to believe him, a promise of leniency if he confesses since as Egan tells him, *You need psychiatric help, Malm,* and a sausage and pepper grinder, too. Malm says a sausage and pepper grinder sounds great and one is ordered for him.

A grinder is the Connecticut version of a hero, a sub, or a po'boy, except that most of the inside of the foot-long sliced-open Italian bread is scooped out and you're left with two thick, chewy, leathery crusts, which are filled with meat, roasted peppers, tomatoes, and shredded lettuce, the entire contraption then sprinkled with olive oil. Before closing it up, the best Italian restaurants, like Luigi's in Old Saybrook, will layer provolone cheese over all and run the open grinder under a broiler for just the number of seconds required to warm and soften, not melt the provolone.

Bob Malm slowly begins to act in a way that indicates he is coming to trust his interrogators. He starts making excuses for his crimes. He says, yes, he was with Pidgie D'Allessio but insists it was a date and as for what happened . . . Well, she liked it.

But right then, an especially large and heavy monkey wrench is tossed into the proceeding and it lands in the interrogation room with a loud reverberating bong. Someone else has confessed to murdering Irene.

JOHN H. WILLIAMS is an Army private stationed at Fort Devens, Massachusetts. He says that he killed Irene after walking around my neighborhood in a drunken stupor, AWOL at the time. He writes a two-page confession after being questioned by the Army's Criminal Investigation Division. This means Chief Godfrey must now convince the police commissioner and many other government officials—meaning a lot of politicians—that the soldier's confession is a hoax. But with this timely confession of Private Williams, the politicians don't want to hear about Chief Godfrey's own suspect, Robert Nelson Malm. After all, Godfrey's had Malm in custody for three days and he hasn't cracked. Now with the soldier's confession, there's no need to crack Malm—they have Irene's killer.

The commissioner says to Godfrey, Let Hartford's kids back outside to play. Time for them to get on with their little lives. And let's not forget this, Chief: *Christmas is coming!*

Chief Godfrey has no choice but to abandon the questioning of Bob Malm, and without waiting for a warrant to be issued for the arrest of Private Williams, grabs a couple of cops and races to Fort Devens in a police cruiser, a trip which normally takes three hours in a car unequipped with a blue dome on its roof plus a siren. The chief is at Fort Devens in two.

Chief Godfrey immediately recognizes Private Williams, remembers seeing him at various police stations in the city, where he was brought in many a time on charges related to drunkenness. The first thing the chief asks the soldier is if he recognizes him, and Private Williams looks toward him in what the chief considers a dim-witted way and says, No.

The chief listens, enraged, as Private Williams calmly explains that he followed Irene and some kids from Charter Oak Terrace to the little grocery store.

He says, When Irene left the other children, I stopped her and she went with me through several streets.

Willingly?

Yes. Then we went down an embankment and I started to molest her. When she screamed, I choked her and she got quiet and I left.

You choked her with your bare hands?

Yes.

The Fort Devens provost marshal takes Chief Godfrey aside and tells him that at that point the soldier's mind went blank though he thought he remembered carrying the body down a dirt path.

The chief questions Private Williams further, knowing that in order to convince the politicians, he must disprove the confession beyond the details that do not match the events of the crime. So Chief Godfrey asks to see the provost marshal and requests that the marshal assign two military police to him in order to take John Williams back to Hartford in his custody so that he can walk him over the terrain of the crime and have him explain in detail what he did. Chief Godfrey knows military reservation law and civil law, as well, so he is aware that he is asking the impossible.

The provost marshal cannot grant the chief's request and suggests he speak to the judge advocate of the fort.

The judge is familiar with the circumstances that brought the chief to the fort. He says to the chief, I am very sorry but the boy is a soldier of the United States Army; he's on a military reservation; he is in another state, and I am sure you understand what that means.

The chief says, I am only asking he be brought to Hartford for a short time. A few hours. He can be returned by the same MPs who bring him.

The judge says, The only way I can let you have him is for you to obtain a warrant from your prosecutor and then I'll turn him over to you and if there is nothing to it we will pick him up and take him back.

The chief is in a Catch-22 dilemma. If he asks for a warrant, he is admitting to the possibility that Private Williams committed the crime. This absolutely can't happen or the cracking wall that braces the chief's predicament will fall. He tries a new tack: Judge, would you accept a breach of peace warrant just to let him come back to Connecticut.

The chief knows the answer the judge will give and listens to him give it: The boy has to be charged with a felony before we can do anything.

The chief has no choice but to call Captain Egan at Hartford headquarters and tell him to go through the opening motions of obtaining the warrant.

Egan says, In the middle of the night?

Yeah.

Egan knows the chief is following orders and also knows that, realistically, there is no getting a motion until morning.

The chief returns to the Army interrogation room exasperated, stands over Private Williams, and asks him, Why are you telling me this story?

I want to get it off my chest.

Are you sure you aren't telling it to me so you can get out of the Army, get out of the court-martial you are facing here?

The private smiles and says, No, I like the Army.

With that, the chief commands the Hartford officer who accompanied him to Fort Devens, Sergeant Ralph McGuinness, to lie down on the floor. McGuinness is taken aback, but immediately does as his chief asks.

The chief says, Private Williams, I want you to demonstrate what you did to that little girl.

I told you, I strangled her.

Show me.

Private Williams gets down on the floor and pretends to choke Sergeant McGuinness with his hands.

Now get up.

He does.

Describe the terrain again. The place where you strangled her.

I have a headache. I'm sick of this.

The chief has been at Fort Devens a long time and his response to Williams is, So the hell am I. The last words the chief utters on his way out the door are directed at the provost marshal. He says, Turn that little shit over to the MPs and see to it that he be court-martialed. *On a charge of AWOL, not murder!*

As the chief is racing back to Hartford, he gets a call on the police radio from the provost telling him that not only is Private Williams still insisting he killed Irene but that he cut off a lock of her hair, which he hid. The soldier wants to tell the chief where he hid it, and he won't speak to anyone else. Chief Godfrey hangs up, radios Hartford, and tells the dispatcher that he will not accept any more calls from Fort Devens.

Within minutes there comes another call, this time from the commissioner telling the chief to go back, find out where the lock of hair is, get it, and arrest John Williams.

The chief explains to his boss that the coroner determined that Irene's hair was intact. He fabricates without the slightest hesitation.

Upon arriving back in Hartford, Chief Godfrey is able to make everyone gathered at the commissioner's home in the middle of the night see that the soldier's confession is a hoax because of the scarf business, and besides that, his own suspect is about to confess at any second.

The commissioner and the Hartford politicians relent ever so slightly, giving Chief Godfrey the rest of the night to get a confession from Bob Malm. He will have till 9 A.M, seven hours. If he doesn't get it by then, he is to charge the soldier at Fort Devens with Irene's murder and arrest him. It is pointed out to Chief Godfrey that Malm was a model prisoner at the Wethersfield State Prison for five years; his parole officer can't say enough good things about him; and his success at his job at the Cedarcrest Sanatorium has proven him to be an upstanding citizen.

Chief Michael J. Godfrey tells the politicians the same thing he told the provost at Fort Devens but in a much calmer tone. He says, The soldier, John Williams, is guilty of being absent without leave.

And then he walks out without another word and heads for the Hartford County Jail.

In his car, he calls his man, Egan, asks him if Malm has heard about Williams's confession. Egan says, Course not.

The chief orders him to see to it that Bob Malm does not hear of that confession no matter what. Then the chief asks Jimmy Egan, Who's with you?

Mancini.

Put him on.

John Mancini is an officer with the Hartford County Police, a jurisdiction that must be represented in a capital investigation taking place within the county. The chief gives Mancini the same order he gave Egan.

Then to Egan again: I'll be over there in twenty minutes and our goddamn time is running out.

When Egan hangs up the phone, Bob's antennae have raised. He asks, You boys got a problem?

Egan's fists are curled and tight. He wants to kill Robert Malm. Mancini can see this and steps in. Mancini has been around, and as a county officer rather than a city cop, he is less encumbered by politics. This gives him the leisure to think rather than connive, and he has been thinking.

He leans toward Bob and says nonchalantly, Girls get to be eleven, twelve years old, ya know? And it's just at that time they choose one road or the other, right, Bob? A girl can take the good road or she can take the road to wayward behavior. We fellows all know about dirty girls, don't we, Bob? I mean, there's a lot of talk in the neighborhood that possibly the girl accosted you, not the other way around. Matter of fact, I had an argument with my wife about that myself. This morning, even.

Egan sees the hint of a smile on Bob's face. Bob, he is sure, is connecting the question to the phone call. Bob senses the break he believes he's finally getting. He raises his hooded eyes. He says, She winked at me.

Mancini doesn't move a muscle. Egan swallows so he'll sound calm and carefully says to Mancini, You continue on here with Bob and I'll be right back.

He saunters out the door, closes it behind him, and runs for a phone just as Chief Godfrey is dashing into the jail. The two come face-to-face. Egan says, We got the motherfucker.

thirty-four

CHIEF GODFREY doesn't waste more than thirty seconds casually apologizing to Bob for having been gone so long. The chief can see that Bob is no longer in the agitated state he left him in. He says to Bob, After the girl winked at you, did she say anything?

Yeah. She said hello to me.

Do you suppose she thought she knew you?

Maybe. Acted like she did.

Then what happened?

Oh, I was just talking with her, walking along, making conversation . . . Bob lights his thousandth Old Gold . . . until I saw some kids coming. I took her across an empty lot and we hid under a boat. Boat was up on a few concrete blocks.

The girl went willingly with you, Bob? Agreed to hide with you? Crawled under the boat and all?

Yeah, she did.

Then what happened?

Those kids I saw came right up to the boat. The little snots started throwing rocks. I yelled at them and they ran away. Then I took the girl out from under the boat with me and we went to the back of the lot and there was a fence.

What did you do?

I helped the girl over the fence.

Helped her?

Yeah.

She was still going along with you willingly?

193

Yeah.

Then?

I took her through some backyards to the next street. Then we crossed that street, and we went down this driveway to the backyard of some house.

Bob takes an especially deep drag on his cigarette. The chief waits. Bob continues: There was this shed in the corner of the yard behind a picket fence and we tried to get in it but the door was stuck or locked, I don't know.

Did she say anything?

Yeah.

What?

She said she had to get home before her brother did.

Anything else?

No.

What happened next?

I helped her take her clothes off and then she laid down on her coat, and we . . . ya know . . . we fooled around.

You didn't rape her?

Nah.

Did you ejaculate?

I think so.

The chief let that one go by.

Then?

Then I left.

You left after you strangled her with her scarf?

I didn't strangle anyone.

You tied a scarf around her neck. You tied it real tight.

Well, yeah, but that was to teach her a lesson.

What lesson?

She said she was gonna tell her mother.

Chief Godfrey thinks, Vera was right. He didn't kill Irene because she resisted. He killed her because she said she would tell her mother what he did. He thinks, Malm has placed the onus of his crime on little Irene. It's all her fault.

He says, So, Bob, she died? I mean, from the scarf?

I figured she could be dead.

What did you do after you figured she might be dead?

I told you, I left.

No thought to resuscitating her?

Bob Malm looks at the chief as if he's hearing a foreign language. The chief asks him if he'll go over the information again so it can be put in writing.

Sure.

Egan dashes out for a typewriter, returns, and puts paper in the roller. All three cops look up at Bob Malm. He repeats what he's said while Egan types like he's never typed before. Chief Godfrey arrests Bob for the murder of Irene based on his confession.

Bob says, The captain here told me I need a head doctor.

The chief stares at his killer. He says, Yeah, you do. And you'll get one.

The chief orders a mittimus, a precept in writing under the hand and seal of a peace officer, which will be handed to the jailer of a prison, commanding him to receive safely and keep the person charged with an offense . . . *herein named in the mittimus until he shall be delivered by due course of law*. The jail where Bob is received safely and handed to the jailer is the Hartford County Jail, where my Uncle Chick works.

THE BAN IS LIFTED; all the kids in the neighborhood can play outside again. No one says Irene's killer is caught, or arrested, or put in jail or anything at all, but I know that must be what happened since my father tells me I can go outside after school and play again and also he doesn't keep the newspapers from me anymore.

He says, Don't tell your mother I'm letting you read the papers again.

Not to worry. I won't remember what I read in the coming year's newspapers for decades when I will see them again at the main branch of the Hartford Public Library. Except for one thing, that is. I know that Dondi does not age during the five days I missed reading the strip, or ever at all.

thirty-five

IN THE MIDDLE of my research, I catch a flu I can't shake. I begin to lose weight and that cheers me up a little. But after six weeks of feeling crummy, I decide I must have diabetes. That's because Tyler, as he enters middle age, catches a flu he can't shake, loses weight, and just won't come around. Then he even begins limping.

He is diagnosed with adult-onset, type 2 diabetes, which my grandfather had, as do my Auntie Palma, Auntie Alice, and Uncle John Tirone.

Tyler has to have his big toe amputated and soon after, retina surgery so he won't go blind. His critter is blind by then, his one remaining black button eye gone. While Tyler is in Hartford Hospital, a number of staff come to gape at him and spread the word: *We've got Rain Man on nine!*

Tyler asks the nurses to pose for him. He's made sure to bring his trusty View-Master to the hospital in addition to the critter whose remaining three limbs hang by threads. Tyler's *doppelgänger* as it turns out. One nurse asks his doctor if the critter can accompany Tyler to surgery. The doctor asks her if she's lost her mind—the critter is beyond filthy. She promises Tyler she will hold the critter for him until he comes back to his room. He doesn't put up too much of a fuss as she's already injected him with a sedative.

My mother visits him once. Tyler asks her would she clip his nails, something she used to do before she abdicated responsibility for his care. She says, No, Tyler, the nurse will do it.

Then she kisses him good-bye and tells him she'll see him at home. My Auntie Margaret and I stare at her back as she leaves.

My mother has detached from Tyler as my father becomes more attached to him than ever. He will not leave Tyler's side, sleeps in a chair in the room at night though the nurses assure him they will see to his care, promise to call him at home if Tyler asks for him. He says, I don't want Tyler to have to ask for me.

When my own flulike symptoms continue, I go to see a doctor even though both my big toes look fine. I go to my obstetrician, obstetrics being the only medical need I've ever had not counting the broken arm when I was three. She tells me that type 2 diabetes seems to affect half the siblings in a family, why, she has no idea. She does a test and that bit of wisdom applies to me; Mary continues to intercede. My doctor diagnoses a sinus infection, prescribes an antibiotic, and I recover.

Then it's back to the library.

I CHRONICLE Robert Nelson Malm's life, find what few facts exist. I don't have to think about him too much if I am scribbling demonically in my notebook. I learn of the terrible circumstances of his birth, his initial arrests, his military career. In articles published by the *New London Day* fifty years ago, I read what Navy men have to say about their fellow sailor. They like him—pleasant enough fellow. Quiet guy. They refer to him as Bob. And I come to think of him as Bob.

Bob, the heinous killer, gradually becomes real to me and soon I know exactly who killed Irene, so I write about Bob from the time he is born until he confesses to killing my friend Irene.

I put it all in a folder and file it hoping I can make this Bob go away. I can't.

I REMEMBER the Allyn Street Theater. In Hartford, every neighborhood has its own little movie house; my friends and I go to the Elm on New Britain Avenue, just over the West Hartford line in a tiny blue-collar enclave called Elmwood, where my father was raised and where my grandfather helped build the Luna Club. We don't go to the downtown theaters except on rare occasions when first-runs are irresistible. I remember going to Main Street to the big theaters for two movies; once with my Auntie Palma, who takes me to see *Showboat* starring Howard Keel and Ann Blythe, and also to the Strand, where, as a thirteen-year-old, I see *Love Me Tender* five times with my best friend, Linda. The manager of the Strand announces on the sound system that Elvis Presley is no different from any other actor and the audience is not to scream when he appears in a scene. But the audience proceeds to scream the minute the lights go down and throughout the entire movie. Then we weep bitterly when the Elvis character dies. I am one of the most enthusiastic screamers but I have to fake the crying part. My friend, Linda, doesn't fake it. She screams and bawls authentically through all five showings. One day, Linda will become a nun, settle for a marriage to Jesus since the love of her life is beyond her charms.

I went to the Allyn once, with my high school boyfriend because he really wanted to see *The Creature from the Black Lagoon.* I remember enjoying it terrifically because the half-man, half-amphibian was so sympathetic.

In the library, I press the little button that moves my *Hartford Times* film along. I start with the article covering Irene's funeral, and I notice a short unrelated article on the same page about the arrest of a man wanted in the assault of a girl on Beaufort Street, which had occurred two weeks earlier. The reporter was onto something.

A librarian who has been helping me taps me on the shoulder and I jump. He says, I can get you the coroner's report. It'll take a few days though—they're at another location.

A few days? Good. I'll need a few days to prepare myself. Also, as my father might put it, a short one will help, too.

. . .

I HEAD TOWARD HOME on I-91 when my car decides to veer right and gets off the highway at the Brainard Field exit and aims west through to my old Hartford neighborhood. I drive down New Britain Avenue, past Hillside, and bear right onto Coolidge. When I get to Broadview Terrace, I don't make a right turn toward Nilan Street, where I once lived, but left, past Sequin Street, and then I take a right at Dart. At the bottom of Dart Street, I park. Across from me on the other side of Chandler Street, Charter Oak Terrace is laid out. It is now home to the Bloods and the Crips, to the truly impoverished; there are fires all the time. Irene lived in the corner of the grid in front of me.

I get out of the car and walk up Dart Street away from Irene's apartment. What had been woods on the right side of the street is now minuscule ranch homes in a derelict state. At the corner, I turn left onto Broadview Terrace until I get to the big iron mailbox on the corner of Sequin. I imagine Kathy Delaney and the other children, joined by Irene, climbing up on it, jumping off. On my right is the parking lot in back of St. Lawrence O'Toole's Church where the kids went on to jumping off the retaining wall. I walk the arcing road onto Coolidge Street. The church where I was baptized, confirmed, and married is a sprawling unfaded blond hulk utterly out of place on the residential street. All the fine Dutch colonial homes on that end of Coolidge, though still very fine, seem small and quaint, smaller than I remember, the usual phenomenon experienced when you try to go home again.

I cross the street, walk along Coolidge, and come to the library, still there, squat and menacing, my refuge. Here Coolidge merges with New Britain Avenue. I walk along that part of the sidewalk, which was once a tiny bridge crossing the brook. The brook is encapsulated by a culvert, which has been covered over with dirt and planted with grass. Too bad. It was a nice place to stick your bare toes on a hot summer's day. The Brookside Tavern is there though the brook is not.

I go into Jack's store, now packed with food imported from Puerto

Rico. Instead of a hotdog, I buy a bundle of cilantro. The clerk doesn't ask me if I'm having a party. He says something in Spanish and I understand by his gestures—holding the bundle to his nose and taking in the citrus fragrance and then holding it out to me so that I can have a whiff too—that the leaves are fresh.

I follow Irene's footsteps out of the store toward her home taking Sequin instead of Dart and then I come to the lot where a boat once sat on concrete blocks. The boat is gone and the house that stands there instead is thirty years newer than the rest of the houses on the street.

I am compelled to walk through that yard and the one backing up to it from Coolidge Street. No one is about. I cross Coolidge and look at the numbers on the mailboxes. I go to Number 80 and peer down the driveway. There is no picket fence, no toolshed either.

I walk down the driveway where Officer Proccacino parked his car and I look at the grassy area where Irene died. I mourn.

Then I open the plastic bag of cilantro, hold it up to my face, breathe in the fragrance again, and leave, not tempted to go and check out my house at 75 Nilan Street. I thought I would, but I don't.

thirty-six

T HE NEXT DAY, I get the autopsy report in the mail.

The autopsy, performed at Hartford Hospital by a pathologist named Dr. Perry Hough, begins with a list he'd typed on his Royal typewriter—a list full of typos and X-ed out misspelled words replaced with proper spellings, and drops of something. Sweat or tears, perhaps. The list describes the items of clothing taken from Irene's body, an act that signals the beginning of an autopsy.

> *red jacket with fake fur collar (small blood stain on shoulder)—*
> *label removed*
> *green slacks—Blue Bell, Girl's Size medium*
> *yellow socks*
> *jersey—white with red and brown horizontal stripes, make—*
> *Flight Club, size small*

Memory cells activate. I hear Irene at the lunch table on our field trip saying, This is Fred's old jersey I'm wearing. He gave me this, too . . . And then she fingered some sort of good-luck charm pinned to the shirt. Gail and I admire it. But I can't remember exactly what it was.

> *white undershirt, Wear-Rite Full Combed 12*
> *reddish-brown, Young Ann Sportmaker shoes with plaid laces*

Plaid shoelaces, all the rage. If we have new shoes they come with plaid laces. If they don't, we beg our mothers (in my case, my father) to buy us a pair of laces and then we restring our shoes with them.

202

Irene has plaid laces before all the other girls as a direct result of her mother's affection for her.

> *scarf—floral design of blue, yellow and white with a red border*
> *pink panties Wear-Rite, combed yarn, girl's size 14, W. T. Grant*
>   *Company*
> *green plastic change purse containing sixty-one cents; two quar-*
>   *ters, one dime and one penny*
> *two brown barrettes, one pink barrette, six bobby pins*
> *good-luck charm, a penny set in a horseshoe, taken from shirt, se-*
>   *cured with a safety pin*

Dr. Hough notes that it was necessary for him to cut the scarf out from where it was embedded in Irene's neck; that her mother identified the scarf as Irene's own; that she was told her ex-husband had agreed to identify the body; that she pointed out her husband hadn't seen Irene since she was seven years old and that she would identify her daughter's body. Which she did.

ON JANUARY 17, 1954, five weeks after his crime, Robert Malm appears in court. He decides on a bench trial rather than a trial by jury. Such is almost always the choice when the testimony will include lurid details that might prejudice the jurors. Three Connecticut Supreme Court judges, who of course are professionals, will not allow lurid details to stand in the way of their seeking justice for the accused. The bench of three will both preside over Bob's trial and decide his fate. The trio's decision, though, does not have to be unanimous; two of the judges can find him guilty and that decision will stand. This is the trade-off.

All trials have transcripts written by court reporters who, in the fifties, were called court stenographers. When I wrote my fifth novel, in order to develop the protagonist, I needed the transcript of O.J. Simpson's trial. That's when I found out that a trial transcript is copyrighted by the court reporter. The court reporter who transcribed

O.J.'s trial will happily turn over a copy to whoever wants it for two dollars a page. (The transcript runs around five thousand pages so I depended on my fellow Hartfordite Dominick Dunne's reporting instead.)

Court reporters, if they feel like it, can sell their transcripts; donate them to a law school; or they can just file them somewhere, whereupon their heirs will eventually throw them out. The trail to the court stenographer who owned the Malm transcript runs cold immediately. He or she is not named in the court records. I am bemoaning that fact to a lawyer friend of mine, who checks out a judicial Web site for me and learns that Robert Malm appealed his verdict.

He says, Even though the trial transcript isn't public record, the appeal rulings are.

I ask him, Why is that?

He says, Who the hell knows?

Then he explains that the appeals panel needs the testimony from the original trial. Meaning that the court reporter chronicling Malm's trial was required to turn over that portion of the original transcript containing the testimony of the witnesses—about 90 percent of the transcript.

thirty-seven

THE TRANSCRIPT of Robert Malm's appeal hearing is 434 pages long, consisting almost entirely of the original testimony. Bob pleaded not guilty to the charge of murder since he never intended to kill Irene. He claimed he panicked when she said she would tell on him and so he choked her to make her understand she was not to tell. And then she seemed to die. Bob's spin on murdering Irene was that it was sort of an inadvertent manslaughter.

I stare down at the appeals transcript lying on my desk, not seeing it. Instead, I am seeing myself at nine years old sitting at the kitchen table reading about the trial of Bob Malm in the *Hartford Times* while my father broils a porterhouse steak. I believe my father canceled the newspaper-reading ban because, what with Tyler, he had so little energy to put up with my harassment. His batteries wore down. Children are always able to sense this vulnerability in a parent.

He knows I won't ask him what rape is, but he also knows our lives have changed and that I will probably ask him *something*. My being an obedient child and not asking why I can't go to the movies is not the same thing as asking why my friend was murdered. He is willing to deal with this.

His back is to me in the kitchen and I say, Dad, the paper says Irene winked at him.

He doesn't answer. I speak very calmly: But, Dad, she didn't wink at him.

He says, I know.

After a little while I say, Irene wouldn't wink at anybody.

Not winking didn't have to do with her being shy. It had to do

205

with the fact that kids did not go around winking at adults. Unimaginable.

My father says, Mickey, I'm busy here.

I leave him be. I don't bring up that there have been whispers at the school yard, where I hear the words, *mature for her years*. I hear the word *reputation* on the street. But I must tread gently.

I say, Irene wouldn't go with him unless he made her.

I know, Mickey.

The paper says she went with him . . . *willingly*.

My father's back stiffens. He says, That's his lawyer talking. You're too young to understand.

I don't ask any more questions because he's annoyed and I can't risk his taking the newspapers away again. He cuts out the eye of the porterhouse steak and puts it in my plate, the rest of the steak on his own. We will have baked potatoes and also a special treat—my father's friend has come up from a stay in Florida and brought fresh radishes. I now connect this gift with the bedtime story my father chose to tell me the night before, "Nanette Visits the Château." Nanette's favorite meal is a slice of French bread, spread with butter and topped by a layer of sliced radishes. (People will say: Where does Yutchie get these stories he tells the kids? No one knows. I know. Out of thin air.)

At the start of our dinner, my father wields the bread knife.

Mickey, he says, this is Italian bread, not frog. But it's the same thing only bigger.

He unwraps a small block of butter: And this is frog butter, got it special.

He spreads the frog butter on the bread. He says, The frogs don't put any salt in their butter.

He holds up the bunch of radishes and I watch him slice them. He lays the dazzling white, moist, red-bordered radishes on the buttered bread. He passes me Nanette's favorite meal. Crunchy, chewy, creamy, all at once. We knock off the entire loaf of bread plus all the radishes that my father's friend told him he should toss into his next salad. My father warns, Now leave enough room for your steak.

But I am not able to leave room for the steak though I stuff it down anyway.

A few evenings later while he is frying chicken wings, I say, Kathy Delaney is in the paper, Dad. She had to go to court.

My father comes and looks over my shoulder while he breaks up a head of iceberg lettuce.

Kathy says she didn't know Irene was under the boat.

He goes back to the sink to wash the lettuce leaves while I go on reading. Then I say, Kathy says she saw a boy twirling a girl.

My father comes back again. Where does it say that?

I point to the line. He reads it. I hear him take in a breath. I cannot picture the murderer twirling Irene. Twirling to me is dancing the polka.

Dad, it says the courtroom was silenced by what Kathy said.

My father sighs. Mickey, what Kathy saw was little Irene trying to get away from the man.

And now he takes the paper away from me.

It is Kathy Delaney—not one other person—who insinuates into the trial proceedings that Irene didn't go willingly with Bob, that she didn't wink at him, that she didn't make conversation with him, that she didn't go along with having sex with him. In fact, even though Kathy thought she was seeing Brenda and Charlie, her observation demonstrates that Irene tried to escape Bob's clutches. Irene was in fact, tortured for half an hour as she was dragged along, shoved under a boat, pushed across backyards and down driveways, pulled over fences, hauled across streets and through hedges, all the while strangling on Bob's hold on her scarf, as he tightened it up here, loosened it there, keeping her alive and ensnared until he finally tied his sailor's knot.

THE THREE-MAN judicial bench finds Robert Nelson Malm guilty of murder in the first degree just two months and twelve days after he killed Irene. Bob is sentenced to be executed. Then he is remanded to prison . . . *where you shall be safely kept until the twelfth day of July 1955, whereupon the punishment of death shall be inflicted upon you.*

The day after Malm is charged and sentenced to die, he files his appeal with the Connecticut Supreme Court of Errors maintaining his innocence. When the appeal is filed, the first job of the clerk of the Superior Court is to deem Bob's court-appointed attorney, James D. Cosgrove, of sufficient financial responsibility to pay the costs of the foregoing appeal and acknowledge being bound to the state of Connecticut in that action.

Attorney Cosgrove is in recognizance of those costs. He writes a check for a sum of $150.

thirty-eight

I READ THE HUNDREDS of pages of testimony. Kathy Delaney is on the stand for over an hour. She is not allowed to sit during her testimony because she will not be visible from the defense and prosecution tables. Kathy says that on the evening of December 9 she saw a boy twirling a girl. At no point does she ever say that she thought the boy and girl were Brenda and Charlie. She says *boy* and *girl*. Incredibly, James Cosgrove doesn't ask her in his cross if the boy and girl might have been someone other than Irene and Robert Malm.

Bob's lawyer exhibits tunnel vision—he focuses on Irene's willingness to accommodate Bob and that his client had no plan to kill her. Cosgrove can save Bob from the death penalty if he can establish that his killing her was an accident—that there existed no intent.

The final defense witness will be Bob himself. The corresponding *Hartford Courant* article describes Cosgrove's frustration with Malm's decision to take the stand. But Bob insists and such is his right. Cosgrove will do his best to lead Bob through his misfortune.

Bob swears on the Bible that he will tell the truth.

Cosgrove calls him *Robert*, as in: Well, *Robert*, I would like to ask you this . . .

And so, Cosgrove, via a large map of my neighborhood set on an easel, prompts Bob to describe his trip to Fox's; to the Allyn Street Theater; to the White Tower; and his aimless walk through city streets "in the general direction of a route to Newington." He describes turning right onto New Britain Avenue from Hillside Avenue. He doesn't say he stopped there in order to catch the bus back to Newington. Presumably, he meant to walk nine miles on a drizzly night growing chillier as a cold front moved in.

Attorney Cosgrove brings him to Coolidge Street in front of St. Lawrence O'Toole's Church.

Q. Now, Robert, at that time were you alone?
A. Yes, I had been alone all day.
Q. Was anybody with you?
A. No, up to that time after leaving New Britain Avenue I had only seen one person.
Q. Where did you see that person?
A. Well, I don't know the names of the streets . . . I don't know where he came from but it was either a soldier or a Marine. I couldn't tell which. There was a uniform on him, that's all I noticed. He was heading toward New Britain Avenue.

The soldier Bob passed was in all likelihood Private John Williams, who would have made a good witness if he hadn't been so drunk that upon reading the account of the murder became convinced he was the one who had committed it.

Q. And as you turned onto Broadview Terrace toward Sequin Street, did you have occasion to see anybody?
A. Well, while I was on that corner I could hear—well, I just got the idea that it was kids somewhere. I didn't have any idea where they were. I could hear them and I started down that street and well, I don't have any actual memory of ever noticing anybody on the street until I started to cross it. That was the first that I ever noticed anybody on the other side.
Q. And as you started to cross the street did you see somebody?
A. Yes.
Q. And who was that person?

A. Well, I didn't—Of course, I had no way of knowing then, but I know now that it was Irene, or whatever the name is.
Q. Did you call over to her?
A. Well, I don't want to give the wrong impression of her . . . but I don't want to make it seem like the girl brought any of this on herself . . . as I was crossing the street she said *Hello,* so I said *Hello* back and walked over to her.

Then Bob describes chatting with Irene, how she didn't bring upon herself what was to follow, but that she was the one who approached him, not vice versa. So, so slick. He tells the court how he and Irene hid under a boat, and then he suggested they *duck the crowd.* So they went off to find a more private spot whereupon he *led* her across yards and a street, *boosted* her up over a fence *more or less hiding from the other kids,* and *helped* her over another fence until they got to the toolshed.

Bob states: She said, *Don't take my clothes off here,* and the word *here* was in there . . . After taking them—not all her clothes, but most of them—off—I am not sure whether I sat down on the ground, or whether she did first, but we both got on her coat on the ground and well, I think I kissed her a couple of times . . .

Then I guess I had my hands on her body . . . I don't remember anything about the panties everybody has been testifying to, but she— I remember her saying something about them, they were muddy or something . . .

She put her slacks back on and I tried to shake out her coat a little bit for her. I helped her with her coat, and as I put it on, I tried to brush it off a little bit on the back for her. Up to that time I had never seen any scarf. She threw it around her neck and put an overhand knot in it . . .

I had my hands on her shoulders trying to clean her coat and I don't remember exactly what she said, but she said something about she was going to be sure and tell her mother when she got home . . .

My hands were on her shoulders and I just grabbed hold of the two ends of the scarf and I threw another knot in and jerked it up tight, but at the time I was kind of confused. I couldn't tell whether she was fainting or was pulling away from me, or what. But she just fell down to the ground and I knelt down and looked at her . . .

I got the impression she was dead. She just didn't look right in some way—I can't place it . . .

I got back up and I took a couple of steps and jumped over the fence that was there and left.

ATTORNEY COSGROVE should have stopped right there. But he will go along with his client to further demonstrate that Irene's death was brought on by some incomprehensible phenomenon having nothing to do with his client's intentions or actions.

Q. Well, Robert, as of the time you met Irene on Sequin Street, when you first joined her, do you recall touching her at all?

A. Well, it wasn't on the street actually. When we started in off the street, as best as I can remember, I had my hand on her shoulder. It might have been her upper arm . . . I was guiding her like you do with a woman, and while we were at the boat, as I indicated to the police, when we were crouched down, I had my arm across her shoulders, and well—other than helping her across the fences and when we were running across the backyard, and when we thought the kids were coming after us again—I think it was her elbow I had hold of; it could have been some other part of her arm, but I am pretty sure it was her elbow. Outside of those times there, I had no physical contact with her at all until it was behind the shed.

And now Cosgrove attempts to show that Bob's ejaculation was yet one more mysterious phenomenon that he had no control over.

Q. And while you were laying there on the ground or while you were there . . . I will withdraw that. While you and Irene

212

were in the rear of what we now know as number 80 Coolidge Street, did you have a discharge?

A. Well, when I gave my statement to the police they asked me about that and I, well, of course, I had to say yes [i.e., *I came off* is what Bob told the police] but I tried to explain it but they put that in there [i.e., into the written confession] and afterwards I talked to the psychiatrist from Mr. Bill's office at the county jail and I told him about it and I stated that it was something that I couldn't understand myself because there was no preliminary feeling to it at all and as a matter of fact at the time I hardly realized that it happened and he told me, the psychiatrist, that an occurrence like that quite often will happen if a person is under emotional strain or stress or anything and that he could understand it happening where no actual contact had been made at all.

Now that Bob has taken advantage of the opportunity to describe the bewildering riddle of what happened to Irene, considering that no contact had been made, he puts a spin on why he had no choice but to take the stand:

Mr. Cosgrove explained to me that I didn't have to if I didn't want to, and I told him that because there was a lot of conflicting statements of witnesses or supposed witnesses and that there seemed to be a lot of doubt in different places, that I felt the Court should have every angle of the case possible, not in any form of defense because I don't guess I have any, but just to give all sides of it I thought that I had better appear on the stand. And that's about all, I guess, I can think of.

And with that, Attorney James Cosgrove turns to the State's Attorney, Albert S. Bill (who is chomping at the bit), and says, Your witness.

thirty-nine

ALBERT S. BILL, Chief State's Attorney for many years, has never experienced the kind of obfuscated, self-pitying, reconfiguration of a horrendous crime into an inadvertent, unintended death that he has just witnessed. And now he must listen to Robert Malm say that he even ejaculated inadvertently. State's Attorney Bill is unable to contain his fury.

He strides up to the witness box and does not precede what he has to say with formalities or niceties. And he does not call Bob, *Robert.* The Chief State's Attorney doesn't use any name at all as he barrages him, right from the get-go, with short, pointed questions to which Bob obfuscates further, replying to every question with either *No,* or *I don't think so,* or *I guess not,* or *Not that I remember,* or a nod, or a shrug. Usually, Attorney Bill doesn't even give him the time between questions to attempt an answer. His staccato is rapid machine gun fire.

When you started out from Cedarcrest did you have any particular *plan* that involved the evening? When you left the Allyn Theater, did you have a *plan* for the rest of the evening? Did you have any *plan* on what you were going to do after eating? When you came out of the White Tower, did you head for the bus stop to go back to Cedarcrest? Did you intend to take a bus back?

What was your *intention* when you left the restaurant? What was your course of procedure for the rest of the evening, if you

214

had one? Did it occur to you that you might take the bus to Cedarcrest after your dinner? Instead, you proceeded to walk, is that correct? You were window-shopping? You had no definite *plan* at that time where you were going? Is that the normal course that you would take, to walk to Cedarcrest? When you got out to the end of any shopping district you took a left turn? And that wasn't getting you anywhere as far as getting back to Cedarcrest, was it? And then when you got down a ways you took a right turn on another street, didn't you?

Well, you'd gotten over onto Hillside Avenue but you don't know *how?* You didn't recognize Hillside until you got down to the corner of Hillside and New Britain Avenue, is that right? And then you knew where you were? Now, does the bus you take to Cedarcrest go by that corner?

Without waiting for an answer, Bill turns away and points to a blown-up map of my neighborhood, which is set on an easel.

Do you see those two objects on the map with red around them? Those are stores. Do you recognize them? You know the tavern? You knew if you continued along New Britain Avenue along the route you were on you ultimately could get to Cedarcrest, right? So what did you go up Coolidge Street for?

Bill is now jabbing aggressively at the map, his motion the same relentless rat-a-tat-tat of his questions.

Do you mean to say when you turned right on Coolidge Street you thought you were heading back to Cedarcrest? And yet you take this turn here that you were unfamiliar with, is that correct? And as you went along there were four or five houses on the east side of Coolidge Street, and there were five or six houses on Broadview Terrace in front of you, weren't there?

You knew it wasn't a business section, didn't you? You knew you were turning from a business district into a residential district, didn't you?

You turned on the arc toward Sequin Street, didn't you? You stopped on the corner? You didn't particularly care whether you were on Sequin Street or Coolidge Street, did you? You didn't know where you were, did you?

Bill leaves the map, approaches the witness stand, and begins jabbing in the direction of Robert Malm's chest.

Did you see anybody on Sequin Street? Well, you saw a little girl, didn't you? You were prowling, weren't you? *You were looking for girls of tender age, weren't you?*

State's Attorney Albert Bill continues to harangue Bob, nonstop, becoming more and more obstreperous, and when he is in a complete state of agitation, he will finally bring himself to address Bob by name.

You mean to say that you can't tell us what your intentions were as you stood there with that little girl and these other children who were coming toward you down the street? You were playing a game, you say? You were playing hide-and-seek with her? *Ducking* the rest of the children. You were getting this girl off *alone!* Isn't that what you're really saying?

As a matter of fact you did get her alone back there, didn't you, by the boat? That's the way you wanted to have it turn out, wasn't it? Get her away from the crowd. Why did you yell *Beat it?* Why didn't you let the other children come up to you? You wanted her alone, didn't you? You didn't think of joining with them and playing a real game of hide-and-seek, did you?

216

Isn't it true that you so wanted to get her away that you put Irene over the fence to get away? Did you tell her where you were taking her? Did you tell Irene that it was a game of hide-and-seek? As a matter of fact, you had your hand on her shoulder all the while, didn't you, *threatening* her?

Did you realize you were dragging this little girl away from home and you mean she didn't protest at all to you? And you mean that she didn't question you at all on where you were going, or what you were doing? Did you say, Oh Irene, let's go over this fence? *The game was over by that time, wasn't it?*

Bill suddenly makes for the prosecution's table and pours himself a glass of water in order to calm himself. He lifts his shoulders and returns to the stand.

You weren't using force, you were guiding her—is that what you are telling us? *Guiding* her? Like a *woman?* And you want us to believe that she never expressed any concern about getting home again until you were in back of the toolshed? And she made no protests at all about going into Sequin Street, over the fence, along the other fence to the back of the toolshed—no protests at all during that trip, is that correct? And you used no force?

Let us see how it was that this little girl who had never seen you before came along with you—can you tell us? You want this Court to believe that this timid little girl just went along with you—allowed you to *guide* her—you, *a thirty-year-old stranger,* over fences, through yards, and along a fence to Coolidge Street, and made no protest and didn't seem to care where she was going, or inquire about it, or care anything about it? Is that what you are trying to tell the Court? You are trying to make this Court believe *that?*

What were you thinking about? Just thinking about getting that girl off alone in some lonely spot—isn't that what you were trying to do? Well, when did that little thought come to your mind—that you were going to take this little girl and take some of her clothes off and molest her—when did that thought come to your mind? You mean you never had a thought of it until you got her *behind that shed?*

State's Attorney Bill's calm has fled yet again. He raises his voice and gets his face as close to Malm's as he can.

If you are going to tell the truth, let us have it now! You went over a fence, came to the shed, and then, all of a sudden it came to you—*I guess I will have this little girl undress.* Is that what you are telling us? Right out of a clear sky you started to unzipper her coat. What was her reaction to that? Did she say anything? What did she say? *Don't undress me here. Here!* Is that the correct language?

She suddenly protested, didn't she? But you went right on doing it, didn't you? You were assuring her you wouldn't hurt her, is that it? So, from what you tell us here, that little girl had no idea of what you had in your mind from your actions? Just a moment before you zipped the coat, was that the first time you had any thought of undressing this girl and molesting her? When you started zipping off the coat you intended to remove all her clothing, didn't you? You had no other reason to take off her coat, did you?

Did she assist you in taking off the coat? You told her to, didn't you? She was frightened by this time, wasn't she? It certainly wasn't warm out, was it? You mean to say you took the coat off this little girl and started to undress her out there by the toolshed on a cold December evening and she made no protest?

She was scared then, wasn't she? And you never did anything after that to relieve her of being scared, did you? You unzipped her pants and you pulled those down, didn't you? You made her do this—you must have said something to her. You said that she was scared by that time. Did you tell her to hurry up and get her pants off? Oh, you were very kind—like all this time, leading her on, taking down her zippers and panties, is that right?

You made her know you meant business and to get those clothes off, didn't you? Did she cry or snivel like a child will when they are scared? And when she fell down did she remain on the ground? She didn't go all the way down, you say?

How did she get down on the ground then? *By herself?* Did you take your penis out at that time? Well, you unzipped your own pants, didn't you? Didn't you? She was on the ground, wasn't she, on her coat? And then you put your hands on her, didn't you? And you kissed her on the mouth? Did you put your finger in her private? Didn't you say that in your written confession? Only that you *touched* her private? Here is what the confession you signed says, *I was feeling of her private.* What about that? And how long did this procedure take, this molesting her, when you took out your penis and felt of her private and kissed her—how long did all that take?

And while all these things were going on—these acts of molestation where you were kissing her and touching her, and had her exposed there, do you mean to tell us that she made no protest at all? She was scared to death, wasn't she? You know that she was, don't you? Did she give you any fight at all? Did she go at you, kicking you or clawing you? No, because you were holding her down, is that right? You threatened to kill her, didn't you? You made some threat to her, didn't you, to scare her?

You want to have us believe that she was scared and frightened but she just lay there passively and let you do these things, is that right? I suggest that you had her by the throat then, didn't you? And you discharged then, before you got up and then you worried about what had happened? Well, as a matter of fact you were worrying what was going to happen to *you,* wasn't that it?

And you want to have us believe that this little girl tied such a hard knot in her scarf around her neck that that knot, all by itself, choked her to death. You put a square knot in there on that first knot, didn't you? Why did you want to put any knots in this scarf at all for? You wanted to get rid of that little girl, didn't you? And you saw your chance with that scarf. That's the answer, isn't it, *Malm?* Isn't it, *Malm?* And you have done acts of violence on persons in the past, haven't you, *Malm?*

Now, for the first time, Attorney Cosgrove stands up and calls out, *Objection!*
Judge Shea asks, The ground of the objection?
Cosgrove says, It is entirely outside the purview of the law, as I understand it, to try to get this accused—
State's Attorney Bill interrupts: I won't press it, Your Honor.
Judge Shea says, We will recess until tomorrow.

forty

THE NEXT DAY, State's Attorney Bill, with Robert Malm's written confession in his hands, will keep Bob on the stand for just one minute and again with no preliminary niceties. He holds the document out toward him.

This is from your confession, Malm: *She dropped on the ground, and a half minute went by. I kind of dropped on my knee. I got the impression that she was dead.*

You had pulled that scarf into a tight knot, hadn't you? And it is reasonable to conclude that you must have known that it was tight enough to choke her, isn't that correct? And that is what you did it for, isn't it?

You didn't try to unloosen that scarf at all—made no effort to unloosen it, did you? And yet you stood over her, put a knot around her neck tight enough to choke her to death, you saw her on the ground, and stood over her. That is correct, isn't it?

And then you say here [he looks down at the confession and reads], *I got the impression that she was dead.* Then, *I don't know whether enough time went by for her to be dead, but it looked like it to me.*

Bill waves the document in Robert Malm's stony, expressionless face.

And still you didn't give her any assistance or try to unloosen that scarf, is that right? As a matter of fact, you stayed there to be sure she was dead, didn't you? And then you left, didn't you?

Now, State's Attorney Bill utilizes a loophole in the law that doesn't allow a defendant's prior record to be introduced; instead of asking Bob if he'd committed similar crimes, Bill quotes from the trial transcript Attorney Cosgrove's question to Bob on the direct: *Have you been convicted of other crimes of violence?* Cosgrove knows he cannot object, cannot object to a question that he himself asked.

Albert S. Bill says, Two days ago, Mr. Cosgrove asked you the following: *Were you convicted in the Superior Court of New London on October 22, 1946, for robbery with violence?* And you answered that, didn't you? You answered, Yes. And you were sentenced to jail at that time, weren't you?

Robert Malm nods.

For the first time, Bill responds to one of Malm's many nods. *Answer aloud!*

Yes.

Bill says, No further questions, and returns to the State's Attorney's table.

Cosgrove stands up. He says, That is all, Robert.

Utterly composed, Malm gets down from the stand. Under the nonstop attack by Albert S. Bill, Bob never admits to murdering Irene, denies all, claims no memory whatsoever of the details spelled out so vigorously to him by the spent State's Attorney.

forty-one

BOB'S APPEAL is centered on three protestations: One, he did not intend to kill Irene; two, the evidence was not the equivalent of two eyewitness testimonies; three, nobody told him about Army Private John Williams's confession.

The presiding judge for the Connecticut Supreme Court of Errors is Justice J. Baldwin. Baldwin is a name everyone in Hartford knows. Judge J. Baldwin is a descendant of three of Connecticut's governors and countless congressmen, and ends up serving the court for decades. The newest bridge spanning the Connecticut River was named after his father. My Uncle Ray Kelley is a toll collector on the bridge.

Albert S. Bill begins with a statement of facts. He describes the events of the crime and then goes on to his triple argument. He starts with the easiest—the failure to disclose the statements of Army Private John Williams, meaning that Malm's confession was not voluntary. Bill argues that the failure to disclose confessions of a third party can in no way cause the accused's confession to be involuntary . . . in fact, to disclose such information might well cause a *suppression* rather than an *inducement* to tell the truth. State's Attorney Bill caustically dismisses the nondisclosure: *It can hardly be expected that an accused would confess and tell the truth once he has learned somebody else had confessed to the crime.*

Bill moves on to the two-witness statute. He submits that the evidence as presented complies with the rule. He says, *However, that is not the point!* He rebuffs the court's prerogative to determine if evidence is the equivalent of the testimony of two witnesses: *Such must be left to the jury!*

Finally, the last point, intent, which is crucial for Bill to demonstrate because if there hadn't been intent, Malm would be guilty of second-degree murder—not first—or worse, manslaughter. Cosgrove had argued that Malm carried no weapon and therefore didn't intend to kill anyone. Bill jumps on that: *You don't need a weapon to kill someone, particularly a child!*

Then he ridicules Cosgrove's argument that Bob didn't have enough time to form a willful premeditation. He argues that there was ample time, based on how long Malm was worried about the consequences of his sexual attack: *He had enough time to formulate plans to extricate himself from this situation even to the extent of killing the girl when his threats and the physical pain he directed at her by choking her, failed. And because he dropped to one knee beside her after she'd fallen, he was undoubtedly making sure he had carried out his intent and that she was dead. Clearly, he wasn't intending to help her.*

Then the State's Attorney elucidates: *The scarf was knotted so tightly around the girl's neck that it was impossible for the coroner to untie or loosen it and it could not be removed without the use of scissors! The accused intended to strangle the little girl to death.*

Bill lets that sink in. Then: *In determining the state of mind of the accused, the court is not limited alone to the accused's own statement as to his intent. As a matter of fact the court has a right to determine his state of mind, and did conclude from the accused's own words that his mind was in a state of worry and this coupled with the actions as he described them justified their conclusion that he fully intended to commit the crime.*

JUDGE J. BALDWIN and the two other presiding appeal justices deliberate a total of one hour and twenty minutes with an hour off in the middle for lunch. Judge Baldwin presents their conclusions in cold legalese.

He begins with the most crucial, intent, picking up where Bill left off:

Considering the evidence from the angle most favorable to the defendant, it could be said that he did not conceive an intent to take the life of his victim until after the sexual episode. This left but a short time for him to deliberate and premeditate before forming a specific intent to kill her. But the length of time elapsed is not the test. The question is whether the court could reasonably conclude that there was sufficient time to enable the mind of the defendant to conceive a willful, deliberate, premeditated intent to kill before the act was done.

As the defendant stood talking with Irene on Sequin Street she said that she had to get home before her brother. She repeated this when they were in the rear of 80 Coolidge Street. While they were lying on the ground she said that her mother would be looking for her. When she was putting her clothes on, she threatened to tell her mother. The defendant admitted that he was worried. There can be no doubt that he knew that he had done wrong and feared detection. And, they were in a dark, secluded spot.

Under these circumstances, the conclusion that he formed a willful, deliberate intent to kill her is reasonable and logical. His crime was murder in the first degree.

There is no error.

I think of Irene, her logic, telling her killer that she had to be home before her brother. It is an excuse you used with your friends to save face when they say *they* don't have to go home yet. And then, after the sexual assault, when her killer threatened to kill her if she told, just as he'd threatened Pidgie D'Allessio, Irene said, *I'm going to tell my mother.* She spoke up because she had courage and spunk. She was just a little girl who was frightened in a way no little girl should be frightened, and still she expressed her only thought, which was to tell her mother. She did not yet have the maturity of seventeen-year-old Pidgie, who comprehended fully that her assailant would kill her if she stood up to him. The final act of Irene's life demonstrated dignity in the face of hell.

Judge Baldwin moves on to the two-witness equivalency rule. He states: *General statute 8799 provides that no person shall be convicted of any crime punishable by death without the testimony of at least two witnesses, or that which is equivalent thereto. Simply stated, the statute requires that proof shall not depend upon the testimony of one witness. The crime was committed in the evening of December 9. The defendant was taken into custody on the evening of December 12. From that time on he was questioned at intervals, first about another incident which had occurred in November, and then about the crime here charged until he confessed at 9:30 in the evening of December 15. The state relied heavily upon this evidence.*

There was much corroborating testimony. Witnesses saw what they de-scribed as a tall boy and a girl disappear down a driveway on Sequin Street at the time the defendant stated he did so. They heard him shout, "Beat it," as he said he had. The bag containing potatoes and cookies which Irene had pur-chased at the store was found in the backyard of 46 Sequin Street. The jacket which Irene wore was identified by some of the witnesses who saw her on Se-quin Street with a boy. The fruit of what is botanically known as Bidens frondosa, *beggar's-lice, which grew in the yards in the rear of both 80 Coolidge Street and 46 Sequin Street, was found on the clothing of both Irene and the defendant. Police officers testified that after the defendant had con-fessed he took them over the course which he had followed on the night of the crime from the motion picture theater to the place where the body of Irene was found.*

These instances of corroboration are but a few of many which could be re-cited. It is fair to say that practically every important detail of the defendant's statements were checked and evidence confirming them offered at trial. Much of the corroborating evidence had been obtained before *the defendant confessed. The requirements of the statute were more than met.*

There is no error.

Finally, the judge treats the third appeal protestation—that the con-fession was not given voluntarily: *The defendant was arrested on Decem-ber 12. He confessed on December 15. The state offered the testimony of Detective Mancini of the Hartford County Police Department as bearing upon the voluntary aspect of the defendant's confession. On cross-*

examination, Mancini was questioned with regard to his knowledge of the statements concerning the death of the child made by a soldier named Williams. The defendant claims that the failure of Mancini to disclose this knowledge to him bore upon the voluntary aspect of the statements made by the defendant.

But Mancini was under no duty to disclose to the defendant any knowledge he might have concerning Williams's admissions. Withholding information concerning other persons who might be involved in the investigation of a crime is no differing in kind from the giving of false information concerning them, and yet the latter conduct, while not commended, has been held not to render a confession involuntarily.

Hold it right there, Baldwin. I read the line about the "latter conduct" again. The judge has slipped an impotent little opinion he holds into his ruling. Okay, the law says you can *trick* suspects—give them false information, withhold information, whatever. And the law also says this is not the same thing as lying to them. Baldwin points out that such conduct is not *commended*. Well, that's nice.

I carry on.

Had Mancini's knowledge been divulged to the defendant it may be that he would not have confessed in the hope that the crime would be laid at another's door and that he would escape. Viewed from this angle, the failure to divulge Williams's statement could have no bearing whatever upon the question whether the defendant's confessions were voluntary.

To fully cover this episode, the defense offered Chief Godfrey as witness. He testified that he had talked with Williams and that Williams's story differed so vitally from the facts of the crime as they had been disclosed that Williams could not have been the person who killed the child.

There is no error.

forty-two

THE END of Robert Malm's appeal document, by some miracle, ends on the left-facing page. My copy therefore includes the right-facing page, the beginning of the very next appeal taken up by the Connecticut Supreme Court of Errors. It is titled: The State of Connecticut v. Patricia D'Allessio.

What in God's name is this? But I can't know; there are no more pages copied. Yet again I head back to the library.

IT SEEMS THAT after Bob Malm was arrested, Patricia D'Allessio tried to claim a three-thousand-dollar reward offered by the state of Connecticut, a reward for assistance in capturing Robert Nelson Malm. Her claim is denied. I look at the dates of the two appeals transcripts. Patricia D'Allessio appealed the ruling against her three days after Malm appealed his guilty sentence.

I skim through her transcript; it isn't over four hundred pages, it's a wispy dozen. No need to copy it and bring it home to read.

I am freaked out right from page one—the three judges are the same three judges who determined Bob Malm's fate when he made his appeal. Judge J. Baldwin will write the ruling. And Cosgrove is representing Pidgie!

Governor Abraham Ribicoff offered the reward to anyone with information leading to the arrest of Irene's killer. When Pidgie claimed the reward eight days after Irene's death, the governor's staff members handling the state's offer deemed that offer to be a simple contract not in force at the time Pidgie went to the police; Governor Ribicoff

hadn't tendered the reward until the day *after* she'd read the *Hartford Times*'s story of Irene's murder. Yes, Pidgie called the police, and yes, she identified Malm in a lineup, and yes, she also endured the trauma of coming face-to-face with him to identify his voice as well, but that all came a day too soon for her to be entitled to the reward.

She is denied the three thousand dollars. Pidgie, a tough cookie according to her father, appeals.

I turn the tissue-thin page to read the appeal ruling and I'm thinking, Okay, Baldwin, set things right.

First, he introduces his qualm: In a nutshell, there is no precedent. Pidgie's appeal is unique. So Baldwin describes how he and the two other state Supreme Court judges reviewed sixty cases having to do with contract law, had to study sixty business contracts to determine whether or not Pidgie was entitled to receive the reward.

The judges then spent four times longer on Pidgie's appeal than they did on Robert Malm's before they emerged from their deliberation.

J. Baldwin's ruling is a single brief paragraph:

The appellant's compensation is the consolation which comes to every citizen from the discharge of a public duty, which is the common obligation of all. The court cannot read into the terms of a (contractual) statute something which manifestly is not there in order to reach what the court thinks would be a just result.

There is no error.

Presiding judge Justice J. Baldwin had looked at the evidence against Bob Malm just a few days earlier *from the angle most favorable to the defendant*—in other words, from a generous angle giving him the benefit of the doubt. He'd even used benevolent phrasing. Pidgie's is a civil case so he can draw a hard, condescending, and dispassionate line when it comes to the brave D'Allessio girl, without whose cooperation Bob Malm would not have been arrested. Basically, in order to avoid setting a precedent, the judge washes his hands of it, a precedent set by Pontius Pilate.

Decisions of justice are based on points of law; there are rules tha

must be followed no matter what anyone might think. Such makes matters pretty easy for a judge, but when no point of law exists, when there needs to be a new interpretation, a judge fears the consequences of his precedent being questioned and being made to look a fool. So judges don't do it, even when it's clear they should. Instead, feeling guilty, they slyly express sympathy to the appellant in a cowardly ruling.

Fuck them.

forty-three

R OBERT MALM is the second-to-the-last person to be executed in the state of Connecticut.

A retired reporter from the *Hartford Courant,* Jerry Demeusy, self-publishes a book called *Ten Weeks of Terror* about the last killer to be executed, Joseph "Mad Dog" Taborsky, who robbed gas stations and package stores (*package* means *liquor* in Connecticut) with the help of his partner, Albert Culombe, who suffered mental retardation. The newspaper reporters, as well as Culombe's lawyer, refer to Culombe as a mental defective.

The two robbers pistol-whip their victims—plus any witnesses—and then shoot them.

My Uncle Chick, my father's oldest brother, the one who worked at the Hartford County Jail, brings us a beach blanket every summer. The blankets are the color and practically the texture of sandpaper so it is always a challenge to find the blanket when we come out of the water. One summer Uncle Chick brings us Mad Dog Taborsky's blanket. It has a frayed corner. Uncle Chick grabs it when they take Mad Dog to Newgate Prison in Windsor, which houses death row and the execution chamber. The other prisoners won't take bedding that belongs to a condemned man taken to Newgate. Bad luck.

Just before Mad Dog's execution, the Connecticut court, at the behest of a number of politicians, decides the state should execute the four other inhabitants of death row in the same week—double executions, where a pair of condemned men will be electrocuted, and then three days later, pair number two. That second pair included Irene's killer, Bob Malm, and his partner in death, a twenty-two-year-old cop-killer named John Donahue.

The idea is to deliberately save Mad Dog for last, to clear the deck in order to place him at stage center, Mad Dog being a killer who is big and mean and unrepentant. He had been sprung on a technicality a few years earlier, which allowed him to kill and maim some more. Politicians want his execution to be as close to a public hanging as possible in order to please their constituents, who detest Mad Dog so. (As for the "mental defective," Albert Culombe, his lawyers take his appeal all the way to the Supreme Court of the United States. Earl Warren writes the ruling determining that his crime was second-degree murder rather than first because of his mental condition. With the conviction overturned, Culombe is released. He steps outside the prison fence, whereupon he is immediately arrested again on the new charge, murder in the second degree. He might have pleaded innocent to this charge with the defense arguing double jeopardy, or that he was not capable of understanding right from wrong, but he chooses to plead guilty so he can remain in prison where he won't have to work or cook. I believe Tyler might have understood Culombe's reasoning. And I do wonder why it is that the Culombe case has never been cited when people suffering from mental retardation are condemned to die.)

In contrast to the bloodlust for Taborsky, people simply want to be rid of Irene's killer because nobody can stand thinking about the poor little girl anymore; just be rid of Malm and then let's put it out of our heads.

In Connecticut, on the day of a scheduled execution, condemned prisoners are granted the opportunity to stand in front of the Board of Pardons at the state prison, presided over by the governor, and ask for mercy. The board then deliberates and decides whether or not the supplicant's death penalty should be commuted to life in prison.

The two men scheduled to be executed three days before Bob Malm and John Donahue choose to appeal for mercy. One is turned down and is executed three hours later, and one has his sentence commuted to life. This man is the only condemned prisoner whose sentence Governor Ribicoff commutes before he resigns his post to become John F. Kennedy's Secretary of Health, Education, and Welfare. The man is a petty thief named Benny Reid, who, like Malm's partner John Donahue, committed murder at seventeen years of age. He shot a clerk during a store robbery.

A Trinity College student writes a compelling editorial in the *Hartford Courant* noting intellectual and legal reasons why the prisoner should serve life rather than be executed; his argument is based on Benny's young age when he committed the crime. Governor Ribicoff invites the student to present his argument at the mercy hearing for Benny Reid. The student accepts the invitation, argues his opinion to the Board of Pardons, and Benny Reid's sentence is commuted to life in prison. (The Trinity College student, George F. Will, is today's preeminent conservative columnist and pundit.)

IN THE LATE AFTERNOON of the day Robert N. Malm is scheduled to die, he makes a last attempt to save his own life. Without legal counsel, he stands before Governor Ribicoff and the Board of Pardons.

Governor Ribicoff says: Let the condemned be heard.

Malm says: Listen, I tried to brush the mud off her. I helped her with her coat. She said something about telling her mother and I knotted the scarf around her neck. She fell down. I think she fainted. So I left.

Bob continues to deny he was responsible for Irene's death.

Justice Edward J. Daley of the board asks, Why didn't you untie the scarf when the little girl fell to the ground?

I couldn't have.

But you knew it was a dangerous situation for her, didn't you?

I didn't think about it.

The committee waits. But Bob has nothing more to say. Irene's death was an accident. Period.

He is led back to his cell. Fifteen minutes later Governor Ribicoff passes the word to the warden that Robert Malm's plea for clemency has been turned down. He will be executed, as scheduled, at 10 P.M. Bob refuses a last meal.

Then, in front of Governor Ribicoff, the lawyer for John Donahue, the second man who will be executed back-to-back with Bob, points out that John was a juvenile at the time of the crime, seventeen years old, and a mental defective besides.

Governor Ribicoff says: Let the condemned be heard.

John Donahue stands and says to the board: For the life of me, I don't know why I did it. I am truly sorry for what I've done. There is no retribution I could make for the terrible thing I've done.

Then John Donahue's father speaks, his wife by his side. He says, I have always felt and still do that something is wrong with my son. But still, I feel I must apologize for John's crime to the people of the state of Connecticut.

Governor Ribicoff, after hearing John Donahue's petition for clemency, and after John is led back to his cell on death row, turns to John's parents and tells them that he and other members of the board have the feeling that they are blaming themselves for their son's crime. He says to Mr. and Mrs. Donahue: I don't want you to go through the rest of your days, irrespective of the decision of this board, blaming yourselves for the homicide committed by your son. I will say that you are normal parents, in fact, wonderful parents, and we want you to know we have a deep sense of compassion for you.

Weeping, they leave the chamber and go to sit just outside the heavy oak doors with their priest. But unlike Benny Reid, John Donahue didn't shoot a store clerk, he killed a cop, and for that there is no mercy. Within minutes the couple receive the news that their son will die that night as planned. They and the priest decide it best to leave without saying good-bye to John.

A COIN IS FLIPPED as to which of the two men—Malm or the cop killer—will be electrocuted first. The cop killer wins. But the state executioner doesn't like the whole idea of a double execution. The executioner, a serious, small man with thick eyeglasses whose identity is kept secret, is an electrician. I guess it makes sense; hangmen of old were usually butchers. Historically, Connecticut executioners serve long careers; only one in the previous hundred years does not retire gracefully after putting in decades of service. He commits suicide.

The Connecticut executioner receives good pay for the up-till-now infrequent gigs and he brags to everyone that he makes a professional, proficient job of it. Actually, he is obsessed with his job: he spends his days studying the effects of bolts of electricity that pass through human bodies. He becomes an expert on what happens when people are struck randomly by lightning. But *he* will breach no such randomness. He is not of the likes of Bob Malm, whose killing was the height of random selection.

The executioner will contain his electric bolts so that the killings he performs will be humane. He makes clear in interviews what a challenge this is. He boasts: I take extraordinary care to see that the amperage and voltage I calculate to complete the job succeeds without overkill. (Presumably, his pun was not deliberate.)

The electrician measures his convicted killers, weighs them, surveys the density of their muscles and body fat, and devises mathematical formulas as to exactly how powerful to set his bolts of lightning. The results of his computation mean that he executes his victims by delivering ten thousand volts of electricity via five charges, one after the other, two thousand volts at a time. The executioner feels one single large surge is too risky as it might blow out the death house circuitry. No one wants to rummage around in their junk drawers for a fuse with the condemned prisoner only half dead. The calculated five electric charges will not be so weak as to leave the condemned alive, yet not so potent as to cause him to combust.

The executioner/electrician says: My job is to determine the precise amount of electricity to kill without mutilating.

Now the executioner explains to the State Prison Advisory Board that, physically, the cop killer and Malm are two disparate body types;

the cop killer is short and skinny—small-boned—and Malm is tall and solid—big-boned and muscular what with his military training, a physique he has maintained.

The executioner is instructed to clam up and just do his job.

The man considers himself, above all, a professional. He feels that strictly obeying the instructions of the state is even more important than his desire to do a consummate job. After all, the state is paying him a bonus beyond just a doubling of his usual excellent fee. He will get the job done as directed so he clams up.

He averages out all the statistics he's come up with on his two victims and bases the amperage on that mean.

Shortly after being denied clemency, with only four hours left before he is to die, Bob Malm asks to speak to the warden and that request is granted. He announces he'd like to donate his body to medicine with his eyes going to the Connecticut Eye Bank. In order for a prisoner to do that, the warden is required to request permission from his nearest kin because the law directs that once he is dead, his body no longer belongs to him; it is not left to Robert Malm to decide what should be done with his body.

Bob knows this. He is, perhaps, finagling a way to put off his execution. But the warden goes to work, calls every service available to him and manages to reach Bob's long-estranged sister in California who tells him that Bob's decision is all right with her. She also tells the warden that she does not intend to claim his body. As for Connecticut's policy to bury unclaimed prisoners in potter's field if he changes his mind about donating his body to science—that's fine with her.

The warden tells Robert Malm that his eyes will be given to the Connecticut Eye Bank and his body to the Yale School of Medicine. Bob Malm says to him, There's a monster inside me. The monster killed the girl. And he did the same thing before, many times, and was never caught. He has to die.

So in his own way, Bob Malm finally, at the last hour, sort of takes responsibility for not only killing Irene, but other unknown girls as well; he blames a monster that resides in his body. He doesn't apologize for the monster's actions, doesn't say the monster is sorry. When asked by a reporter what other girls the monster might have killed when he was a resident of California or as a seaman in the United States Navy serving in World War II, the Pacific Theater of Operations, he declines to say.

Bob is fully integrated with the monster.

Neither Bob nor the monster has any idea what remorse is. Neither did my brother, Tyler. When Tyler pushed the kid off the stool at the Lincoln Dairy, my father made him apologize and he did, but he wasn't sorry, he was annoyed. Tyler did, in fact, have a monster that lived inside him. The monster's name was autism. So maybe sociopathic behavior is within the ever-widening spectrum of autism. Maybe a sociopathy that requires murder to assuage the internal demon-monster is a developmental anomaly that someday will be diagnosed and treated. Who knows? Therefore, a theory—now defunct— that killers should be studied, not executed, in order to predict such sociopathy in others so they can be treated before they kill, makes sense to me.

forty-four

THERE ARE TEN WITNESSES waiting in the death chamber where the two consecutive executions are to take place. It is the only time in Connecticut's history that this will occur. The witnesses include four reporters, including Jerry Demeusy of the *Hartford Courant*, two physicians who will declare the condemned dead—one for each man—and four prison officials. There are no law enforcers who were involved in the case present, and no family members either to witness the executions as there may or may not be today. No one's considered such a thing yet.

The ten men sit on two wooden benches, nothing separating them from the electric chair gerry-rigged of two-by-fours a few feet away.

The young, brain-damaged cop killer is led into the death chamber accompanied by the warden, a priest, and four guards. The slight fellow is strapped to the electric chair crying. The guards place the electrodes at various points on his body; they fit a metal helmet lined with a wet sponge on his head. They drape a black cloth hood over the helmet. It is not the tradition in Connecticut to ask condemned men about to die if they have any final words. The warden, the priest—reading the Catholic prayers for the dead from a missal—and the guards back away and stand silent. The electrician seems bothered, as if he is thinking, *Let's get the show on the road.* The warden touches his glasses, giving the signal for the executioner to commit what the law refers to as state-sponsored homicide.

Upon the signal, the electrician turns to his oversized instrument panel, which is just a few feet to the left of the electric chair. He closes one large switch after another while he turns a rheostat control back and forth, watching his two meters carefully. The five two thousand-volt shocks drive a nine-ampere current of electricity through the metal helmet on John Donahue's head, which passes swiftly through his body before exiting out the metal clamp around his ankle. His black hood catches fire. If his hair hadn't been shaved off, it would have caught fire, too. His eyeballs explode, and blood and the liquid of his eyes run down his shirt from under the tattered, burnt remains of his hood.

Jerry Demeusy says that the stench was even more unforgettable than the two popping noises and the blood and the flames and the smoke.

One of the two physicians approaches the chair, puts a stethoscope to John Donahue's chest, and unnecessarily pronounces him dead.

Directly after the poached murderer is wheeled hastily out of the execution chamber, Robert Malm is led in surrounded by the same four men who had accompanied John Donahue. The stench remains; the blood hasn't been wiped up off the floor; the whole room is full of smoke; and a peculiar ash is still floating about.

All the witnesses now want out as they can barely keep from vomiting. But they hold on.

Malm catches a glimpse of the chair and a half-smile forms on his face as opposed to the wide-eyed terror exhibited by Donahue. Perhaps he has detached himself from the monster and feels that he will not be executed after all—the monster will. His words to the Board of Pardons reflect such delusion: When Irene fell to the ground, dead, Malm was an innocent bystander.

Bob is strapped into the chair, which is smeared with the previous fellow's body fluids as well as his waste—his diaper hasn't contained all that it was designed to. Before the hood is placed over his head, Bob Malm closes his eyes and the four men back off.

The warden taps his eyeglasses, the executioner goes about his chain of actions for the second time that night. When he fires the quintuple bolts, Malm springs up, his big muscular body straining against the leather straps that harness him to the chair. He makes an inhuman noise and then he sags. Though limp in the chair, the inhuman noise persists in coming out from under his hood. The doctor goes to him, places his stethoscope against Bob Malm's chest, and declares him alive.

The second physician jumps up, tries his stethoscope on Bob, and also declares him alive. This one says to the warden, What do we do now?

The warden just keeps staring at the condemned man, who continues to make his god-awful noise. Then he looks to the executioner, a take-charge guy, who pulls himself up to his full height of five feet two and says sternly, Just wait—this man will die.

The warden's eyes dart to the doctors. The one who was supposed to declare Bob Malm dead says nothing at all, appears to be in shock. But the doctor who declared John Donahue dead steps up and says, It's likely.

The noise Bob Malm is making grows softer, he jerks a few more times, he goes limp again, jerks some more, and after a minute, begins grunting. Everyone waits. After another three minutes, he finally expires, something both doctors confirm. The witnesses are ordered to leave. A surgeon enters the death chamber with instruments and a metal box lined with dry ice. He takes the hood off Bob Malm's head and removes his eyes.

In the *Hartford Courant*, Jerry Demeusy writes: *Bob Malm died hard.*

In all the articles the *Courant* and *Times* reporters had written about his crime, none of them ever said Irene died hard.

Part IV

What Goes Around . . .

forty-five

Peace Corps, Buea, Cameroon

LIFE GOES ON: I finish college much to the joy of my family and then I join the Peace Corps much to their consternation. I receive an engraved invitation from Sargent Shriver to train at Columbia University for service in Cameroon. When my father breaks the news to Gramps, he says, They grow good grapes in Africa.

I serve in a town five thousand feet up the side of Mt. Cameroon, an active volcano that itself rises more than thirteen thousand feet above the equatorial sea. The first white man to climb the mountain was Sir Richard Burton. In keeping with a tradition he began by leaving an empty cognac bottle at the summit with his name on a piece of paper plus a copy of *Punch* sealed inside, I make the climb and leave

243

behind an empty beer bottle with my name and a copy of *The New Yorker* inside. The first black man to climb the mountain, centuries before Burton, was a honey harvester. When I climb the mountain, I go with a group of honey harvesters.

I come home from Cameroon two years later, get a job, get married, have children, write during the wee hours, and sell my first novel to Doubleday in 1985.

In 1990, what goes around begins to come around. My mother is seventy-five, complaining that she can't keep food down. She is diagnosed with stomach cancer. I am in the hospital corridor eavesdropping when she tells her sister the news of her diagnosis.

She says, Margaret, why is it always cancer?

Auntie Margaret says, I don't know, Florence, I just don't know.

There is a pause and then my mother says, So guess when the doctor decided to tell me?

When?

Right smack in the middle of *Oprah!* I missed the whole second half of the show.

They both laugh. Auntie Margaret proceeds to tell her who Oprah had on during the second half and they chatter away, gossiping about the celebrity guests.

The doctor opens my mother up, finds she is loaded with cancer, and doesn't sew her back together again until he first removes 80 percent of her stomach. The doctor says to her, The surgery plus mild doses of chemotherapy will keep you out on the links for an extra year.

But my mother, thinking positively, chooses to dismiss the last four words the doctor says. When she returns to the hospital a year later, no longer able to play golf what with the cancer having spread to all her other organs, she stops talking to me plus several people who love her. She believed that the operation made her all better, and since it turns out she is hardly all better, she blames us. I think, why isn't she blaming the government?

I blame the Reverend Dr. Norman Vincent Peale.

When my Auntie Palma comes to visit, my mother closes her eyes and looks away. Auntie Palma always refers to my mother as her best buddy and she is crushed.

I'm feeling a little crushed myself. Once I had children of my own, my mother and I formed a new relationship; she became friendly toward me, the way she was with her friends. Not her close friends as there was no hope I'd ever be a golfer. But we would chitchat on the phone now and then, or go to dinner. I knew I was in her inner circle when she called one day with the news that my father was going on a business trip. My father had evolved into a self-made metallurgist, a ball bearings expert, and Wade Abbott began sending him off to consult with customers. So my mother said, He's going to Mexico.

A perfect straight man, I asked, Why?

She said, Because the Mexicans are having trouble with their balls.

So I say to my mother's doctor, Can you do something for the depression?

He looks at me like I am a moron. He says, She has *terminal* cancer.

The bound galleys of my third novel, *The Port of Missing Men,* arrive a short time after my mother is hospitalized. Each day, my Auntie Margaret reads a chapter to her. Auntie Margaret tells me how much they both love it. The book is set in their era, the twenties, thirties, and forties. Auntie Margaret says, Mickey, you brought us back to great times—we were humming "I'll Never Smile Again" all afternoon.

She is the one to tell me all this because, of course, my mother is not speaking to me. I have failed her. I can't stop her dying. But I know that she is at least smiling with Auntie Margaret.

I log the seventy-five miles from my home to Hartford a couple of times a week over the next ten years beginning when my mother's cancer renders her unable to play golf. One afternoon, I get stopped for speeding on I-84 by a state cop. I am racing home from Hartford so that I can get my daughter to a high school gymnastics exhibition and my son to a Babe Ruth playoff game. I tell the cop my excuse and I am shaking with such distress. Incredibly, his eyes grow moist and he says, I know, I know.

Once I am calm, he tells me the main thing I have to do when driving is to concentrate on the road. The road and nothing, else, ma'am, nothing else. I promise him I will. I thank him.

I DECIDE to do something about my mother's depression. I take her out of the hospital to the Branford Hospice on the shoreline; the Connecticut shore, after all, is Shangri-La.

The hospice is designed on the British model. She will have comfort and pain control in a lovely place without medical intervention. She doesn't agree to go but she doesn't disagree with my plan either since she's not talking to me. She asks Auntie Margaret to pack one of her scarves so she'll have something from home to look at. I choose one of my mother's Vera scarves—black with an avocado green border. The pattern is silhouettes of running horses, nine in the avocado green, three in white, and three in a beautiful shade of blue-gray. Next to the name Vera in the corner of the scarf is Vera's signature ladybug.

Her room is full of sea breezes and flowering plants. The walls are mostly glass, the property full of hundred-year-old maples. The ceiling is wainscoted with finely grained wood. The director explains that since almost all of the patients are bedridden, they can study the grain of the wood instead of just staring at a blank white ceiling.

Once my mother is settled in, the nurse tells her that if she would like something to eat or drink, she can have whatever she likes. She has only to ask. My mother says, I don't want anything.

The nurse asks, Then how about just a cup of coffee?

No.

Are you a tea drinker then?

My mother snorts.

Before she was depressed, my mother was always polite to strangers not counting Sandy Duncan.

The nurse looks at me. She is an experienced hospice person who is therefore able to read my mind. I am psyching a message to the nurse: My mother loves coffee but she won't have any because she's depressed.

The nurse says to my mother, Will you excuse me for just one minute, Mrs. Tirone?

My mother nods and I notice the flare of her nostrils. If only she could storm out of the room.

The nurse returns with three cups of coffee on a tray plus a white ceramic pitcher and a blue and white china sugar bowl. She says, My coffee break is coming up. Maybe you girls would like to share it with me.

The coffee smells really good. She gives me my cup, and passes another to my mother, who takes it. She says, Cream, girls?

We nod. She pours. It is actual cream as we are on the British model.

Sugar?

My mother asks, Do you have Sweet'n Low?

The nurse smiles and says, We don't have to bother with diets, do we?

My mother responds to that. She smiles back. She says, Three spoonfuls, please.

The nurse piles the sugar into my mother's coffee.

We all drink. The nurse says, Isn't this lovely?

It is.

Then the nurse says, Are you a widow, Mrs. Tirone?

My mother gazes out the window. No.

The nurse looks to me, unable to read my mind this time. I say, My brother is autistic. My father is his caregiver.

The nurse opens her mouth to say something no doubt along the lines of, Can't someone relieve him? But a perky woman has come in the room carrying a guitar. She smiles at my mother and says, Would you like a song, Mrs. Tirone?

My mother nods, this time incredulous rather than annoyed.

The woman begins playing *Love Me Tender.* I catch my mother's eye

Mother and Dad on their honeymoon

and we both burst out laughing. When we gain control, she says to me, Wait till I tell Margaret about this one.

Then she apologizes to the singer, telling her that Elvis always made her laugh. The nurse, meanwhile, having noted my mother's gold crucifix and St. Francis of Assisi medal says to the singer, Perhaps Mrs. Tirone would like something less secular.

My mother says, Something *Catholic.*

The woman immediately segues into "Oh, Lord I Am Not Worthy," a hymn that has always depressed me.

Fortuitously, my daughter arrives. She scopes the situation and asks if there's a piano. The hospice nurse says, Of course, and goes and sees to one. Again, my mother expresses to me how much she is looking forward to Margaret's visit so she can tell her about that too: Mickey, they're going to bring a piano! My mother has now addressed me directly for the first time in a year.

Her granddaughter does not play a hymn once the piano is rolled to my mother's door. She plays one of my mother's favorites, "Bewitched, Bothered and Bewildered." Somewhere in the middle, my mother closes her eyes and falls asleep. Now my daughter plays more gently and the old Rodgers and Hart tune becomes a lullaby. I can't imagine what life would be like without my sentimental, pure-of-heart, take-the-bull-by-the-horns daughter.

A FEW DAYS after entering hospice care, my mother is dying. I hear a snippet of conversation between her and Auntie Margaret: *Margaret, don't you wish Liberace had lived long enough to be on* Oprah? *Wouldn't they have been a hoot together?*

Within twenty-four hours of my eavesdropping on her and Auntie Margaret, she is unconscious. A half-minute passes between each labored intake of her breath. I am taking in long slow cleansing breaths myself, the kind I learned to do in Lamaze class. Cleansing breaths accomplish nothing toward relieving labor pain but they give you something to do other than scream, which ticks off the nurses as they are always in deep conversation about, say, Princess Di. When not in labor, I come to find that cleansing breaths keep me from passing out, which I am afraid I am about to do. My mother, my daughter, and I are fainters. My mother faints on the sixteenth hole at the Greenwich Country Club when she has a tournament just about sewed up. I faint in front of an audience of 250 people come to hear me and Howard Fast talk about our respective books. Howard is so impressed. He says later he enjoyed laying his head against my chest because everyone thought I had dropped dead and he felt it was up to him to verify that. When my daughter is a high school senior, she faints at an airport in South Carolina and ends up in deep shit. She's saved her baby-sitting money to go to Parris Island, where her boyfriend is becoming a U.S. Marine; she's supposed to be sleeping at her friend's up the street.

At the Branford Hospice, I watch my mother draw her last breath. I don't faint. I stand up and tell her good-bye.

I bring the Vera scarf home.

It is a struggle to get my father to agree to attend my mother's funeral. He won't leave Tyler even though Auntie Palma offers to stay with him. Auntie Palma missed my wedding to stay with Tyler. Uncle Guido manages to convince my father to go. Uncle Guido says to me, Your father is taking this very hard.

At my mother's wake, a large number of men—young and old—shake my hand and recount mixed-double golf tournament victories at various country clubs across the state, victories they attribute to their talented partner, my mother.

Do you play? several ask.

No.

Too bad.

But one says, Too busy writing?

Yes.

MY MOTHER is dead two years before my father is diagnosed with Alzheimer's. Here is Alzheimer's in a nutshell: After my Auntie Palma and Uncle Guido check on my father one evening, get him into bed, sure he is safe, they leave him. They will come back in the morning. That is the routine. But on this night, a few hours later, the first snow of winter begins to fall. My father becomes aware of the snow. When I am a child and we have our first snow of the season, it always seems to happen at night. If it isn't too late and my father knows Tyler and I are both still awake, he comes up and gets us out of bed, brings us down to the kitchen, opens the back door, and with a bit of a flair switches on the porch light. Tyler and I watch the clouds of white flakes whirling and swirling in the glow of the bare bulb. It is such a huge thrill. (Even now, the season's first snow gives me a rush.)

On this night, this Alzheimer's night, when my father somehow feels the arrival of snow in his bones, he goes to the back door, turns on the porch light, gazes at the thick flakes, and then goes outside. He goes outside barefoot in just his pajama bottoms. He never wore pajama tops. He closes the door behind him and locks himself out.

By some great good fortune, our neighbor, a reclusive fellow whose name is Eddie, sees the back porch light go on next door. He goes to the window, and there is my father walking around the house bare-chested and barefoot in the snow. He dashes to his door and calls my father into his home. No one I know has been in Eddie's house.

Eddie is a year older than me. Growing up, he would watch the neighborhood children play from his window. He never came out of the house except to go to school (and later to the Aetna, where he worked as a bookkeeper for decades). One summer day, we children become audacious and knock on his door and ask his mother if he can come out and play baseball with us. His mother is reclusive too. She says, of all things, Yes. The next thing we know, Eddie is walking toward us up the driveway that separates my house from his. He is carrying a bat. He tells us, My mother says I can play, but only if we use my bat.

The bat is a Statue of Liberty souvenir bat. It is twelve inches long. He is serious.

I say, Play ball!

My other neighbor, Alan Griggs, the smartest boy there is, suggests we use a wiffle ball instead of my father's softballs from his days playing second base for Hartford's Industrial League. We consider Eddie's bat and agree. Alan runs across the backyards to get one from his house on Coolidge Street, two doors from where Irene's body will be found the following December.

The outfield moves way, way in. Although we are having a great time, Eddie never gets a hit because he swings his bat one-handed and only after the wiffle ball is already nestled in the catcher's hands. Then, without our noticing, Eddie segues from his position in right field back into his house. When we do realize he's gone, we just continue on with the game because it is such a great challenge to try and smack a wiffle ball out of the infield using Eddie's bat. (The rule we make up for the game is that an infield hit is an out.)

When the game's over, we return the bat to Eddie's mother. She tells us he had a lovely time.

The police no doubt questioned Eddie as well as Tyler when they were looking for Irene's killer. Two teenaged boys next door to each other, both dealing from decks of their own unique designs.

The night my father locks himself out of the house in a snowstorm, Eddie is watching and rescues him. Then Eddie calls my Auntie Margaret. She gets in her car and races over. Eddie meets her at his front door and she brings my father home, gets him back into bed. The next day, she calls me and tells me what happened.

I drive the seventy-five miles to Hartford, sit in the kitchen drinking coffee with my father, which he makes on the stove in an old tin percolator with a little glass ball perched on the lid. When the coffee bubbling up into the glass is approaching the color of mahogany, my father deems it's brewed. Chock Full o' Nuts. Delicious.

I ask him why he went out in a snowstorm. He says sternly (as he is the father and I am the child), Mickey, how can I get *into* my house if I don't go *out?*

Alzheimer's in its initial, relatively easy stage, when all that's missing is the car keys and logic.

I send my old neighbor, Eddie, a bouquet of flowers. He sends me a thank-you note telling me the flowers are beautiful, so special to have them in winter.

forty-six

TYLER'S DIABETES continues on its destructive path. He has to have his foot amputated. Within months, his leg below the knee. My father's Alzheimer's, on it's own destructive path, prevents him from understanding that he can no longer take care of Tyler. I try to find services for my brother and he is given intelligence tests. A state psychologist tells me with Tyler's pools of knowledge he doesn't score low enough on the tests to qualify for services. Foolishly I ask, What do I do?

The psychologist says, Frankly, unless you care for him yourself, the only alternative he has is to live homeless on the streets.

That's nice.

Finally, a social worker named André tells me that since Tyler has no assets, he qualifies for Title 19. I don't know what that means. André explains and I apply in Tyler's behalf. Because of the diabetes, Tyler is also qualified to go to a nursing home and I won't have to sell my house to pay for it. Even more important, André says to my father: Tyler now needs insulin shots to control his diabetes—he has to have twenty-four-a-day medical attention and will have to be admitted to a nursing home.

My father protests as he's always done when someone so much as hints at putting Tyler away. Finally, though, knowing he won't be able to see to measure insulin into a syringe, he gives in. Eyeglasses with a stronger prescription haven't helped him because he is forgetting the mechanics of an important skill—seeing. He tells everyone that he has no trouble managing Tyler—he's managed him for fifty years—but he's not a doctor so he can't take care of his son's diabetes. Face saved, thank you, savior André.

My father wasn't always in such a parasitic relationship with my brother. When Tyler was five, he toured the state hospital for the mentally retarded and simply made the decision that it was up to him to care for his little boy. It was during the time the retarded were kept in pens, naked.

André also sees to getting my brother out of a wheelchair and fitted with an artificial leg. I tell André I wish he'd been around for my grandfather. When my Italian grandfather's leg was amputated he told his doctor to get him a wooden leg. The doctor said—in that condescending way they learn so well it's as if they take ten courses in medical school on condescension—Mr. Tirone, it would take too long to fit you and construct a prosthesis.

How long? asks my grandfather.

A year.

My grandfather says, I can build you a house in a month and who says I'm going to die tomorrow?

The doctor slithered away.

André gets Tyler admitted to St. Mary's Convalescent Home in West Hartford and I get him admitted to a research program at Yale–New Haven Hospital. Tyler informs the research psychiatrist there, Dr. Chris MacDonald, that he'll be summering at St. Mary's in West Hartford instead of Chalker Beach. Dr. MacDonald notes that on Tyler's chart. While the doctor is noting, Tyler swipes a photograph of the man's children off his desk and sticks it into his shirt, giggling.

Dr. MacDonald says, Tyler, did you take a picture from my desk?

Nope.

Put it back.

Okay.

Tyler puts it back. The doctor reaches into his wallet and takes out his kids' school pictures. He hands them to his patient.

You can have these. They're old.

Tyler is dazzled by the gift. I say, What do you say to the doctor, Totsie? (Totsie was the nickname my mother called him until he reached adolescence.)

254

Tyler looks past Dr. MacDonald's shoulder and says, *Fanks.* (He never could pronounce *th*.)

While Tyler happily studies the pictures, Dr. MacDonald says to me, He misses life when the two of you were children.

The doctor accepts that his patients have no morals.

TYLER IS PUT ON fluoxetine (Prozac to the rest of us), a drug the Yale psychiatrist has found to relieve, somewhat, the autistic's drive to perform obsessive compulsions. Within weeks of taking the drug, Tyler, when frustrated, continues to raise his wrist to his mouth but miraculously, stops short of chomping down on it. Thank you, Dr. MacDonald. (When Dr. MacDonald observes Tyler's "rounds"—the kishing and shoe tapping—he says to me, Your brother's rounds are a lot more productive than many of my colleagues'.)

Dr. MacDonald suggests a support group for me. He smiles: Better late than never.

I think, What the hell?

My group consists of siblings of autistic adults. Not autistic *children*. Autistic children suddenly have more services available to them than you can shake a stick at, as opposed to adults previously deemed to be retarded, now deemed autistic, who have none. Our group leader tells us our purpose will be to explore the damage done to us.

I say, I don't feel damaged, and I'm thinking, If he wants damage, he should check out my childhood friend, Joyce, whose father ate scraps of paper while the police broke her door down.

Turns out, none of us feels damaged. Leader is skeptical. To show us that we are in denial, he begins the first meeting by suggesting we jump right into the deepest end of the pool and discuss the humiliation we endured. The group, as one, lowers its eyes. Leader's specific topic is anal digging, something certain mentally disabled people—and others I would have to guess—take great pleasure in. Sort of a side dish to masturbation.

Our sibling group talks about the tight-waisted pants, the pulled-to-the-limit belts, the homemade restraints utilizing Ace bandages, none of which sways an autistic person bent on anal digging or whatever other pleasure he might find in his body. I say my brother had to wear a bathing suit when he took his bath and another sibling says her sister was bathed fully clothed. Which was nothing compared with her menstruating from one end of the house to the other. Another, a young lawyer, confesses to the group that she was the one who brought up the anal digging problem to Leader earlier. Now she apologizes to us. We forgive her. She says she told Leader how nothing could get her brother to stop. She describes to us a trip to the Special Olympics where he participated in the fifty-yard dash and the broad jump. The lawyer noted that when he jumped, his sneakers might as well have been glued to the ground. She says, During the fifty-yard dash, he stopped and sat down ten seconds into the race unlike the Down syndrome kids who zipped past him like a herd of elephants.

Her brother is still declared a winner, though, as are all participants, in both events.

The lawyer then describes the scenario driving home. She says, Up front, my parents were beaming, so happy that my brother had won a gold medal *and* a silver one. And I'm in the backseat trying to keep him from cramming the gold medal up his ass. He knew gold from silver, let me tell you. Gold would get the prize spot.

I don't know who is the first to snicker. I think me.

My support group, soon in hysterics much to the wonder of Leader, decides our war stories won't help us as much as heading for the nearest bar. Leader makes an excuse not to join us. We go to Toad's Place and drink and laugh the night away while rastas play ska. It is clear that all of us love our deranged siblings, because we begin telling loving tales and I impersonate Tyler's rendition of Cinderella. Even though these brothers and sisters make our lives complicated, often miserable, they also make us happy.

One fellow says, My brother will practically kill himself to stop a bout of anxiety, but, I'll tell you this, he'll kill to protect me too. But yet, he's as sweet as a teddy bear . . . well, in his own way. He's my Boo Radley.

We all drift for a moment or two, into memory. I had a cat named Streakie for a short time until she was hit by a car in front of my house. My parents extended their sympathies to me but Tyler kept saying, Sister, don't commit suicide. Please don't commit suicide.

For days I'd hear him mumbling to himself, Good thing we don't have any howitzers in the house.

Poor Tyler was imagining me blasting myself into oblivion with a howitzer.

My fellow siblings and I leave Toad's Place after some serious all-around hugging and I reread *To Kill a Mockingbird* and decide, too, as my fellow support group members had, that Boo Radley was autistic, sequestered by his father for his own protection, but not successful enough to keep Boo from killing a bad man to save a young neighbor boy. Autistics demonstrate love oddly, as oddly as they do everything else, but their love is mighty just the same.

MY FATHER VISITS Tyler every day, twice a day, at St. Mary's until he injures himself in a fall at one o'clock in the morning in front of Jack's store at the corner of Hillside and New Britain Avenue. He'd probably gone out to buy a couple of Dutch Masters. A woman coming out of the Brookside Tavern finds him. She cradles him in her arms until an ambulance arrives and takes him to Hartford Hospital. Since he has forgotten his wallet—forgotten where he put it, forgotten he owns a wallet, forgotten what a wallet is—he has no identification, but a forbearing person at Hartford Hospital gets his name out of him and then someone says, Hey, that's Margaret Kelley's brother-in-law!

Auntie Margaret to the rescue.

I make the dash to Hartford, where my father is still in the emergency room. I pour out my soul to some poor innocent nurse, telling her that my father will be killed if he keeps wandering, and then she sighs and says, I hear you. She calls the nursing home of my choice and claims some kind of life-threatening emergency. I hug her.

Within hours I am settling him into a nursing home on Hillside Avenue, a mile from his house in Hartford. I park his last Ford, a Taurus, in the lot across the street and ask permission of the nursing home director to leave it there. She says it'll be okay. My father keeps his car keys in his pocket; he will now check out the existence of his car a thousand times a day, which gives him comfort.

Neither Tyler nor my father agrees to visit one another at their respective nursing homes, I don't know why. When I'm with my father, he always says, How is Tyler doing? I tell him Tyler is just great, which is true—he's adjusting and his wrist is no longer chronically infected; it's actually healing.

My father is not adjusting to Alzheimer's: He reaches a point where he forgets how to walk: Look, Yutchie, says Uncle Guido, you put one foot in front of the other like this.

Uncle Guido demonstrates and my father follows, taking one step. But then he forgets the rest of the demonstration as to his other foot following suit. Uncle Guido is crestfallen. He can save an entire freezing, starving platoon's life with weeds but he can do nothing for his closest friend.

A year later, my father forgets how to talk. My daughter, who is now studying to be an RN, says I should bring up a topic from long ago and see if maybe he can talk after all. Okay.

I say, Dad, remember the hope chest you bought Mother?

He doesn't respond.

Did you buy it in a store or did you have a carpenter make it?

Sternly, he says, I bought it at the *furniture store* on Main Street!

I take a deep cleansing breath: This was during the Depression?

Nineteen thirty-two.

So how did you pay for it?

Guy let me give him a buck a month. Fourteen months.

It cost fourteen dollars?

He says, That's right. But I never told your mother I was paying on time.

I have only recently had the beautiful, walnut, cedar-lined chest restored. The restorer, a lovely Hungarian, talks to the hope chest and calls it, *old fellow,* when he examines it. I tell my father all that. He is gazing into my eyes. I understand what he wants to know. I say, Guy charged me over four hundred bucks. Had to pay it all at once.

He smiles. He says, You're the one who's lost their marbles.

One day, Freddie Ravenel comes to visit him. Right after Freddie leaves, I arrive. The nurse tells me there's been an African-American gentleman sitting in the lobby crying his eyes out.

She says, He'd just had a visit with your father. He told us your father gave him a job when no one else would, that he filled out the loan application for his first car, that he cosigned a mortgage or he'd never have had a house, that he helped him with his income taxes every year.

My father helped everyone with their income taxes. I never knew he helped Freddie even.

I go down to my father's room. I crouch next to his chair.

Hi, Daddy.

The noise of my voice attracts his attention, which is far, far away. But his eyes are able to find my own, not usually the case anymore.

It's me, Dad, Mickey.

He concentrates. Hey, Mick.

I kiss his cheek and then I plant my face directly in front of his to keep his gaze steady. He struggles but he stays with me.

Freddie Ravenel was here to visit, Dad.

That's right, he says.

I wait for more and he actually says more: Freddie didn't know who I was. He kept saying, *Mr. Mawse, oh, Mr. Mawse . . .* But he couldn't find me.

Did you try to speak to him?

I know that is too hard a question even as I'm asking it. My father looks to the light, the window, and stares out.

For about a month, he is able to converse if I bring up old events, and then he can't. He has a meeting with representatives from all the departments at the nursing home who are determining a new course of care. I am invited to attend. The head of nursing asks me, What is his normal weight?

I turn to my father and say, Dad, what do you usually weigh?

He says, One forty-two.

I say to the staff, Could you not give up on him?

I never hear my father speak again. His last words to me: one forty-two.

Soon after, his aide, whose name is Rosa, and who acts as though he's her own father–kissing him, hugging him, patting his cheek–says to me, Your father keeps saying, My son, my son.

I want to kill myself for giving up on him. I lean down next to him and I say, Tyler is great, Dad, he's great. He misses you a lot but he's really doing so well at St. Mary's.

Now, this is a lie.

ONCE A WEEK. I've been taking Tyler out to various libraries, where he goes to read the same books he owns. He's only brought a half-dozen of his books to St. Mary's since he'd planned to be there for a short holiday.

We go to the libraries in Hartford, West Hartford, New Britain, Farmington, Avon, and Simsbury. We hit libraries the way barflies hit gin mills. Everybody knows our name. Tyler's favorite is the New Britain library. He gets to check the photo file of Jean Marie Kabritsky, who is still singing and continuing to gain weight. I show him all the cards referencing my own books in the card catalog. He could care less.

Tyler claims a table right next to the section on military history and peruses the latest two *Jane's* volumes. After my mother died and my father was fairly out of commission with the onset of Alzheimer's, it fell to me to buy the annual *Jane's* books for Tyler. At Books on the Common, my local bookstore owners, the Silbernagles, out of the goodness of their hearts, ordered them for me and charged me what they paid rather than retail. Today *Jane's All the World's Aircraft* costs six hundred dollars. The service I received from the Silbernagles is not available at Amazon.

Tyler walks the stacks and finds a couple of new acquisitions—a book describing the struggle for Kwajalein, the other the route General Hobart's Desert Rats took from Mersa Matruh to Berlin.

Tyler talks to his books while he reads. His unseen antenna diverts him from the books when a child comes by. Then he grabs his forty-year-old Brownie box camera. My mother had hid the camera when he started taking pictures of children walking up Nilan Street, but I have since found it. I remember the day my mother hid the Brownie hoping he'd stop hanging out the front door and asking passing kids to pose, but he switched photographic equipment and utilized his View-Master. I have been dismantling the house on Nilan Street; I found the old Brownie in the basement and gave it back to him. He grinned at it and held it all day long and I retired the View-Master. Now at the library, he aims the Brownie at the child, and whispers, Say cheese.

Before my father was rendered psychotic by Alzheimer's, he was the one to take Tyler on his weekly library jaunt. He did not demand Tyler whisper in the library. However, he did insist that Tyler take a picture of only one child, not every single one of them. That is the compromise our father worked out with Tyler. Tyler got his pictures and my father only had to deal with one angry parent per library visit.

When I come to be Tyler's library chauffeur, I tell him he has to keep his voice to a whisper at all times, and then he can take all the pictures he wants. This means that the children don't hear his instructions—Say cheese—and since a Brownie is held at chest level as opposed to pressed up to his eyes, the children generally don't notice he is photographing them.

The question arises: Why not explain to Tyler that he shouldn't take a strange child's picture because the child might become frightened? Tyler, incapable of empathy, has always ignored such advice. I can come down harder and tell Tyler there will be no library if he takes children's pictures with his Brownie, but that would break his heart. Not that he'd bite on his wrist—the fluoxetine and the heroic Dr. MacDonald at Yale–New Haven have taken care of that—but I'm not going to have his heart broken either.

We stay at the library for a couple of hours. When Tyler gets up to select a new book, I try to get him to keep his damn kishing to a minimum. He goes back and forth to the shelf three times, kishing away. Fluoxetine only takes you so far. I say, Tyler, please kish more quietly. He tries, and to compensate for that effort, which proves disruptive to his rounds, he must add something new, so he begins winking his right eye then his left, three times. This requires a great deal of physical effort and manipulation since he's never tried winking before: His facial muscles contort outrageously just as a two-year-old's will who attempts to wink. I whisper, Tyler, what the hell are you doing?

He says, I'm imitating the signal at a train crossing when the train is approaching the guard rail. If I do that, I'll be able to whisper.

Do I want the winking or the kishing? Doesn't matter what I want. Tyler's kishing is soon back to its annoying decibel and guess what? There will be a train approaching the crossing every fifteen minutes from here on in.

While Tyler reads, so do I. Sometimes, other patrons sit down at our table. When they do, Tyler takes up his Campbell's soup can, which he carries with him in the Brownie camera bag, and calls into it, Enemy approaching, men. Keep low.

Our new neighbors look at their watches like they're late for appointments and scurry away. Every once in a while, a patron will stay, smiling at me to show he understands. A fairly large problem arises when Tyler has to go to the bathroom. Then he will stand, salute, and announce in a General Patton kind of voice, Urination time!

Once, after I accompany him to the men's room and back, a kindly woman sitting at our table coincidentally reading the bathroom chapter in Martha Stewart's *How to Decorate*, leans over and whispers to me like I'm a lifelong friend, As soon as he said that I had to go, too!

Tyler looks at her with some curiosity. Then he whips out his Brownie and tells her to say cheese. I whisper to her, He's from *People* magazine.

She is suddenly late for an appointment, too, having realized I'm just as demented as the general.

On one library day, when it is time to return to St. Mary's, Tyler decides to exit by the service door instead of the front entrance. As we pass a *Staff Only* door, he hangs back and then scurries out before I can grab him. I dash through and then clamor down the metal stairs behind Tyler. A librarian opens the *Staff Only* door above and calls out, You can't go that way!

Tyler ignores her and, therefore, so do I. Tyler is now lumbering along at a fairly good clip, favoring his artificial leg only slightly. Once he reaches the service area, a custodian is at the bay shooting the breeze with the UPS man. He gapes at Tyler and says to him, Sorry, pal, you can't go out this way.

The custodian and the UPS man form a phalanx, not wanting Tyler to fall off the delivery ramp. Then the security guard appears. He's come to know Tyler. He looks at me.

I say, Sorry. I couldn't stop him.

He says to Tyler, Listen, Commander, we have to go upstairs and use the front door.

Why?

The loading platform is dangerous. You could fall off.

I won't.

See, it's a matter of insurance.

Tyler grows curious instead of single-minded. The fluoxetine.

The guard says, The insurance company's rule is that patrons can't use this entrance. If they do, they won't cover the library. Then the library will have to close.

Tyler asks him, Are you a commissioned officer?

The security guard says, I certainly am.

Tyler salutes and says, Good man, and heads back. I salute the security guard, too. He says, You're a saint.

I say, Don't I fucking know it.

He laughs.

Our next stop is the West Hartford Barnes & Noble, where I follow in my father's habit of buying Tyler one book and two magazines each month. Tyler goes along with this rather than three books per month because his room at St. Mary's has only three shelves and he won't agree to the idea of putting his new books in St. Mary's library, which could easily use a few extra editions.

Tyler picks a book called *Destroyers*. Fifty bucks, not bad. One of the two magazines he picks is *Wings*. I explain that *Wings* is actually a soft cover book, not a magazine, and costs twenty dollars, which will put him over budget.

He says, It's a pulp. He calls magazines, pulps.

I say, No, not arguing price because he has no concept of what money is as it holds no interest for him.

He says he has to have *Wings*. I tell him to pick out two magazines and put *Wings* back. He picks two magazines and holds on to *Wings* hoping I won't notice. I do. His wrist comes up to his mouth. This tells me that he truly can't manage without *Wings* even though the fluoxetine is doing all it can.

I say, Listen, Tyler, next week is September. *Wings* can be your September book. We'll buy just two magazines for September so you can have *Wings* on our next library day.

He says, Buy it today. Please, Sister, please.

Sister Barbara, one of the head nuns at St. Mary's, finds it's so adorable that Tyler thinks I'm a nun too.

I relent. I'll compromise. I say, Okay, I'll buy it today but you're not getting it until your September book day.

He smiles. His smile is one of those thousand-watt jobs.

I take out my MasterCard.

He keeps the Barnes and Noble bag in the backseat with him. I say, Tyler, take *Wings* out of the bag and put it on the seat next to you and I promise to bring it next time. I don't back down on my promises and you know it.

He giggles. Not getting away with a form of thievery continues to amuse him. He puts *Wings* on the seat next to him.

In the parking lot at St. Mary's, as he's pulling himself out of the car, getting his artificial leg caught as usual, he eyes *Wings* wistfully. I almost grab the damn book and say, Here, take it. But I don't because if you give Tyler an inch, he takes a mile. He will start demanding extra books. I've got two adolescent kids. Once you give into a demand such as hundred-and-fifty-dollar sneakers, you're cooked. Tyler learns from people like General Hobart and his desert rats; teenagers learn from their strongest influence, each other.

I see Tyler back to his room and he doesn't respond when I say, Good-bye, because he's already plopped on his bed engrossed in *Destroyers*.

I walk down the hall, past the nursing station, and wave to the staff. One of them says, Tyler so looks forward to his trips to the libraries with you.

Yeah, he does. Then I hear Tyler call out, Sister!

I turn. He's standing in the hallway outside his room. What, Tyler?

Sunday is September first.

I know.

It's the new month. He says, Bring me *Wings* on Sunday and we'll get the two magazines on our next bookstore day.

I sigh. That will mean on our next bookstore day he will try to schnauzer an extra book. Also, I hadn't intended to visit this Sunday—it's Labor Day weekend. I'd be at Chalker Beach in Old Saybrook. But Tyler is standing there looking so hopeful, so earnest.

Okay, Totsie, I say.

He grins at a fixed point over my head and turns back into his room.

I call out, What do you say, Tyler?

His head appears. He says, *Fanks.*

From St. Mary's, I drive to Trinity Hill Health Care Center to visit my father. He is in his Gerry-chair at the end of the hallway gazing out the window at his car. I tell him about my adventure with Tyler.

He stares past me out the window but he doesn't really see the car. In fact, he doesn't know why he's looking out the window.

In my own car, heading home down I-84, I feel happy because even though I won't have my father much longer, I'll still have the Tyler I've always known, that he's safe. Then I feel guilty for all the times I thought: Why can't Tyler be normal? Why can't he be a scholar-athlete? Why can't he be a student at Trinity College and fix me up with one of his frat brothers? Now I have to smile to myself; I'm thinking the frat brother might have been George F. Will.

At ten o'clock that night, I get a call from Tyler's charge nurse. I am at the cottage at Chalker Beach and I have just come from Burgey's Barn, which my Uncle Ray and Auntie Margaret bought for a thousand dollars in the sixties. My Auntie Margaret, my husband, my cousin Rita Belch, and I have been playing some setback. Auntie Margaret is nearly as cutthroat as my mother, but unlike my mother, she is able to tolerate her two nieces' poor playing abilities. As for my husband's setback skills, Auntie Margaret can't control rolling her eyes.

The nurse on the phone says to me, Mary-Ann, Tyler fainted this evening.

By law, in Connecticut, a nursing home must notify family if a resident has had an emergency. The previous time they called to notify me of an emergency was when Tyler pulled the fire alarm. He felt no one would guess the perpetrator's identity since there were so many residents at St. Mary's. A fire at a nursing home is a very big deal, so the firefighters from West Hartford, Hartford, and six surrounding towns stormed St. Mary's in full gear from helmets to axes. When the first firefighter arrived on Tyler's floor, he shouted, All hands on deck! Kamikaze attack!

Staff was able to figure out that Tyler preempted the battle.

Tonight, on the phone, the nurse goes on: Tyler fainted as he was heading to the library, right in front of us at the station. (St. Mary's had come to keep the library open at night for Tyler since that's when Tyler chose to use it. His head nurse, Anne, argued for his right to do that. She said to the board, St. Mary's is Tyler's home. He should be able to go to the library whenever he damn well pleases. Case closed.)

The charge nurse says, Mary-Ann, he regained consciousness immediately. And he persisted in telling us he intended to go on ahead to the library so we knew he was fine. All the same, we talked him into going back to his room and getting into bed. We told him he'd fainted and when you faint—that's the rule, back to bed. An order from the commander-in-chief, we told him. The doctor came in just a little while later and examined him. He told us Tyler just needed a nice glass of orange juice and a little rest—fifteen minutes—and then he could go to the library. Tyler was very happy to hear that. He told Doctor that I'd already given him orange juice and that he *was* resting. This doctor is such a nice fellow. He saluted Tyler before he left.

Then she says, An aide had a peek at him five minutes ago to see if he felt well enough to go back to the library. Mary-Ann, I'm so sorry. Tyler died. The entire staff is devastated.

I am calm because I am convinced there is some kind of mistake. That my father died, not Tyler. I look up at my husband, who is staring at me.

I say, Tyler died.

Hearing the words come out of my own mouth, I know it isn't a mistake. I see that I am holding a phone. I speak to the nurse again. I say, Thank you.

THE NEXT DAY, I bring Tyler's September book, *Wings,* to Fisette's Funeral Home and ask Mr. Fisette to put it in the coffin with Tyler. He tells me there is no problem there. He is looking at me, though, in a strange way. I say to him, What's wrong?

He says, Mary-Ann, I have bad news.

I think, But I already have the bad news.

The state came and got Tyler. They intend to autopsy him.

I freak out. Mr. Fisette gets me some coffee. He says over and over again that there is nothing he can do. Tyler died under suspicious circumstances.

I am so appalled. The law says a nursing home has to call a family member in an emergency, but the state can require autopsies at will. Connecticut gave my brother nothing, starting with an education. Now they intended to mutilate him in death after he'd been so mutilated in life with his diabetes that my father and everyone else couldn't prevent.

I insist on calling someone, anyone. Who should I call, I ask Mr. Fisette.

The coroner's office.

I freak out some more.

Then I pick up the phone and I speak to a very polite woman. She explains calmly that Tyler was on Title 19. This means he is state property. She says they are, therefore, not required to notify next of kin when an autopsy is in order. She says it's too bad the nursing home didn't inform me.

I call St. Mary's. Sister Barbara is crying. Mary-Ann, we just found out an hour ago. We tried to call you. We had to leave a message on your machine.

Then she says, Please let us have Tyler's funeral Mass here in our chapel.

I agree.

Within a few months, Malcolm X's widow, Betty Shabazz, dies in a fire at her apartment in New York, a fire set by her young grandson. Her family refuses to allow her to be autopsied claiming religious privilege. I wasn't given the opportunity to claim anything.

Tyler's funeral is postponed for a day.

The next morning Mr. Fisette calls me and says, Tyler is back. Then he says, Only his head was autopsied.

Wonderful.

The cause of death, arteriosclerosis.

I don't say to Mr. Fisette that the cause of death was criminal indifference to disabled people. I do blame the government this time.

Soon I am back at Fisette's, and there is Tyler in his coffin, just like

Jackie was decades ago, same exact spot, embanked in flowers, a pair of rosaries twisted in his hands. The first time Tyler ever touched rosary beads. Rosary beads are standard issue at Fisette's. He is wearing my husband's suit. He looks pretty sharp.

Wings is somehow attached to the coffin lid as if when it's closed, Tyler will be able to read his book. I take the critter out of the bag I'm holding. I nestle him into the crook of Tyler's neck and shoulder, just where Tyler would put him when he was finally able to go to sleep after those hours of rounds and kishing.

I ask the priest from St. Lawrence O'Toole's Church if he will say a Mass of the Angels for Tyler instead of a regular funeral Mass. A Mass of the Angels is celebrated for children who die before the age of seven. I explain that Tyler was denied the sacraments and the explanation to my parents was that he would never attain the age of reason (seven years old), not mentally anyway. I explain to the priest that according to the Church, Tyler is therefore still an angel. The priest gives me a look that I would have to describe as *imploring* and asks, Would you go along with my just saying the special prayers from the Mass of the Angels?

I am a sucker for *imploring*. I tell him that will do.

Staff at St. Mary's chapel outnumbers relatives ten to one. I don't know who is with the patients. Eddie, my Nilan Street neighbor who played baseball only once on a summer day, who rescued my father from death by exposure, sends a massive basket of flowers to St. Mary's for Tyler's Mass. Now it is my turn to write him a thank-you for the beautiful flowers.

MY FATHER FORGETS how to swallow food. Then he forgets how to breathe. One day, I come to visit and I see that he is dying. Rosa, his aide is crying. I sit by his bedside for twelve hours. He doesn't die. Rosa tells me to go home, that there is no telling how long he'll hold on, that he won't be alone. He dies that night with Rosa standing in for me. I am filled with guilt and sorrow.

Sitting in front of his coffin, I wonder how he could have possibly endured his son's death. How could he have survived the news of Tyler's autopsy? The Alzheimer's has been a blessing is what people say to me at his funeral.

I DECIDE TO SELL the cottage in Old Saybrook. More guilt. I know my father figured I'd keep it and go there every summer with my family. It is a four-hundred-square-foot shack with a leaking roof, leaking sink, and leaking toilet pipes. It smells like the inside of my childhood treasure box, the Dutch Masters humidor. (My son says to me that once in a while he catches the odor of a cigar and thinks Grandpa is coming down the street. Only it's someone else.) Cleaning out the kitchen cupboards, I find a box of LaRosa number 8 spaghetti hidden behind a box of broken dishes. There is a price on it—twenty-five cents. It's from Jack's store. Tyler liked spaghetti number 8 and Jack always kept it in stock for my father. I decide to keep the box of spaghetti, put it on my cookbook shelf at home.

When I leave the cottage for the last time, I stop at an antique shop because a walnut dresser with a marble top is sitting in the yard in front of the store and it catches my eye. It reminds me of the one that was in my Italian grandfather's bedroom. My father told me it had been my grandmother's pride and joy.

I buy it and pay a lot to have it delivered sixty miles away. When the deliverymen arrive, I have them put it in my bedroom. They leave and I begin putting my clothes into it. There's something in the bottom drawer that rolls around when I open it. I pull it all the way out and a large shiny ball bearing rolls toward me.

I am now one of those whackos who say things like: After my mother died a butterfly landed on my shoulder and I knew she was all right because she loved butterflies.

My father has channeled a ball bearing to me; it's all right that I sold the cottage.

Part V

The Future Is Now

Dad and Mickey

forty-seven

Dad and Mickey dancing with her cousins. Paul with back to the camera.
New husband, rear left, dancing with Auntie Kekkie

WHEN I FINISHED this memoir, I thought about Irene's brother, Fred. I wondered if Fred couldn't help but be overprotective of his estranged daughter and so she chafed. Maybe something as simple as that. Or was it a kind of vicarious survivor's guilt? Did he, unconsciously, feel bitter that his daughter survived childhood but his sister did not? Maybe as complicated as that. Or was it something in the middle: Did his daughter feel an uneasiness in him and interpret it as rejection?

Well trained, I stopped thinking about that. Instead, I fantasize that Fred has reached out to his daughter, or her to him, and they have established a new relationship. My fantasy includes a grandchild for Fred, a girl who is named Irene in honor of her great-aunt.

I take a vacation. I go to visit my husband's cousin and his wife and their dog, Thurber, in the Georgia mountains near the Tennessee border where the land is pristine and the pine trees tower over all. One day the four of us are out riding around looking for a piece of property the cousins are considering buying. But they can't find it, can't figure out where the turn is. My husband's cousin asks over his shoulder, Do y'all shoot out road signs up North?

We have such a swell time, exactly the kind of break I needed.

From there we take a quick trip to Charleston because I've always wanted to visit Charleston. When we get there, I stand by the harborside looking at all the piers, and find myself wondering where Bob Malm's ship, the *Charles F. Osborne*, was berthed when it was decommissioned before Bob was sent off to New London to train at the sub school.

We tour Fort Sumter. There is a plaque listing the members of the company who defended the fort during the attack by the Confederacy. Many of them, I learn, were with the regiment's marching band. The list includes:

> First Sergeant John Renehan
> Musician Charles Hall
> Corporal Christopher Costolan
> Musician Robert Foster
> Private Edward Brady
> Musician James E. Galway

There is a woman's name at the bottom of the list, Anne Weitfieldt—her title, Matron. The park ranger tells me that matron meant married woman and no one has any idea who the woman was.

On the National Park Service ferry returning to the city, I take my pen and notebook out of my purse. I start writing a new novel. I will make up who Anne Weitfieldt was and what she was doing at Fort Sumter when the first shot was fired. Me, writing a Civil War novel, of all damn things. I am so excited I start to cry. Crying is such a luxury; people have no idea.

All writing is therapy. To some extent all writers seek their craft to heal a wound in themselves, to make themselves whole.

GRAHAM GREENE

Better to have a miserable childhood than a miserable adulthood. The first is so much shorter.

BETTE MIDLER

notes

Mary-Ann's fourth-generation Sox fans

The Charter Oak was purportedly felled by a thunderstorm in 1855. However, a few days earlier, Samuel Colt presented his top five gun dealers with sidehammer revolvers; the grips were carved from a large branch of the tree, lopped off by Colt's good friend on whose land the tree stood.

Uncle Guido, who served in World War II as a combat engineer, had two duties: defusing explosive devices (booby traps) and laying mines. As any fan of *The English Patient* knows, Uncle Guido was, therefore, a sapper. One day, on the road to Bastogne, the GIs came to a footbridge and although the men couldn't see an explosive device in the bridge, Uncle Guido—by then attuned to the German mind-set—was sure it was booby-trapped. His commanding officer, who had become a good friend and whose job it was to get to Bastogne, disagreed and proceeded to the bridge to show his men there wasn't a bomb. As soon as his foot hit the bridge, he disappeared in the explosion.

There has always been discussion as to Harry Truman's decision to drop the atomic bomb. I asked Tyler why Truman dropped the bomb. Tyler said, To end the war. Then he said, But the tactic failed—Truman had to drop a second bomb. That did it.

When Daddy Welch died, Mrs. Auerbach sent twelve cars to carry Fox's employees to the funeral. A record number of cars. A tribute to her loyal employee.

The federal government decided Connecticut needed a major interstate road parallel to I-95, fifty miles to the north, which would cut through Hartford—another way to get from New York to Boston. A major cloverleaf of exits and entrances into and out of Hartford was a bit of a stumbling block because they'd have to figure a way to get around the state capitol building, the state armory, and the second-oldest high school in the United States, Hartford Public. The solution was simple—my alma mater was bulldozed.

All my family served as an extended employment service. Auntie Margaret could get you into Hartford Hospital; my mother could get you into C.G.; my father could get you into the Abbott Ball; and my Uncle Ray could get you into the state, where you'd have great benefits and plenty of vacation days. Today, my Auntie Ida who is eighty-seven can get you into the Civic Center as a temporary usher if you need a few extra bucks or want to see the UCONN girls play for free.

When my daughter turned sixteen—about to take her driver's license test—my mother advised her to be sure to know how to make a

Y-Turn. My daughter—tall, slim, and with gorgeous jet-black hair like my mother—said, Don't worry, Grandma, I've got everything under control. At the Motor Vehicle Department she said to the inspector as she walked out to the car with him: How about we just bypass all this and go get a couple of Big Macs instead? The man gaped at her. She laughed and said, Just kidding, and she nudged him with her elbow. When they came back, she was sucking up a chocolate shake; she'd passed the test and she got her Big Mac too. She told her grandmother that she got to do her Y-turn in a McDonald's parking lot so it was a snap.

I finally drove by my old house on Nilan Street. My Auntie Palma told me that the Puerto Ricans who bought it must be well-off as they'd surrounded it with a brand-new chain-link fence, which is a status symbol in some circles. The fence was hideous; my little Cape Cod house looked like a mini-penitentiary. But the lawn was neat and trim and new shrubs have been planted. I looked up at the two dormered bedroom windows, mine and Tyler's.

After I sold the house, my daughter walked me out of the lawyer's office with her arm around me and said, Some other little girl is sleeping in your bedroom and she's so happy to have a room of her own. I could only hope that if the little girl had a brother sleeping in Tyler's room that he wasn't a manipulative lunatic. While I drove down the street, past Eddie's house, I heard a rumbling. At the stop sign at Chandler Street I watched a line of bulldozers beginning a new job: disappearing Charter Oak Terrace. Sweet Jesus. I skedaddled on home, happy to note that the big church and the tiny library across from each other hadn't yet fallen victim to progress.

At a very posh nursing home in West Hartford I had lunch with retired state Supreme Court Judge, Douglass B. Wright, who was the Assistant State's Attorney to Albert S. Bill at the trial of Robert Malm. He became a preeminent torts authority, wrote a book called *Wright's Wrongs*, which is still used by law schools today. Jerry Demeusy, the retired *Hartford Courant* crime reporter arranged the lunch. The two men joked how the Connecticut Supreme Court of Errors had to have a name change because it was so often referred to as the Connecticut Court of Supreme Errors. The official title is now the Appellate Court. Judge Wright slipped a little flask out of his pocket and offered me some "schnapps"—he didn't think much of the nursing home's ban on alcohol. The judge is the person who revealed to me that Robert Malm told the cops Irene winked at him. When it was time for me to leave, the judge invited me to come back on any Saturday night when he and his band played American standards for the residents and guests. He'd also named his band Wright's Wrongs.

Jerry Demeusy and I discussed why people confess to crimes they didn't commit, as did Army Private John Williams, who claimed to have killed Irene. People confess to murders all the time for lots of reasons, one loonier than the next. (The soldier's father told Jerry that a bureau had fallen on his son's head during his last leave home and it made him goofy.) When police accept false confessions, the term *hoax* is no longer used to allow the police to deny accountability. Cops are supposed to know a hoax when they see one. Actually, they do. Any mystery writer worth her salt will attest to that based on conversations over a few beers with a couple of chatty officers. Cops are trained to be success-oriented or face the wrath of the hungry State's Attorney.

Chief Godfrey did not rely on the *State of Connecticut v. Palko* when it came to extracting a confession from Bob Malm, did not trick him into thinking his mother had asked him to confess, or that someone had seen him kill Irene. But State's Attorney Albert Bill relied on the *Palko* decision when it came to Malm's appeal. Yes, it was true that Malm was not informed of Private Williams's confession, but according to the *Connecticut v. Palko* decision . . . *the object of evidence is to get at the truth and a trick which has no tendency to produce a confession except one in accordance with truth is always admissible.*

Bill turned to another case when it came to the two-witness statutory rule, *Connecticut v. Poplowski*. He described every bit of evidence the state had against Robert Malm. He submitted that the evidence as presented complied with the rule—that the evidence was the equivalent of eyewitness testimony from two people. Then he stated: *The whole duty of the court is to call the attention of the jury to the statute and instruct them that the case must be proved by the "testimony of at least two witnesses or that which is equivalent thereto" leaving them to judge entirely for themselves what constitutes sufficient evidence, whether it be direct or circumstantial, or made up of both.*

Bill pointed out that in counsel's brief, counsel relied on the two-witness equivalency rule in *State of Connecticut v. Poplowski, to the effect that facts cannot be established by not believing witnesses who deny them.*

My initial reaction was, of course: *Say what?*

Bill summarily dismissed any idea of the Court proving if evidence is the equivalent of the testimony of two witnesses. Such must be left to the jury.

Executions by electrocution often went awry. When the current didn't get the job done, curtains might be drawn and the first of the autopsy procedures begun immediately. Or in less genteel prisons, a corrections officer might be ordered to strangle the prisoner. I found this out when researching methods of execution for a novel I was writing. I asked a Texas prison official why the executioner couldn't just throw the switch a second time. He said, *You could blow the whole circuitry out. A maximum security prison without power? That would be a place no man wants to be at. Now, course, we just give 'em the stick. Thank the Lord above for that.*

The United States Supreme Court has recently ruled in *Roper v. Simmons* that the execution of those who committed crimes as juveniles violated the Eighth Amendment's prohibition against cruel and unusual punishment. George F. Will was fifty years ahead of his time.

Connecticut now has another governor who is a woman. She was Lieutenant Governor under Governor John Rowland when he decided to give away state contracts in exchange for a hot tub; he resigned to avoid impeachment and she inherited the title.

Execution in Connecticut has been in the news again. After the Taborsky execution, new legislation removed the viability of the death penalty—the numbers and kinds of appeals allowed would take forever. But after forty years of no executions, an inmate in the number 1 position on death row stopped the appeals process and his newly hired lawyer went along with the plan. The man was assigned an execution date. However, a federal District Court judge did not go along. He determined that a lawyer's job is to consider what is in the best interest of his client; committing suicide may or may not be in his best interest. The execution date was postponed while other people filed appeals on the killer's behalf claiming he was mentally incompetent to make such a decision. The governor-by-default said she wouldn't grant the condemned man a temporary reprieve while things got sorted out. She made that determination after reading the details of his crimes, which caused her to lose sleep. In a television interview she announced that she had no sympathy for him. (As if that has anything to do with the price of rice, as my mother would say.) On Friday the 13th of May 2005, the State of Connecticut allowed the killer his suicide by medically assisted lethal injection, which took place just after he received the sacrament of the Holy Eucharist. Coincidentally, on this same day the Bush administration announced the closing of the submarine base in New London, a decision later tossed by the BRAC Commission.

When my father was dying of Alzheimer's, he referred to my writing as typing, and my income as winnings. I have discovered that many people think in those terms when I tell them what I do for a living.

My son cataloged Tyler's books and I offered them to the American Military Museum in Danbury, Connecticut, which is a small museum with dioramas of battle scenes using life-size mannikins in vintage uniform carrying authentic weapons. There is also a display of gifts sent back from our GIs to their family and friends. (My cousin Donald Grogan, Auntie Yvonne's son who served in Japan with the occupying forces, sent me a bisque baby doll in a red kimono.) The museum also has a parking lot full of tanks. After receiving the makeshift catalog, the director called and was filled with emotion. He wanted to make sure I knew that many of the books were one of a kind. I told him I didn't think the books were valuable as they were all dog-eared and spotted with root beer soda and Chef Boyardee spaghetti sauce. He said they were valuable to the museum. I said, Good; they're yours. I didn't donate my baby doll in the red kimono.

My Italian grandfather learned English listening to the Boston Red Sox on the radio. He did not live long enough, and neither did my father, to hear the Sox shellac the Yankees in the 2004 American League Championship Series. But all five generations of Tirone Red Sox fans were there in front of our TV sets with my father and Gramps, who definitely hovered. While the gentlemen/idiots of Boston won the World Series we savored the divine fragrance of a Dutch Masters cigar and homemade wine.

When I found myself writing this memoir, I contacted Irene's brother, Fred. He was pleased to hear about it. Fred and I met, and now we're friends. His employee said to me, *This is like a miracle.* Talking with him, I got a feel for what it might have been like to have a normal brother. Often he speaks of a stepdaughter; he has a loving relationship with her. He ends our conversations with questions such as, *Do you remember pineapple cream pie?* I do, so I get out my mother's recipe card file filled with nothing but desserts. Here, Fred, is the recipe—so simple, so fifties:

Pineapple Cream Pie

Bake a pie shell and let it cool.

In a large saucepan bring a 15 oz. can of crushed pineapples to the boil.

Pour in a box of pineapple Jell-O.

When the Jell-O is dissolved, remove from heat.

Spoon a pint of vanilla ice cream into the mix and stir till melted.

Put the pan in the fridge and let the mix set until a mound rises in the center.

Spoon the mix into the pie shell and put back in fridge for at least two hours.

Before serving, spread with whipped cream.

(Yum.)

Irene and Fred Fiederowicz

acknowledgments

A$_N$ ACKNOWLEDGMENT TO Jessica Auerbach, Sarah Clayton, Ethel Paquin, and Jere Smith for reading, etc.; Margaret Kelley, Cleasse Sullivan, Patty Sullivan, and Rita Belch Giacomazzi for family lore; Bobby and Jackie Tirone for generosity of spirit; Jerry Demeusy and Judge Douglass B. Wright for insight and entertainment; attorney Rick Vaccaro for taking the time to open some crucial doors to the judiciary; Mark Davis, political correspondent, WTNH TV–Channel 8 News, Connecticut, for a last-minute leap to the rescue; the librarians at the Hartford Public Library, the Connecticut Historical Society, the Connecticut State Library and the *New London Day* for ferreting out so much; the Connecticut Commission for Culture for their liberating grant; my agent, Molly Friedrich, and my editor, Liz Stein, for their literary tango; Paul Cirone for acts of faith; and Amanda Jene for her prescience.

about the author

Mary-Ann Tirone Smith is the author of eight novels. She has lived all her life in Connecticut, except for the two years she served as a Peace Corps volunteer in Cameroon.